Reshaping Ethnic and Racial Relations in Philadelphia

Immigrants in a Divided City

JUDITH GOODE AND JO ANNE SCHNEIDER

Reshaping Ethnic and Racial Relations in Philadelphia

Immigrants in a Divided City

TEMPLE UNIVERSITY PRESS

PHILADELPHIA

Temple University Press, Philadelphia 19122
Copyright © 1994 by Temple University. All rights reserved
Published 1994
Printed in the United States of America

The paper used in this publication meets the minimum requirements of American
National Standard for Information Sciences—Permanence of Paper for Printed
Library Materials, ANSI Z39.48-1984 ⊛

Library of Congress Cataloging-in-Publication Data

Goode, Judith Granich.
    Reshaping ethnic and racial relations in Philadelphia : immigrants in a divided
city / Judith Goode and Jo Anne Schneider.
    p.   cm.
    Includes bibliographical references and index.
    ISBN 1-56639-140-7—ISBN 1-56639-141-5 (pbk.)
    1. Philadelphia (Pa.)—Ethnic relations.   2. Philadelphia (Pa.)—Race
relations.   I. Schneider, Jo Anne, 1959–   .   II. Title.
    F158.9.A1G66   1994   93-17959
    305.8′009748′11—dc20

To the people of Kensington, Olney, and Port Richmond—both new neighbors and old—who live the joys and challenges of a changing neighborhood, and to the local organizations that work unceasingly to create the best possible communities

CONTENTS

MAPS

ACKNOWLEDGMENTS

The Philadelphia Changing Relations Project was a group effort involving a number of researchers working on independent projects. Judith Goode and Jo Anne Schneider led the project, but study findings were discussed in group staff meetings. The research presented here includes the work of Sandra Andino, Suzanne Blanc, Cynthia Carter Ninivaggi, Carole Cohen, Louise Duhamel, Elzbieta Godziak, Juvencio Gonzalez, Lynn Hall, Hong Joon Kim, Saku Longshore, Jay Longshore, Maria Mulero, David Marin, Juana McCormick, Aparajita Mitra, Marilyn McArthur, Carmen Rolon, and numerous students in fieldwork classes. We are extremely grateful for their efforts. The research effort also depended on the help of Caitlan Evans, Sarah Peck, and Daniel Santiago. We also thank David Bartelt, David Horowitz, and William Rickle, S.J., for their advice on the research. We are grateful as well to Muriel Kirkpatrick, administrator of the Temple University Anthropology Lab, and to Scott Snyder of the Social Science Data Library for creating maps for the project.

The Changing Relations Project relied on the support of a number of organizations and individuals in the local communities who opened their institutions, neighborhoods, and homes and who shared their insights about living in a multicultural community with us. Our work would not have been possible without their time, kindness, and support. Many community leaders and several teachers and their students in neighborhood schools worked collaboratively with the project for several years. We hope we accurately reflect what we learned from them. We also thank the many staff members of Philadelphia's museums and cultural institutions and the organizations promoting improved human relations for providing access to information and for helpful suggestions.

The Philadelphia project was one of six sites in a national project, which was overseen by a project board. Our work was enriched by the insights of the researchers on our sister projects and the board members. As members of the board, Robert Bach, Louise Lamphere, and Roger Sanjek visited the project and provided helpful insights. Our coresearchers from the other six cities were especially helpful at a national project meeting held in Philadelphia in 1989.

Funding for the project came from the Ford Foundation through the Research Foundation of the State University of New York.

Reshaping Ethnic and
Racial Relations in Philadelphia

Immigrants in a Divided City

Introduction

The after-school program at a Catholic school in the Olney neighborhood of Philadelphia had taken a particularly chaotic turn one afternoon. The students included children from South India, Puerto Rico, Central America, U.S.-born African Americans, and Portuguese emigrants. The children were playing a game, and it was not going particularly well. The Latina student commented on the color of a South Indian boy's skin; he called her "yellow"; she screamed back that she had a suntan. Later, two native-born African American children made fun of the Indian boy, telling him that he looked like an Indian. He told them not to ridicule his nation. Then he resorted to an appeal for general racial equality; a statement that stopped the argument cold.

In the aftermath of the highly publicized murders of a white boy by a group of Puerto Ricans and a Puerto Rican boy by several whites during the summer of 1989, a Puerto Rican nationalist group called a meeting in Kensington to gather support for justice for the Puerto Rican community. The mother of one of the youths accused of murder sat at the table in front of the packed hall. She told how Puerto Rican boys were rounded up after the killing and how her son was kept away from his parents in a police car for several hours and presumably beaten. The organization's leaders made impassioned speeches calling for equal justice for their community. Representatives from other organizations—an African American woman from West Philadelphia, a rabbi, representatives of several white organizations—all made speeches supporting the Puerto Ricans' cause. The rabbi and the African American woman talked about the oppression of their own groups to signify solidarity with the Puerto Ricans. In many ways, the language, subject matter, and tone

*of the meeting echoed similar events from the heyday of the civil-rights and
Black-power movements. Yet the mayor and the police chief who represented
the "oppressive" power structure in the city were African Americans.*

Each of these examples shows intergroup relations to be complicated and
confused. Each draws on a range of structural and historical information to create
a view of people from different groups. Disentangling these many factors in
intergroup relations is itself a complicated and confusing task. This book draws on
two years of study in three Philadelphia neighborhoods—Olney, Kensington,
and Port Richmond—to address an emerging and vital issue: How do racial and
ethnic dynamics change once the country is no longer Black and white?

Answering this question requires looking at current events and historical
experience at the national, citywide, and local levels. It involves examining
several catagories of economic and political structures. How do changes in the
economy and political programs nationally affect Philadelphia, and each of its
neighborhoods? Addressing this question means looking at power: Who
controls a particular event, neighborhood, or institution? It also involves
examining the influence of ideas on actions and of actions on ideas.

Ideas and structures such as the economic system and the government
interact—ideas come from experience in the world. But experience means two
things: the concrete images and situations people directly encounter as they
move through the city—boarded-up neighborhoods, children playing happily
on integrated playgrounds, immigrant store owners—and the ideas they
receive from the media, formal institutions, the family, and school (Williams
1977). Then each individual reinterprets these multiple messages through his
or her own life and agendas.

Rather than focusing only on the role of macrolevel structures in placing
newcomers and established residents in the social structure of Philadelphia or
only on individual actions and beliefs, this book takes a middle ground. Both
structural conditions and public discourse influence the behavior and actions of
people as they live out their lives in a multicultural city. Social structure and
public discourse are themselves contested elements that are sustained and
changed through dialectical interaction between varying ideologies and structure. Macrolevel structure and discourse set the stage for individuals' life
chances and belief systems. But within the constraints of their lives, people are
free agents working to maintain their position or to change society. The
constant dynamic between individual action and structural factors both repro-
duces and changes the social and economic structure. This book examines the
ways that individual beliefs and actions, neighborhood dynamics, citywide
power structures and concerns, and national economic structures and ideas all
interact to create and change intergroup dynamics in these Philadelphia
neighborhoods.

The Philadelphia Changing Relations Project was not conceived as a community study. Instead, it assumed residential segregation and concentrated on interaction among newcomers and established residents in arenas that naturally bring people from different areas together. Yet we found increasing residential integration in all neighborhoods except Port Richmond. In addition, the combined dynamics of class, race, and the neighborhoods' vision of themselves and one another became an increasingly important point in the study. We found ourselves comparing three neighborhoods, not as bounded entities, but as places where particular kinds of people lived and held particular views of place and space.

The Changing Relations Project

In 1988 and 1989 the Ford Foundation sponsored research on changing U.S. communities. The foundation established a project board of social scientists to oversee six independent research projects in different parts of the country addressing the same questions. The project board was concerned about general perceptions that new immigrants were being met with hostility as they moved into U.S. communities. The board questioned whether the presence of new immigrants strengthened boundaries among existing ethnic and racial groups, created new formulations of group identity or difference, or improved relations across groups. The original mandate of the project involved discovering ways that increasing numbers of new immigrants changed both general social understandings of ethnic and racial categories and the nature of social and economic power relations in the areas under study.

Most investigations of race and ethnicity in the United States look at one community. In contrast, the Changing Relations Project focused on the interaction among people from different racial, ethnic, and immigrant communities. For this reason, each study concentrated on communities, institutions, or settings where people from many different groups come together.

The research project, *Changing Relations: Newcomers and Established Residents in Philadelphia, PA,* began in January 1988 as part of this national Ford Foundation effort. Philadelphia was the Northeastern site in an investigative effort that included independent research projects in Monterey Park, California, Miami, Florida, Chicago, Illinois, Garden City, Kansas, and Houston, Texas. As an older East Coast industrial city with a rapidly changing economic base, Philadelphia contrasted with Garden City, Kansas, where meat packing is a major industry, and the commercial centers of Miami and Monterey Park. Each study focused on neighborhoods where new immigrants and established residents, as well as people from many different backgrounds, came together regularly. Chicago was the closest match to Philadelphia within the national research effort.

Large sections of Philadelphia remain highly segregated. While African Americans worked with whites throughout the city, the African American population, especially its low-income segment, lives in neighborhoods segregated from many Philadelphians. According to the 1990 census, 72 percent of African Americans live in census tracts that are 90 percent or more African American. Exceptions to this pattern are Southeast Asian refugees placed in African American neighborhoods by the voluntary agencies that resettle them and Korean merchants, who own stores in all African American neighborhoods.[1] Much of the Puerto Rican community lives within a narrow strip east of Broad Street, starting around Spring Garden Street and moving toward the Northeast. Much of the Northeast and the areas near the rivers that border the east and west sides of Philadelphia remain mostly white. Yet there are also a number of notable integrated communities in Philadelphia, including Germantown, Mt. Airy, and Olney. Kensington, South Philadelphia, and other neighborhoods are becoming increasingly diverse. The Philadelphia Changing Relations Project focused on these more integrated neighborhoods.

Since the basic questions of the Changing Relations Project required a focus on settings where several races and nationalities come together, we increasingly found that African Americans were a minority in the areas where we worked. African American people from throughout North Philadelphia shopped on the shopping strips observed in this study, but only a few middle-class and established working class African Americans lived in the neighborhoods we examined. Unlike the situation in most of the schools in Philadelphia, African American children were the minority in both public and parochial schools included in the study. African Americans, however, became an important symbolic presence. Our work traces the way that established dynamics of race affect interactions in an increasingly diverse community.

Although the fifth largest city, Philadelphia is only the sixteenth largest receiver of new immigrants in the United States. Newcomers have been far less important to its dynamic than at other research sites like Houston and Miami. The presence of a large, geographically isolated but socially and politically important African American population had a profound effect on how immigrants viewed themselves and positioned themselves vis-à-vis the political and socioeconomic structures of the city. By focusing on the communities where people from varying backgrounds come together, this book explores the dialectic among different kinds of diversity and the way that new and existing patterns come together in Philadelphia to create change.

Interaction Patterns and Research Focus

Since the study traced interaction patterns among people from different groups, we looked for places where people of diverse backgrounds mixed. The sites where new immigrants and established residents and members of minority groups and majority groups come together greatly influenced the focus of our research and the results we report. Noting the people who were absent from integrated settings says much about the social and economic situation in Philadelphia. In general, we found that residents had very different experiences and expectations of people from other groups, depending on their own socioeconomic background and place of residence. Differences reflected differential effects of race or immigrant background, class, previous experience with persons from other groups, and current contact. We identified people who were extremely isolated from all other races and nationalities, as well as those whose acquaintance with people from different races and countries ranged from casual, intermittent contact to intimate relationships.

People from these various groups experience and understand diversity very differently. Unlike many studies that focus on thoughts and actions of people from one group, our research deliberately concentrated on what happens when individuals from different backgrounds come together. This concentration yields a number of unique insights into changing dynamics in U.S. cities.

Defining "Newcomer" and "Established"

As we began work, we quickly realized that date of immigration had little to do with local definitions of newcomer and established resident within Philadelphia neighborhoods. People who had lived in the United States for generations—such as African Americans, Puerto Ricans, or some whites—were sometimes considered hostile newcomers. For instance, rowdy whites reportedly caused problems in Olney, and New Yoricans (people of Puerto Rican descent born in New York), who are well established in the United States, became a significant newcomer presence within the Philadelphia Puerto Rican community. Our research focused on these new definitions of newcomer.

Definitions of established resident also had little to do with living in a particular neighborhood for a long time. Being defined as an established resident hinged on three factors: (1) where the person was born, (2) how long a person had lived in a particular place, and (3) how much the individual participated in the social networks and activities considered important in a particular setting. In many cases, such participation far outweighed the length of time someone had resided in a neighborhood or worked at a company, where a person was born, or the color of her or his skin.

Within relatively new groups like Poles and Koreans, demographic characteristics, expectations, and behaviors differed between people who had been in the country for ten or fifteen years and more recent arrivals. In some cases, distinctions between "newcomer" and "established" depended upon participation in community activities and personal style rather than on time in the United States. We found that people were defined as insiders or outsiders or as minority or majority group members based on a variety of social characteristics, levels of participation in a given context, and power dynamics. People became insiders through playing by established rules and participating in the community.

Quite often, "newcomer" became equated with race or nationality. This tendency involved both fear of different races and attempts to fit new immigrants into the existing dynamic of race and ethnic politics within the city. For instance, Koreans and Cambodians learned to organize as nationality based interest groups and compete for city resources. Puerto Ricans have also used the language of racial politics when working for their own constituency. At the same time, long-term residence has come to take priority over racial categories. For example, residents of the two historically African American blocks in Port Richmond are considered as much a part of the community as their white counterparts.

Geography and Methodology

Within Philadelphia, the project concentrated on interaction among various newcomer and established groups living in the eastern part of North Philadelphia. (This area extends from Broad Street on the west to the Delaware River on the east, with Girard Avenue as the southern boundary and Godfrey Avenue as the northern border.) As the project progressed, the geographical focus centered on the neighborhoods of Kensington, Olney, and Port Richmond (Map 1). While the territorial delimiters were quite large, the research concentrated on activities in workplaces, schools, business strips, and neighborhood organizations. Although these activities drew participants from the larger area, they took place in such discrete localities as a school or a ten-block shopping strip.

Historically, anthropologists change the names of the people, places, and institutions that they study in order to protect the identities of those who opened their lives to in-depth research. Throughout this book, we have changed the names of all individuals and organizations in the interest of privacy; however, we have used the actual names of the neighborhoods throughout it.

The project concentrated on interactions among five groups who live and work in the greater North Philadelphia area: whites, African Americans, Puerto Ricans, Koreans, and recent Polish émigrés. Originally, the project defined whites and African Americans as established, with Koreans and Polish émigrés being characterized as newcomers. The Puerto Rican population included both established and newcomer individuals. When appropriate, the white population was further differentiated into self-defined ethnic communities. As we encountered individuals from other groups (such as Indians, Portuguese, Vietnamese, Chinese, Cambodians, Lao, Cubans, Guatemalans, Nicaraguans, and Colombians), we expanded our research design to include comparison of interaction between members of these groups and our primary-focus groups.

A team of researchers learned about the interactions among newcomers and

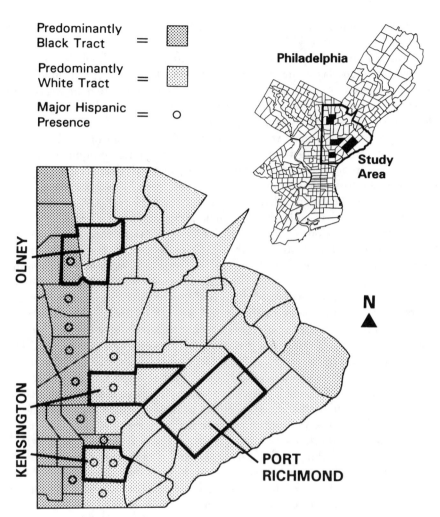

MAP 1.   The study area in Northeast Philadelphia.

established residents by watching and participating in activities at a number of sites. (Anthropologists call this research technique "participant observation.") Research in schools started in the early spring of 1988 and continued through the 1989 school year. Throughout the study period we observed and conducted interviews in four schools: a parochial and a public school in Olney, a public school in Kensington, and a parochial school in Port Richmond. All schools served students between kindergarten and eighth grade, with the exception of the Kensington school, which began as K–6 and now is K–5. Observations addressed activities and perceptions of professional and volunteer staff, parents, and such outside program providers as counselors and school nurses, as well as the interaction among children. In addition to weekly observations, we interviewed principals, key teachers, and involved parents about their own backgrounds, the history of the site, and activities at each school. As appropriate, we observed classes in English as a Second Language (ESL), lunch and recess, after-school programs, gym classes, and some regular classroom activities. Later in the study, research was expanded to involve several other elementary schools and two high schools.

Like many of our sites, the schools proved to be a springboard to other research opportunities. As time went on, we modified our perception of each site to encompass its variety of activities and the larger context that influenced events in the school setting. For example, research at both parochial schools was quickly expanded to involve the parish as a whole. For the public schools, we expanded into the community organizations that held programs in the schools.

Philadelphia developed a concern with human relations early in its history. Several established institutions within the city, as well as many community efforts, exist to facilitate interactions among groups. As we contacted community organizations in an effort to conduct interviews with people involved in community affairs, we discovered that a coalition of these citywide entities was orchestrating a series of human-relations projects in the neighborhoods we were studying. Given the importance of both intracommunity work on human relations and citywide efforts on this issue, human-relations activities quickly became important in our study. A large part of this book focuses on that topic.

This aspect of city dynamics quickly brought the project into contact with a number of community and citywide organizations, as well as local churches. Field-workers regularly attended meetings of neighborhood organizations in all three communities. We continued work with these groups throughout the next year of the project.

In addition to working with local ethnic- and neighborhood-based groups, researchers attended citywide ethnic and human-relations events. These included festivals by and for the various ethnic communities, World of Difference seminars, interethnic training conferences, and city-sponsored ethnic parades. Activists in key ethnic and human-relations organizations were interviewed, and we collected written material and newsletters from a variety of institutions.

We did research in a large unionized factory, a small garment factory, and a supermarket, observing activities and interviewing key figures in these institutions. We also conducted research on three shopping strips. In addition, staff at several job-training and placement agencies were interviewed to provide background information.

Beyond observing activities and conducting interviews in a variety of settings, the project conducted formal, structured interviews with both newcomer and established households representing all groups included in the study. Data collected in the communities were combined with analysis of newspaper and other media reports from the Philadelphia area, collection of materials on human-relations issues created by or for Philadelphians, and comparison with other secondary-source materials.

While the project covered a wide range of research sites and communities, our access to people from different groups varied. Even though we were careful to include researchers from Korea, Puerto Rico and different sections of India in our research team, we found that their work was limited by their own middle- or upper-class backgrounds or by their own perspectives on the differences between the cultures of their homelands and people from those countries who had emigrated to the United States. We had very little access to the newest and most isolated Puerto Rican, Polish, and Korean immigrants. However, we had good, ongoing relationships with working-class and middle-class whites, Puerto Ricans, African Americans, and Poles in the places that we studied; this was also the case with more-established Koreans. Work in this study was augmented by contacts with Puerto Ricans and Polish émigrés initiated before the Changing Relations Project began.

National Forces and Community Dynamics

Most of this book concentrates on the various structures, ideas, and interactions within Philadelphia and the particular neighborhoods that we investigated. Yet what happens in even a single school or neighborhood organization is shaped by historical events and the current structures of the country and even the world. Before examining the many different factors that influence intergroup dynamics in Philadelphia, we will outline some of the important nationwide influences on individual and neighborhood beliefs and actions.

This outline is not meant as an exhaustive recounting of immigration history, racial dynamics in the United States, political economy, government policy, ethnicity, or U.S. ideology—each of these subjects requires many books to understand. Nor do we intend to provide a literature review on any of these topics. The outline here provides a framework for understanding the structural and ideological dynamics that became important in comprehending events in Olney, Kensington, and Port Richmond. We also describe how we are using concepts like ethnicity and race in this book.

Government Poverty Programs and Neighborhood Organization Structures

In the last thirty years, the U.S. economy has gradually shifted from manufacturing to service. Large factories that had provided relative security, decent wages, and benefits to many Americans since the 1930s moved first to the South and then overseas. The jobs that sometimes replace factory work often require more education than did those of earlier decades. While the new service economy has created opportunity for some, many jobs now pay less than in previous decades, are frequently part time, offer fewer benefits, and are located in smaller, less stable companies. This is particularly true for less-skilled employment. Chapter 2 discusses changes in the economic system in Philadelphia in detail. These economic shifts played a significant role in both the life chances and the expectations of the people documented in this book.

Government antipoverty programs also affected the structures, strategies, and resources of the organizations and neighborhoods that we examined. The War on Poverty of the 1960s created a series of programs in neighborhoods defined as poor. Many of these efforts, such as the Model Cities program, the Housing and Community Development Act of 1974, and the Economic Opportunity Act, stressed community participation in programs to combat poverty. Unlike most government-assistance programs for the poor, which pass money to individuals through the states, these plans allocated money directly to city governments or other local agencies to fund local neighborhood programs. The legislation stipulated that housing, community-development, and community-services funding would only be granted to locally based nonprofit organizations with significant participation from community residents. A dense web of community development corporations (CDCs), neighborhood action councils (NACs), and community action agencies (CAAs) developed in response to these programs in neighborhoods like Kensington that fit the profile of impoverished or at-risk communities. The governing structures of the organizations (and, to a large extent, the kinds of work they do) was mandated by government regulations. In later years, Philadelphia went so far as to designate the geographical boundaries of organizations funded through this legislation.

The initiatives of the Johnson-era War on Poverty were replaced by the Community Services Block Grant (CSBG) and Community Development Block Grant (CDBG) programs. While funding levels have decreased dramatically since 1980 and the focus of the programs has shifted to a certain degree, the basic format for funding and the nature of the governing bodies of the local groups has not changed since the 1960s. We found that these organizations played a significant role in some neighborhoods; the interface between antipoverty programs and efforts to create opportunity for people of color also created a significant dynamic. Chapters 4, 6, and 7 address the ways that these programs contributed to changing intergroup dynamics in Philadelphia.

Immigration Law, Civil Rights, and Changing Economic Structures

Immigrants

Last year we enacted the historic Civil Rights Act of 1964, which was designed to wipe out the last vestiges of racial discrimination against our own citizens.

As we reappraise the relationship of citizen to citizen under this law, it is also good for us to re-examine this same relationship of man's equality to man with respect to peoples of the world.

For as we move to erase racial discrimination against our own citizens, we should also move to erase racial barriers against citizens of other lands in our immigration laws. (Senator Hiram Fong, statement before the United States Senate Subcommittee on Immigration and Naturalization, hearings on immigration reform, February 24, 1965, 45)

The 1960s and 1970s witnessed historic changes in the nature of U.S. society, the kinds of people that make up the country, and the ways that they relate to each other. The magnitude of these changes compares to the upheaval of the Civil War and the combined effects of the Industrial Revolution and the massive immigration from southern and eastern Europe that restructured this country at the turn of the century. After a decade of agitation, Congress passed the Civil Rights Act of 1964. This landmark legislation intended to equalize African Americans' place in the United States by declaring discrimination in housing, employment, and public accommodations illegal. Affirmative action was instituted by executive order in 1965 to ameliorate historic discrimination.

One year after passing the Civil Rights Act, Congress enacted the first major change in immigration legislation since restricting immigration from southern and eastern Europe and from Asia in the first quarter of this century. By eliminating the national-origins quotas, the United States admitted immigrants from Asia in large numbers for the first time since the early years of the twentieth century. The 1975 airlift of Vietnamese out of Saigon began an exodus of refugees from Southeast Asia that still continues. The Soviet Union's brief opening to the West in the late 1970s and current changes in eastern Europe created a migration of Soviet Jews and other eastern Europeans to the United States. The military crackdown on the Solidarity movement brought Poles to the United States as refugees as well as visitors.[2] The combined influx of immigrants and refugees in the next two decades altered the racial and national face of the United States.

The nature of the post-1965 migration differed from the turn-of-the-century immigration waves in important ways. Although the earlier immigrants included among their number some people with either considerable education and skills or aspirations to middle-class status, the majority were peasants in the process of being transformed into an industrial working class (Thomas and Znaniecki 1927; Hourwich 1912). The 1965 immigration law restricted the possibility that new immigrants would be the "tired, poor, huddled masses yearning to breathe free" of Emma Lazarus's poem "The New Colossus" (1883). The 1965 law gave preference to relatives of U.S. citizens and resident aliens and to workers with skills needed by the United States. For countries like South Korea or India, where immigration had been severely restricted for nearly a century, the first new arrivals were primarily educated and skilled individuals. While the family members that these first immigrants later brought to the United States could be less educated than they, the class level of this new migration generally exceeded established residents' expectations of poor, ignorant newcomers.[3] Some educated immigrants from all countries moved into professions and the ownership of small businesses quickly. A number brought capital to start businesses here; others pooled their resources and used their knowledge of business practices to succeed rapidly in the United States.

The refugee population varied enormously, ranging from the elite leaders of Vietnam, Cambodia, and Laos to preliterate tribesmen. Such variation created much confusion, as some refugees became the stereotypical "model minorities," working hard to move up in their new country, while others fell into poverty.

Research on the economic incorporation of immigrants into the United States almost universally confirms that newcomers generally start near the bottom of the economic hierarchy and that immigration often means taking jobs below the occupational level achieved in the country of origin (Sassen-Koob 1980; Grasmuck 1984; Gitelman 1984; Hawks 1977; Hershberg et al. 1979; Panish 1981; Simon 1985; Marshall 1987; Foner 1987; Stafford 1987). But the preference for skilled immigrants in the 1965 immigration law altered this expected pattern. We found numerous paths for new arrivals as they adapted to U.S. society. Present-day immigrant experience often clashes with established residents' expectations of newcomers. Throughout our research, native-born Americans repeated notions that immigrants or refugees "lived on one bag of rice for a week" or "came with the clothes on their backs." While this remains true for some newcomers, the middle-class immigrants that we encountered most often in mixed settings defied the pattern. This study takes a careful look at how immigrants who live and work in mixed settings encounter the culture and socioeconomic structure of the United States.

Scholars of the U.S. economic hierarchy generally confirm that the majority of immigrants and people of color find work in the more informal, lower-paid, and unstable secondary sector of the economy, while whites and an increasing number of African Americans and established Latinos are employed in the more secure, unionized, and larger firms known as the primary sector (Gordon, Edwards, and Reich 1982; Sassen-Koob 1980; Reich 1981). Recent studies have noted the existence of immigrant enclaves as a third economic option for newcomers (Portes and Bach 1985) and the importance of the interaction between modes of incorporation and immigrant resources in placement of newcomers in the labor hierarchy of the United States (Portes and Rumbaut 1990). In our study, some Koreans formed an ethnic enclave, and many Puerto Ricans and new Poles worked in the secondary sector. Since we studied workplaces where whites, African Americans, Latinos, Asians, and others worked together, we focused mainly on primary-sector employers and the more established immigrants. While we were aware of Korean visitors doing piecework in their homes for other Koreans, Polish visitors working "under the table" in cleaning and construction, and Puerto Ricans working in a variety of small factories and in the informal economy, we excluded them from the study because these newcomers worked in settings that included only new immigrants. However, we did encounter the children of these newcomers in schools and saw whole families shopping together.

People of Color

Our nation is moving toward two societies, one black, one white—separate and unequal. (*The Kerner Report: The 1968 Report of the National Advisory Commission on Civil Disorders* [(1968)1988], 1)

Legislation combined with changes in the economy to create several paths for African Americans in Philadelphia and throughout the United States in the last few decades. Civil-rights legislation brought important changes for the middle-class African American community. The combination of affirmative action and antidiscrimination legislation helped middle-class African Americans and Latinos to enter historically white colleges, move into formerly all-white areas, and to begin entering managerial positions in traditionally white institutions. But new opportunities for the African American middle class proved a mixed blessing. African American movement out of the ghetto reportedly had a destabilizing effect (Wilson 1987; Carter 1991; Anderson 1990) and led to debate within the African American community over strategies and ideology (Bell 1987; Carter 1991; Steele 1990; Sowell 1981). Civil-rights policies also failed to dispel the historically developed view of all African Americans as lower class, which continues to form the basis for much of whites' expectations of African Americans they encounter in everyday life.

Skin color and nationality became an important aspect of political consciousness, leading groups to organize along racial and ethnic lines and to demand power, resources, and recognition. As the Puerto Rican population in Philadelphia continued to grow, and as immigrants from Asia entered the political and economic scene, both groups adopted the political stance and expectations of equal access developed by the civil-rights movement. African Americans reacted to these other groups reviving the language of the civil- rights movement and receiving some of the benefits of affirmative action on the grounds that the program was begun to reverse the effects of slavery.

Expected opportunities failed to materialize for many people of color. The economically based structures that maintain a small number of whites in control of most of society and relegate most people of color to the lowest levels of the economic hierarchy could not be erased by simply announcing that the doors were now open. Nor could the historical structures that gave immigrants priority for employment over African Americans (Lieberson 1980) and that shaped the generalized expectations of immigrants and African Americans be changed simply by court edict. As industrial jobs disappeared, working-class people of all colors found themselves competing for an ever shrinking economic pie. Established minorities reacted as new immigrants from Asia took over many businesses in poor African American and Latino neighborhoods. The poverty statistics for these two communities are still staggering. In 1987, a full third of the African American population lived below the poverty level (Dewart 1989, 18). Figures for Latinos parallel the African American situation. Overall, 25 percent of Latinos and 37.9 percent of Puerto Ricans lived in poverty (Marger 1991, 292–93). As the effects of the Reagan era curtailed many of the programs begun in the late 1960s and early 1970s to develop skills in truly disadvantaged populations, the poor fell farther and farther behind (Wilson 1987).

Models and Social Structure

Socially constructed models regarding immigration and minority groups became a critical factor in determining the ways that newcomers and established residents negotiated the political landscape, thought about their futures and the prospects of people from other groups, and created and transformed individual and group identities. These models also were essential in developing organized programming intended to incorporate newcomers into society and to improve interaction across all groups. Expectations of others influenced the ways that the people studied here interacted with individuals perceived as different.

We outline here three primary models of immigration and race. Each draws together a series of assumptions regarding intergroup relations and U.S. society. Aspects of each model appear in academic discourse, popular images, and individual action and thought. In most cases, individuals use pieces of a model in a particular context. These models are not mutually exclusive. We present them as composite summaries in this section to provide a reference for discussion below. Later sections show how models are used and changed in various contexts and interactions.

These models are public discourses on a particular group of people or an issue. They involve a mixture of historical fact, data from current social and economic conditions, and present-day interpretations, which provide a framework for understanding the behavior or expected paths of people from a particular group. Like all public ideology, content is created and changed through a dynamic relationship between scholarly presentations, media and public images, and current social, economic, and political exigencies.

The dialectic between academic research and public images provides an example of the kinds of relationships described throughout this book. The scholars who study immigration and racial or ethnic relations are products of U.S. society. As such, their ideas reflect their own upbringing and the information that they have absorbed as they go through their lives. Academics are also political creatures, reflecting the interests of their class position, their teachers, and their peers. Research questions are influenced by funding sources and the concerns of the larger society. And yet, scholars are not simply reflections of the world around them. They come to a particular topic with questions developed from their own intellects and learn new things as they investigate their chosen topics. Their findings alter the existing picture of an issue and stimulate dialogue that pushes current images in new directions.

The experience and ideology of the many social actors that we discuss are formed and transformed in the same way. New immigrants and established residents of all races and nationalities negotiate their lives in a world framed by the existing social and economic order and by the recent history of race relations and immigration. Yet the actions and expectations of these individuals change their world as they attempt to make their way though an increasingly complex social structure. Our book explores this process.

The "Good Immigrant"

As with all models, this picture combines fact and expectations.[4] This ideology of immigrant incorporation draws on historical experience of turn-of-the-century immigrants in the United States, the fact that many present-day newcomers start out in menial jobs upon arrival here, and the persistent ideology of economic opportunity and step-by-step progress toward social and economic incorporation into U.S. society. All newcomers are measured against this expected path toward adaptation to the United States. People who succeed too quickly or too slowly are both considered "bad immigrants," deviants from the expected norm.

The image of the good immigrants rests on two sets of assumptions: the background experience of newcomers in their country of origin, and the mechanisms for incorporation in the United States. As with Handlin (1951, 7) all new immigrants are expected to resemble somehow the image of turn-of-the-century migrants: peasants who leave the traditional, solid society of the home country to seek opportunity in the United States. In some way, all newcomers are expected to be less educated and less familiar with modern technology than established residents. This expectation takes many forms: newcomer Puerto Ricans are considered "jibaro" (peasants from the mountains who are badly educated and unfamiliar with twentieth-century life), the education of Polish professionals is seen to be decades behind that of their U.S. counterparts, and Koreans are seen as steeped in Confucian culture that keeps them separate from the customs of the United States. This image of the backward immigrant is usually combined with assumptions that newcomers bring with them centuries old cultural traditions that provide a nurturing familial backdrop to incorporation. Cultural traditions are sometimes seen as leading newcomers to misunderstand the informality and fast-paced modernity of American life.

Once in the United States, newcomers are expected to adapt to its society in the same way as imagined for their turn-of-the-century forerunners. In this view, typical newcomers enter the labor market at the bottom of the economic ladder either because they lack the skills to compete in the U.S. economy or because they do not speak the language. From these lowly beginnings, newcomers are expected to move toward economic success and social incorporation. Along the way, they are expected to learn English and to acquire U.S. dress styles, material goods, and cultural habits. At the same time, immigrants are expected to retain part of their heritage, usually in the form of food and holiday traditions.

Progress toward success in the United States is expected to be slow. In most cases, the immigrant generation is expected to struggle both economically and socially in the United States. Their children become the recipients of their parents' expectations of mobility, achieving Americanization and a measure of economic success. It is here that the "good immigrant" story takes one of several possible paths. In one version, the second and subsequent generations move slowly up in the economic hierarchy behind the descendants of previous generations of immigrants.

Other renderings perceive prospects for newcomer children as completely open. In this variation, the success of immigrant children verifies the possibilities of mobility and the importance of individual effort in the United States. The "model minority" images so often ascribed to Asian immigrants is just one example of how established Americans assure themselves that anyone coming to the country can make it if he or she works hard enough. In this way, the ideology of the "good immigrant" affirms the American belief in equal opportunity, which is central to a generalized understanding of democracy in the United States.

The "good immigrant" model is familiar to Americans from a variety of sources. It appears in popular entertainment like the animated film *An American Tail*. It underlies the many stories of immigrant struggle and success in the news media. Policymakers, when designing regulations, assume that immigrants will follow this path to success. Some academic studies, like *The Uprooted*, by Oscar Handlin (1951), and Ivan Light's *Ethnic Succession* (1981), use the "good immigrant" model as the basis for their findings. Other researchers react to this understanding of immigration history by writing about the continued struggles of legal immigrants, refugees, and undocumented migrants in this country.

Models of Race

The civil-rights movement assumed that African Americans would quickly move toward economic opportunity, given equal access to housing, employment, and other social arenas. Much of the premise behind integration rested on the view that stereotypes and prejudice were based on lack of personal interaction with people from other groups. If African Americans and whites mixed in the workplace, schools, neighborhoods, and public buildings, white fear of African Americans would disappear. In the words of Martin Luther King, "I have a dream that my four little children will one day live in a nation where they will not be judged by the color of their skin but the content of their character" (1963).

But the events of the last twenty years are complex and contradictory. In some cases increasing interaction across groups increased harmony, while bringing people together caused more friction in other situations. Mandating equal access allowed some people of color to move up in American society, while others fell into increasing poverty. The resulting confusion led to a host of strategies and public discussions on how to create a truly open society in the United States.

The public discourse on race and inequality is far more complex and contentious than the understanding of immigrant adaptation. There is far more variation within a particular understanding of the problem. Several models appear over and over again, however. They are defined here as "structural racism" and "cultural pluralism." "Structural racism" is often called "institutional racism." Primarily we use the term "structural racism" throughout this book, but we refer to "institutional racism" or "institutional inequality" when discussing historic arguments on this topic that use these terms. While adherents of the structural-racism model often disparage the expectations of cultural pluralism, neither model is mutually exclusive. In reality, most organizers working with a cultural-pluralism model to encourage tolerance will subscribe to aspects of the structural-racism model. In both cases, popular discourse is based on scholarly documentation and argument. Our research found that the popular interpretations of research became key elements in the ways that newcomers and established residents approached the problem of intergroup relations.

Structural Racism

The primary principle of this model draws on the reality that the economic structures of U.S. society are under the control of a white minority and that people of color are often at the bottom of the social and economic hierarchy. In their classic statement of the premise for Black Power, Stokley Carmichael and Charles Hamilton defined the problem as follows:

> Racism is both overt and covert. It takes two closely related forms: individual whites acting against individual African Americans, and acts by the total

white community against the African American community. We call these individual racism and institutional racism. The first consists of overt acts by individuals which cause death, injury or the violent destruction of property. ... The second type is less overt, far more subtle, less identifiable in terms of specific individuals committing the acts. But it is no less destructive of human life. The second type originates in the operation of established and respected forces in society, and thus receives far less public condemnation than the first type. (1967, 4)

The institutional-racism model assumes that all whites participate in the domination of people of color by living their lives in a society dominated by whites. The concept of institutional racism draws on the idea of "internal colonialism" (Hector 1975), which describes the powerful as preying on subjugated populations in their midst. This is comparable to the way that colonial powers used the raw materials and labor from their colonies while squashing any independent enterprise developed there. Racism, then, "is not merely exclusion on the basis of race but exclusion for the purpose of subjugating or maintaining subjugation" (Carmichael and Hamilton 1967, 47). In this view, all whites benefit from institutional racism, and therefore all whites are guilty of racist behavior. Adherents of this theory state that the solution to institutional racism is to change the structure of society.

The structural-racism model draws on a vast and well-established literature on inequality in the United States and throughout the world. For example, such studies as Reich's *Racial Inequality* (1981) document structural inequality in the work force, and a whole genre of education research following Leacock's *Teaching and Learning in City Schools* (1969) shows how assumptions about poor African American children reinforce structures of inequality across generations.

The academic debate about the persistence and significance of racism in the post-civil-rights era was revived with the publication of William J. Wilson's *Declining Significance of Race* in 1978. Wilson emphasized the importance of the political economy (i.e., the historical and contemporary position of African Americans in the economic structure) in explaining continuing poverty. He continued this theme, in *The Truly Disadvantaged* (1987), looking at the growth of the African American middle class, its movement away from the inner city, and the increasing concentration of isolated poor African Americans to explain the persistence of what he called the "ghetto poor."

In response, strong arguments were made that a separate historical formation and continued operation of ideas about race existed alongside class position in explaining discrimination (Omi and Winant 1986). Such writers as Marable (1983, 1992) and West (1991, 1993a, 1993b) examined the complex relationships between the economy, political movements, and racism in the post-civil-rights era.

As Black power gained currency in the 1970s, popular versions of the structural-racism concept quickly boiled it down to a simple equation of race with class. All whites had power, and all people of color were victims of white oppression. Popular literature on institutional racism continues in this vein today. For example, to make up for what Wallis calls the sin of racism, whites should repent; such repentance, "if genuine, will always bear fruit in concrete forms of conversion, changed behavior, and reparation" (1987, 8).

The overarching connection of all of white society to structural racism also appears in some current academic research and policy studies. A recent National Urban League report (Tidwell 1990, iii) bases its discussion on the premise that "white Americans have continued to enjoy material advantage based on the racial exclusionary practices of the past and the operation of institutional discrimination in the present." Lowy (1991, 445) defines "yuppie racism" with the observation that "many Americans do not view racism as a major problem in contemporary society." Both studies rely on an assumption of structural racism.

This model has led to a number of creative efforts to empower people of color and to change the structures of society in this country. It has also spawned the development of programs to get whites to "recognize their racism and seek to change their thoughts and actions" about people of color. As we shall see, newcomers also use structural-racism arguments to obtain services for their communities.

Cultural Pluralism

This model combines a number of strands of thought about intergroup relations in the United States. It refers to U.S. society through a variety of metaphors: mosaic, tapestry, salad, quilt. It views the country as a combination of peoples from many different cultures, each with their own proud heritage. Creating equality in the United States involves allowing each ethnic group to explore and celebrate its own independent culture. Academic and quasi-academic expositions of cultural pluralism include "A Blueprint for a Pluralistic Society" (Gaymon and Garret 1975), as well as numerous writings supporting ethnicity, such as *The Rise of the Unmeltable Ethnics* (Novak 1971) and Glazer and Moynihan's *Beyond the Melting Pot* (1970).

In practice, organizations dedicated to increasing intergroup harmony attempt to teach about the many different groups that make up the United States. In attempting to place all groups on an equal footing, the model favors the concept of ethnicity and downplays race. The cultural-pluralist strategy focuses on informing both newcomers and established residents about their own cultures and those of others. By celebrating diversity, the various groups that make up U.S. society will learn to respect each other's differences and live together amicably. This model assumes that providing positive information about people from other groups will lead to equality as individuals learn to value the various cultures that constitute the United States and to treat each other as equals. As discussed in detail in Chapter 3, the cultural-heritage programs often draw on outmoded, idealized elements of home-country culture despite the overwhelming social science literature that describes ethnicity as a variable phenomenon created as much by conditions in the United States as by the backgrounds of immigrants (Yancey et al. 1976, 1985; Gans 1982; di Leonardo 1984; Waters 1990; Schneider 1990a; Hurh and Kim 1984).

Cultural pluralism generally focuses on the thoughts and actions of individuals, positing that they become prejudiced because they lack information about other groups. It assumes that people develop low self-esteem if they do not have a positive understanding of their own background and culture.

The increasing political focus on hate crimes incorporates this view. Hate crimes are often defined as anonymous acts of violence against people because of their race or nationality. Media and political images of cross burnings, people painting Nazi symbols on synagogues, or gay bashing involve faceless perpetrators attacking representatives of another group. People who commit hate crimes are often described as uneducated youths or members of isolated extremist groups. For example, a National Institute Against Prejudice and Violence report (1986, 3) states that "while racially or religiously motivated violence is not limited to the relatively small number of members of organized hate groups, their rhetoric may well stimulate the young people who commit the majority of these incidents." The solution to hate crimes and other acts of prejudice includes educating the perpetrators about the people that they fear because they are different. This view assumes that changing attitudes can lead to changed behavior.

The definition of prejudice as "an attitude of favor or disfavor . . . related to an overgeneralized (and therefore erroneous) belief" was most thoroughly discussed by Allport (1988, 13). Originally published in 1954, *The Nature of Prejudice* examines the development of prejudice and the movement of idea to action that leads to discrimination and ultimately genocide. While Allport recognizes that all people hold prejudices, and that some prejudices are positive, common usage equates prejudice with negative ideas about a person or group. Mack (1963, 118) notes that Americans frequently use "prejudice" and "discrimination" interchangeably and that in popular usage "discrimination is against a minority." The primary way to combat prejudice expounded in this literature is to teach people about minority groups. This notion fostered numerous popular programs to help people define and combat their prejudices, ranging from the 1944 program for high-school students entitled *Probing Our Prejudices* (Powdermaker 1944) to the ongoing national Anti-Defamation League/B'nai B'rith "World of Difference" program.

While the more sophisticated efforts (like the national World of Difference curricula) recognize the combination of structural factors and experience that leads to discrimination, popular parlance often equates any negative thought or action to harmful prejudice that must be rooted out of the offending individual. At the beginning of *The Nature of Prejudice* Allport describes two situations— a case where an anthropologist keeps his children away from the Indian village he is studying because tuberculosis is rampant there, and a case where a Canadian researcher writes two identical letters (using names that appear Jewish and non-Jewish) for reservations at resort hotels and gets very different results. The first case is not defined as discrimination—since the anthropologist kept his children away from the villiage because of a health hazard, not because he thought less of the people he was studying. The second is a textbook example of prejudice in action—many of the resorts tell the "Jewish" correspondent that the resort is full, while "non-Jews" are regularly told that there are vacancies (Allport 1988, 4-5). As discussed throughout this book, some community organizers, media presentations, and people in the community in Philadelphia would often consider both cases as harmful prejudice. Saying anything negative about people from another group is racism; any action that excludes people from another group is considered an example of prejudice.

What is Race and Ethnicity?

Many popular discussions of race and ethnicity assume that an individual's "group" is fixed at birth. Race is understood as an immutable, unchanging category. Ethnic identity is viewed as based on unchanging cultural traits that influence preferences and behaviors. Individuals are born into a given group: membership in it defines their habits, life-styles, and life chances. Furthermore, racial and ethnic identity is considered a key part of self. Everyone in the United States is assumed to have an ethnic identity, and those who deny it are losing an important part of self.

But a vast array of scholarly literature denies these definitions of race and ethnicity as being natural, unchanging, and primary. Early in this century, the founders of the Chicago school of sociology described the shifting nature of identity for new immigrants (Park 1928; Thomas and Znaniecki 1927). Later social scientists have provided innumerable studies showing how people from specific villages and regions are molded into an ethnic identity in the United States.

Ethnicity in this country is a product of the history and current social and economic structure of the United States. As described in a wide range of literature, Polish Americans, Irish Americans, and other U.S. ethnic groups are a melding in this country of people who came from different regions. Ethnic culture combines traits and habits from the country of origin with U.S. ideas of progress, idealized views of the "home" country, and a whole host of economic and social conditions in the United States. Ethnic identity can be all-important for some individuals from a particular background and irrelevant to others. People stress ethnicity or ignore it depending on the situation. Many native-born Americans can claim multiple ethnic identities, and they can pick and choose whether to be "Polish," "Italian," or simply American in a given context.

Race is also a socially constructed category. While the idea of biology determining capabilities and temperament continues to reappear throughout U.S. history, scientists have continually proved that people defined as "Black," "White," or "Asian" have a variety of capabilities and that every racial group includes much mixing between people defined in different racial categories (Montague 1963 and 1979; Myrdal 1944; Gould 1981). Even the kinds of groups called "races" have changed over time. In a turn-of-the-century attempt to refute the ideas that people from different heritages have different inbred capabilities, Franz Boas prepared research on the different "races" of people from southern and eastern Europe (e.g., Italians, Germans, and Poles) proving that the bodies and IQs of emigrants from various places changed once they came to the United States. At that time, Europeans whom we would now label as "white" were considered to be of different "races." The Poles and the English were consigned to separate biological categories, complete with their own temperaments, physical abilities, and mental capacities—just as some people view black and white today.

While both race and ethnicity are ever changing, socially constructed categories, the two terms have very different social meanings in the contemporary United States. Unlike the situation in the early decades of this century, ethnicity has far fewer social and economic consequences than does race. In many situations it does not matter if one is Italian American or Polish American, but being African American or white is of vital importance. One's color is noted and categorized by other people, modulating behavior in most contexts. Ethnicity matters less often, and it is usually a self-defined characteristic, not a range of expectations ascribed by others. Even though the two populations are mixed biologically, black and white are defined as rigid boundaries. For a person of mixed white and African American heritage, "passing" has profound psychological, social, and (sometimes) economic consequences.

New immigrants find themselves attempting to fit into the idea of ethnic identity and fixed race in the United States. Skin tone for Puerto Ricans ranges from very dark to very light. Depending on individual physical traits and social dynamics, Puerto Ricans in this study define themselves as Black, white, or "other." Koreans and other people from Asia sometimes use the racial category "Asian," but they shift between highlighting race, nationality, or ethnicity depending on social and economic contexts.

New immigrants also discover that they are expected to have an ethnic identity in the United States. As described in Chapters 3 and 7, nationality has particular importance for people emigrating to this country. Throughout the book, we explore the ways that nationality and meanings and uses of race and ethnicity touch the lives of new immigrants in the United States. We also look at how the presence of new immigrants changes dynamics for people long established in this country.

A Note on Group Labels

The names used to describe groups of people from different backgrounds and countries are themselves a subject for debate and possible change. Individuals who emigrate to the United States generally prefer to be labeled as people from their home countries and are surprised to find themselves lumped with very different people who come from the same region of the world. As with the debate over the terms "Latino" or "Hispanic" (Hayes-Bautista and Chapa 1987; Trevino 1987), terms for people considered similar in the United States quickly develop political connotations. The transition from "Negro" to "Black" since the 1960s, and the current debate over "Black" versus "African American," reflect similar issues. The differences between concepts of race and nationality or ethnicity are also controversial.

We struggled with these problems throughout our research. We generally use country of origin to refer to new immigrants (e.g., Puerto Ricans, Koreans, Poles), "white" to refer to established Americans from European backgrounds, "African American" for descendants of peoples from Africa, and "Latino" as a generality for Spanish-speaking populations. Since the preferred label for descendants of African slaves changed somewhat during our research and writing, we generally use "African American" throughout our text, while many of the people quoted in this work use the term "Black." Peoples from Asia are called by the group label "Asian" when necessary. Self-defined labels like "Polish American" are used when we discuss a subgroup identity for established residents of the United States that is considered appropriate for a particular context. Throughout our research we discovered street terms for different groups. Anyone who speaks Spanish is often called "Spanish," while Asian immigrants are all referred to as "Chinese." When quoting people from the community, or discussing contexts where these terms are relevant, we use colloquialisms as well. Finally, we use the term "Hispanic" in quotes where others use it or in references to accounts of events that use "Hispanic" as opposed to "Latino." While we recognize that people from Central and South America and Canada object to U.S. citizens appropriating the term "American" to describe themselves, we have chosen to use that word when necessary to refer to people in this country in an effort to keep this book as free of jargon as possible.

Such words and terms as "minority," "nonwhite," and "people of color" also have political meanings. We have attempted to avoid words like "minority," which often have a negative meaning. However, we do employ "minority" and "nonwhite" when they are the primary terms used by individuals in particular contexts or when they describe a group in a given situation. For example, African Americans constituted a numerical minority in most of the residential contexts in this study and are frequently labeled in this way.

Tracking Intergroup Relations in Philadelphia

This book examines how newcomers and established residents struggle to define themselves and make their lives in ever-changing Philadelphia. Macro-level social, political, and economic conditions combine with historically developed ideas about race, nationality, and social hierarchy to influence the thoughts and actions of people from different groups in their day-to-day lives. Our book starts with a discussion of macrolevel economic and political structures; we then look at the interaction between larger societal factors and contexts and events that occur on the local level. The first part of the book outlines the political and economic changes that have occurred in Philadelphia in the last few decades. This section also describes citywide efforts to enhance intergroup harmony, outlining the dominant actors and models that people encounter in their daily lives.

Individuals from different backgrounds attempt to make lives for themselves amid a changing economic and political scene. Citywide institutions and pervasive societal messages influence individuals' expectations of each other and the possible responses to people from different groups in a given situation. The second part of the book concentrates on neighborhoods and daily interactions among people from diverse groups. Chapter 4 describes neighborhood structures and organizations. Chapter 5 looks at intergroup dynamics in everyday life. We found that patterns differ between children and adults. The power relations of a particular institution or setting also influence interactions among people from different groups. Definitions of "insider" and "outsider" are illustrated within each context.

Chapter 6 focuses on critical events in these neighborhoods. The influence of citywide human-relations organizations plays an important role here. The ways that people structure festivals to celebrate difference incorporate both individually developed understandings of culture and dominant-society models. Community responses to crises involving race and nationality reflect internal community practices and definitions. Neighborhood residents also react to citywide attempts to define these communities by how they respond to crises or structure strategies for change.

The final part of our study examines the ways that macrolevel social and economic factors and societywide models of difference play out in the thought and action of individuals in these communities. We explore the contradictory messages that people encounter in their lives and how individuals use experience and ideas as they move through different settings. Chapter 8 suggests ways that community organizers and policymakers can use the complexity of intergroup relations described in these communities when they are developing plans for change.

PART I

The Citywide Context

CHAPTER 2

The Political Economy of Philadelphia

Several structural factors distinguish Philadelphia from other cities in the national Changing Relations Project, among them the historical dynamic between African Americans and white ethnics. In recent decades, the city has been almost evenly divided in terms of standard racial categories, a template that plays a strong role in views of difference. Yet African Americans are very diverse. Included are a disproportionate number of very poor people living in the largest number of highly segregated census tracts in the country, as well as a very large and visible middle class that has achieved increasing prominence in Philadelphia's power structure. The newcomer population is relatively small, but it is growing rapidly. While few in number, immigrants are becoming increasingly visible in the life of the city. This chapter describes how this has come about.

The very presence of immigrants, along with the relationships between new arrivals and established residents in Philadelphia, are profoundly affected by the shifts in the political economy of the city, which shape the social space and the labor market. This overview provides a history of the interrelations between economic transitions, immigration waves, settlement patterns, and politics in Philadelphia before the current influx of immigrants. In many ways, the experience of these earlier immigrants frames comtemporary interactions. The city has been constructed by an interplay of large-scale economic forces and local responses to them by business and political leaders. Recent immigrants move into this context.

Philadelphia was a major port during the colonial period and the largest industrial center in the United States until the construction of the Erie Canal in the nineteenth century. It was, in fact, one of the dominant industrial centers on the East Coast. The city continued to play a major role in the expansion of industrial capitalism in the late nineteenth century with the entry of European immigrants into an expanding economy between 1880 and 1920.

In the period between the two world wars, massive foreign immigration halted as legal barriers to it were created. At the same time, industrial expansion came to an end, and the city faced depression. It was then that a massive number of African Americans from the depressed economy of the rural South came north to the city looking for industrial jobs and entered a declining economy.

Recently, the Philadelphia Standard Metropolitan Statistical Area (PSMSA) has lost jobs and population to other regions and to other countries as a result of deindustrialization. This was followed by an economic restructuring in the region (Summers and Luce 1988). Yet this restructuring has benefited mainly the suburbs, further widening the gap between them and the central city. The misfortunes of the city (symbolized by a fiscal crisis in 1990) has generated class conflict, usually expressed as city against suburb, downtown against neighborhood, and race against race.

The city of Philadelphia has been hit harder by decline than other rustbelt cities because of the nature of its manufacturing, the extent of suburbanization, and the degree of its fiscal dependence on state and federal resources. The former manufacturing base relied on the production of nondurable goods to a greater degree than was the case in other cities. These enterprises were more sensitive to labor costs and had more movable infrastructures than durable-goods producers. In 1950, 30 percent of Philadelphia's manufacturing jobs were in nondurable goods, as opposed to a national average of 19 percent (Summers and Luce 1988).

The impact of suburbanization is relatively greater here. Much of the city's population, jobs, and tax base has relocated in the seven surrounding counties in the PSMSA. While this pattern of dispersal is typical of old manufacturing cities, a recent comparative study shows that Philadelphia has lost many more economic activities to the suburbs than forty-two comparable standard metropolitan statistical areas (SMSAs) nationwide (Summers and Luce 1988). Between 1970 and 1980, the city lost 11.9 percent of its jobs, while there was an overall gain in the SMSA. This compares poorly to a 6.2 percent average loss for central cities nationwide, showing that suburbanization has had a greater impact on Philadelphia. The exodus of residents has left the city with a population that is older, poorer, and more nonwhite than the suburban ring.

The resulting shrunken tax base has been coupled with a drastic decline in federal funding during the Reagan years. In 1979, federal revenues amounted to 25.8 percent of the city's tax base; in 1988, they were only 7.5 percent (Peirce 1990). This and a low rate of state legislative support brought about a fiscal crisis in the fall of 1990 necessitating drastic bailout policies. One contributing factor was the fact that Philadelphia relies more on its local tax base (as opposed to state or federal moneys) than any of the other largest cities in the United States. In fiscal 1980, 72 percent of the city budget was financed by its local taxes, as compared to 37 percent for Boston, 43 percent for Baltimore, 54 percent for New York, and 65 percent for Chicago (Pennsylvania Economy League 1980).

Hard hit by decline, the city also faces difficult obstacles as it plans for restructuring. With the exception of the enterprise zones, most of the current development strategies relate to high technology and the service sector as the area of greatest growth potential. Philadelphia is using the same strategies to combat deindustrialization as the other, similar cities that are its competitors. The region's history, however, illuminates some unique features that limit the possibilities of high-technology or service restructuring.

One feature is the poor position of the city vis-à-vis other cities in the Northeast megalopolis. Philadelphia competes for a dependent hinterland with obviously stronger economic or political centers like nearby New York and Washington in many potential service industries. In this contest, it has not been able to turn its central location in the megalopolis into an advantage. Instead, location becomes a disadvantage in an international strategy to revive import–export, as air transportation favors Washington and New York and bypasses the city.

Unlike Pittsburgh, the second largest city in Pennsylvania, it does not have a clearly defined region to serve, which would enhance its position as a corporate control center and help it retain locally oriented financial and manufacturing institutions. Furthermore, because of a long-term negative relationship with the state legislature and strong community opposition to new highways, the construction of statewide road and rail systems has left Philadelphia poorly situated as a port or major transportation hub for the region in comparison with such smaller cities as Baltimore. In attempts to revive decaying ports, New York and Baltimore have an advantage because of the nature of highway linkages initially created by state legislative action (Boldt 1991).

In tourism, Philadelphia lags behind Washington, D.C., Baltimore, New York, and Boston. At the time of this study, the city had no adequate supply of hotels or convention space, although the Pennsylvania Convention Center opened in 1993. The high-tech strategy of creating a research-and-development center like those in Boston and Raleigh–Durham has aided the suburbs (as in the Princeton corridor and the new industrial parks of Route 202 near King of Prussia, a secondary central business district) but not the city.

Finally, the history of Philadelphia's political-interest groups, the break-down of important alliances, and the unintended outcomes of particular local policies have weakened the glue that held the city together. Here again, while Pittsburgh has been able to forge public–private alliances to retain local capital investment, Philadelphia has been less successful. Always a place of divergent interests and heterogeneous populations, earlier forms of economy created local linkages between classes and interest groups that held the city together.

The new postindustrial economy, oriented to national and international systems of exchanges, no longer provides these linkages (Adams et al. 1991).

Economic decline in the city has not had a uniform effect on all neighborhoods, groups, and industrial sectors, however. Declining markets create opportunities for new investment in housing and small retail businesses for some newcomer groups. Increases in housing costs have made it impossible for many residents to leave their homes in the city, since they cannot afford the more rapidly increasing prices of houses in the suburbs. This stems the flight of population and slows neighborhood turnover. Smaller, more flexible manufacturing has expanded, creating jobs for many displaced factory workers. There are frequent bright spots in the overall picture of gloom and sliding indexes.

Rise and Decline

The political-economic history of the city has been well documented in the works of Sam Bass Warner (1968) and Theodore Hershberg (1981) in terms of several transformations. Each period of economic change is characterized by different patterns of immigration and spatial patterns of settlement. Seen from the perspective of the immigrant, each wave of newcomers entered a different opportunity structure in the labor and housing markets.

There are two reasons to talk about these demographic facts. First, they give us a larger view of the emerging social-interest groups in the city by showing many significant shifts: from the dominance of industrialists to bankers and insurance firms, from locally oriented capital to conglomerate capital managed elsewhere, from unionized industrial workers to nonorganized, increasingly part-time, two-tier service workers (both professional and minimum wage). Second, these trends have an impact on individual career directions, the way people perceive opportunities for themselves and their children, and how they view competition with other groups.

Originally a colonial port city, the focus of trade with England, Philadelphia developed its spatial center with residences and economic activities densely packed along the Delaware River. The original city laid out by William Penn comprised only what is today considered the downtown, popularly known as Center City. The industrializing city (1830–1880) contained one of the largest concentrations of textile, garment, carpet, printing, publishing, foundry, and machine manufacture on the Atlantic littoral (Hershberg 1981). Industrial development was confined to the original city and to the areas along the Delaware and Schuylkill rivers. In the east, industry stretched out along the Delaware just north (Northern Liberties, Kensington, Richmond) and south (Southwark, Moyamensing) of the original city. The neighborhood names refer to separate municipalities that existed before city consolidation. Other industrial activities clustered along the Schuylkill River farther west in Manayunk; these original mill towns have remained working-class enclaves.

Immigrants from Europe entered this expanding job market, with Irish and Germans coming in particularly large numbers. By 1880, 30 percent of the city's population was of Irish stock, with 16 percent being of German stock. Entering the densely packed area of the old city along with domestic rural migrants, European immigrants found that the overcrowded city provided no opportunity for ethnic clusters. Instead, the population "filled in" wherever vacancies were found. Ethnicity was relatively unimportant in accounting for settlement patterns (Greenburg 1981).

By 1880, Philadelphia had shifted from an "industrializing city" to a full-fledged industrial center with newly rationalized production systems, innovative technology, and large-scale bureaucratic organizations and a growing managerial class. The city's pride in its leadership in industrial innovation was symbolized by its selection as the site of the National Centennial Exposition of 1876, which celebrated technology.

In the 1870s, massive homebuilding occurred in delayed response to the population influx of previous decades. The existence of horse-drawn omnibuses and the new practice of multiple-home construction (tract development) brought about the rapid expansion of bedroom communities, or "streetcar suburbs," to the north and west of the former population concentration. The new middle classes emerging to manage the increasingly large manufacturing and financial institutions began to move away from the noise and nuisance of the industrial area to this newer, larger housing. Most of the existing housing units in Philadelphia were built between 1870 and the Great Depression.[1]

The new suburbs were in sections of the city that had been consolidated in 1854, when the city boundaries were enlarged to include the entire county, creating the city limits of today. The late nineteenth century was characterized by the development of citywide systems in the enlarged territory; it was then, for example, that the police and school systems came into being. With transportation networks developing around the horse-drawn omnibus (and later the electrified trolley), the rest of the new city continued to be developed.

As the labor market expanded during this period, the great immigration from southern and eastern Europe transformed the space and society of Philadelphia once again. The new immigrants clustered in ethnic enclaves around their industrial work sites. Nationality parishes provided Catholic mass in native languages and served as a basis for the proliferation of such localized neighborhood institutions as clubs, shops, newspapers, and the like (Golab 1977; Schneider 1990a).

Deindustrialization

In hindsight, the demographic trends of slowdown and loss are noticeable in the 1930s. Analysis indicates that the growth of manufacturing was reversed during the Great Depression. Industry revived briefly during World War II, but it continued to decline in the postwar period (Binzen 1970; Adams et al. 1991).

Philadelphia reached the pinnacle of its population in 1950, with a total of 2.1 million. By 1970, the number of residents was down to its 1930 size of 1.95 million, and it has continued to fall with each census. In 1940, six out of ten people in the eight-county metropolitan region lived in the city; today, the figure is three out of ten. The city lost 10 percent of its population between the 1970 and 1980 counts, and it appears to have lost another 9 percent in the past decade (*Philadelphia Inquirer*, September 16, 1990, A1, A16).

Although job loss lagged behind population redistribution, it was just as significant. While the city had almost 50 percent of the employment in the eight-county SMSA in 1970, its share had decreased to 40 percent in 1980 and to 35 percent in 1986. Moreover, this loss affected every industrial sector but one. Only in professional services was there less than the nationwide average loss of jobs in Philadelphia (Summers and Luce 1988).

Loss of population and jobs was not a matter of noticeable governmental or popular concern until the late 1960s. In industrial Kensington, the largest factory, Stetson Hats, employed five thousand people and occupied five square blocks. Its closing at the end of the 1960s was seen as a turning point, even though the downturn was several decades old. The mounting blight that accompanied the closing of factories in Kensington—high turnover, housing abandonment, dirt, vandalism, decay, graffiti—entered public discourse only in the 1970s (Seder 1990).

During the Great Depression, when economic expansion in the city was waning, a massive in-migration of African Americans from the rural South was under way. While African Americans had always lived in Philadelphia, their presence grew significantly in the 1920s and continued to grow for the next four decades. This process contributed to the construction of a racial dyad (Lieberson 1980).

African Americans accounted for 221,000 city residents in 1930 and as many as 654,000 in 1970. Since the total city population was the same in both years (1.95 million), the contrast in the proportion of African Americans in the city is striking. In 1930, one-tenth of the city was African American; by 1970, they accounted for one-third of the population. As the white population disproportionately left the city for the suburbs, by 1980 the African American population had grown to 40 percent. By 1990, the African American population in the SMSA had risen another 5 percent, and its proportion had increased slightly in the city itself. The proportional increases in the last two censuses are not due to continued in-migration but to continued abandonment of Philadelphia by whites in the context of overall population loss.

The in-migration of African Americans from the rural South occurred as the opportunity structure of the city constricted. Moreover, discrimination by employers throughout the city's history meant that African Americans were never important in the expanding industrial economy (Hershberg 1981). It is ironic that this pattern was only reversed as whites left Philadelphia and remaining industry began to recruit African Americans as industrial labor. At the very point when employment in manufacturing became most vulnerable, African American work forces expanded in industry. Thus they were less likely to benefit from the gains in job security and income achieved by the earlier labor movement.

Manufacturing was indeed hit hard, with a loss of 75 percent of such jobs between 1955 and 1975 (Adams et al. 1991). The severity of the period is partly exaggerated by the recession of the early 1970s, but 35 percent of the manufacturing base was lost between the 1970 and 1980 censuses alone. Some of the loss of industry has occurred because of general global and national trends. Many analysts point to the 1970s as the point at which a new global economic integration markedly changed the nature of the U.S. economy (Goldsmith and Blakely 1992). In Philadelphia, locally owned firms were bought by large multinational corporate concentrations of capital, and executives decided to seek cheap and nonunionized labor by relocating to the Sunbelt or offshore.

An analysis of half of the 126,000 jobs lost in Philadelphia between 1969 and 1979 revealed that while conglomerate, multinational, and absentee-owned firms accounted for about half of all industrial jobs, 68 percent of the job losses were incurred in such companies (Hochner and Zibman 1982). Other firms, severely affected by the competitive international economy, simply closed down. The garment trade was hit particularly hard by both these trends. It was once the core of Philadelphia industry—in 1880, 40 percent of the city's work force was employed in the textile and clothing sector (Adams et al. 1991). In the late 1960s, there were still 700 apparel firms in Philadelphia, with a work force of 48,000; today, there are only 14,000 workers in 200 firms (Haines 1982; Power 1988).

Other losses occurred as locally rooted firms moved to the suburban ring in search of less tax pressure and cheaper land to accommodate new production technology (Byler and Bennett 1984). The labor force was also moving to the suburbs. Familiar public policies accounted for much of the redistribution of population to the suburbs after World War II—investment in new roads and corresponding disinvestment in public transportation, and the favoring of new-home construction by federal mortgage subsidy programs and corresponding redlining or disinvestment in city neighborhoods. Ultimately, the loss of population and jobs to the suburbs has critically wounded the city's tax base, creating the decline in quality of life.

The Restructured and Restructuring Economy

The Service Sector

Today, 75 percent of Philadelphia's work force is engaged in nonmanufacturing activities in the service sector. The five major components of this sector have become increasingly important as employers in the city: FIRE (finance, insurance, and real estate), services (business, legal, health, education, and other), trade (wholesale and retail), construction, and TCPU (transportation/ communication/public utilities). The first two components are areas where Philadelphia has grown or held its own. However, the city competes with stronger corporate control centers and faces a constant threat of loss of corporate headquarters. For example, the reorganization of the banking industry through mergers has led to the loss of most locally controlled banks.

Philadelphia remains especially important as a health-care center, in higher education, and in other professional services. The city is second only to New York as a location for medical schools, with five training centers supporting more than twenty-five hospitals and ancillary institutions. Higher education is also a major industry, with Philadelphia's largest employers being two major universities. There are also a large community college and numerous small colleges.

The fastest-growing industrial sectors are services to business and legal services. Philadelphia's role as a regional corporate control center accounts for this growth. Yet here, there remains a constant threat of capital flight. As the city's tax base and job market shrinks, the credit market has also been transformed. The takeover of most major banks by corporations headquartered notably in New York, New Jersey, and Pittsburgh has both decreased local control over capital and the number of corporate headquarters in the city.

All of these service activities are symbolized by the skyscrapers that house large-scale bureaucratic structures. Employment in finance, insurance, and real estate, and in health, educational, professional, business, and other services, tends to involve two-stratum labor forces. Here, professional, managerial, and technical workers are on one level; increasingly, deskilled white- and pink-collar workers (clerical and technical information-processing workers) are on the other. Thus, service work creates different sources of interest fragmentation than existed in the old manufacturing settings. Unlike unionized skilled work, the deskilled clerical jobs provide low pay, few career ladders, and little job security.

The populations we studied worked largely in increasingly threatened manufacturing jobs or in the volatile sectors of the service economy. For the most part, they were not sharing in the gains of the professional segments of financial, health, legal, and higher-education sectors of the service economy. An exception were Indian, Filipino, Korean, and other Asian middle-class professionals who worked in health-care and engineering.

Competition for the less desirable clerical jobs tended to be between white and established African American women who entered these jobs in recent years. The workplaces in this sector had few Asians or other recent immigrants. Nor is this a significant source of employment for Latina (Ericksen et al. 1985), although we did encounter several Latina women employed in these corporate bureaucracies. In every case they had gone through public job-training programs in the 1970s. Interviews with high-school students and counselors indicate that these jobs are highly prized by contemporary Latina graduates.

Direct Services

Many Philadelphians work in activities that provide direct services to the local city population, such as retailing or social services. The large retail sector is a major city employer,[2] and it is very significant to Asian newcomers. Retailing is very sensitive to population size and has become volatile during recent population declines; between 1970 and 1980, the city and the suburbs lost 20 percent of the jobs in the sector. Two national department-store chains, two large discount-store chains, and two major food chains closed their operations in the region. Altogether, ten major retailers left, accounting for more than one-third of the 27,643 retail jobs lost. The major retail union, the United Food and Commercial Workers (UFCW), has seen a significant drop in membership. Sales jobs have also become increasingly part-time and nonunionized (Hochner et al. 1988).

The structure of retail activities has shifted as well. The development of suburban malls that attract city residents hurt both center-city department stores and specialty shops and the local shopping strips. The recent attention to revitalizing the downtown and the neighborhood strips, and the development of in-city malls, have provided incentives for both independent mom-and-pop investors and for small chains, often locally owned. Thus, in-city commercial activities are showing some new life after long decline, especially in relation to such frequently needed goods and services as food, eating and drinking establishments, hardware, dry cleaning, and the like. Immigrants are playing a major role here. The relationships between newcomer Koreans and other newcomer merchants and the established white and African American communities in which they set up businesses is heavily influenced by these commercial encounters.

Direct social services to the local population by such public-sector or nonprofit employees as teachers, social workers, postal workers, police officers and firefighters, street and sanitation workers, and other government employees provide further opportunities. However, as the population and the tax base declines, so does employment in these jobs. Direct-service jobs require some bilingual workers to serve the needs of the growing non-English-speaking populations. Latinos are heavily employed in the nonprofit social-service organizations specifically directed at their communities, which are funded by public and foundation grants. However, as hearings by the Philadelphia Human Relations Commission demonstrated, they are severely underrepresented in public-sector jobs (*Philadelphia Inquirer*, December 9, 1990). There are few Latino teachers, school administrators, police officers, firefighters, workers in the corrections system, or holders of other municipal jobs, while they are a growing presence as recipients of service from these institutions. The situation is even worse for Asians.

Construction in the region follows the trajectory of other economic activities. There was an industrial-growth spurt in the suburbs, a building boom in the city center, and a lot of work in repairing the decaying infrastructure in and around Philadelphia during the period of our research. However, this has been followed by a low occupancy rate, a glut of overbuilding, and a decline in building trades. Suburban housing has been cyclical, following interest rate cycles. Minorities, while involved in public construction as a result of "set-aside" regulations, still face exclusion in some sectors of the building trades. Like immigrants (often undocumented ones, such as Polish "visitors" or Central Americans), they tend to be involved at the lower end of the construction chain in nonunionized subcontracting work. Often, undocumented immigrants are recruited to monolingual work crews largely through personal ties.

There has also been a general decline in transportation, communication, and utilities, which directly followed crises in public funding. While established African Americans have made advances in employment in public transportation and the postal service, for example, there have been some complaints about the underrepresentation of newcomers here.

Continued Manufacturing

While it has declined as an economic activity, work in factories is still of major importance for the populations we studied. In fact, it is the most important sector of the economy for the Puerto Rican population. (Ericksen et al. 1985). Yet the kind of manufacturing that employs these workers tends less and less to be characterized by union-related protections of wages, working conditions, and job security.

Philadelphia is still important in petrochemicals and pharmaceutical manufacture, but these jobs tend to be disproportionately professional, managerial, and high-skilled technical. Furthermore, both work sites and corporate headquarters in these industries continue to be suburbanized. During the period of our study, ARCO petroleum moved its headquarters to the suburbs, and Smith Kline and Beecham (pharmaceuticals) announced plans to relocate many white-collar and manufacturing jobs.

Conglomeration, absentee ownership, and the threat of relocation still exist. Today the heart of the zone of large-scale industry is located in two centers, both near the neighborhoods studied. One focus is the Midvale/Hunting Park West zone west of Broad Street in North Philadelphia. East of Broad, there are factories north of Kensington between Erie and Hunting Park that stretch eastward from 5th Street to the strips along Aramingo and Frankford in Port Richmond. Here, many large, medium, and small factories continue to function.

Some of these (like our research site, Summit Lighting) were once locally owned but are now owned by conglomerates; Summit has just been taken over by a second conglomerate. It is feeling the results of some relocation of functions and resulting layoffs, as well as the threat of more to come. While the work force is nominally unionized, the specter of impending layoffs has reduced the clout of the union (Cohen 1994).

Two other kinds of manufacturing organizations remain important as employers. Both are related to the incipient adaptive shift in U.S. industry to flexible manufacturing, which emphasizes small plants, changing product lines, small quantities of custom-designed goods, short product runs, and augmentation through subcontracting—all of which allows the firm to minimize risk and take advantage of shifts in demand.

The first type consists of businesses that remain locally owned independents. They tend to be small and have adapted through flexible product runs. Metal fabrication and the garment industry are important examples. Many such concerns are still in the hands of families of the 1880–1920 European immigration wave, often owned by people of Jewish, Italian, and eastern European ancestry. (Very few are minority owned.) One typical metal-fabricating firm, employing 150 workers, recently celebrated its fiftieth anniversary; its leadership is being shifted from a group of second-generation brothers to the third generation. Such enterprises, while small, are much larger than those described below and are unionized. Their work forces tend to be tripartite—white, African American, and Latino, with seniority in that order.

These plants, along with several distributor/warehousing enterprises, are typical of the participants in "enterprise zones." They are the beneficiaries of a local economic-development policy involving tax breaks and other subsidies that has given them new life and political access. The zones have provided breathing room for the owners of these small manufacturing businesses, which are still vulnerable to cyclical layoffs, increasing capital intensity, and buyouts by larger firms. There are three enterprise zones in Philadelphia. Our fieldwork in Kensington involved one of these zones and its problems in relating to the surrounding community (Ninivaggi 1994).

The other kind of manufacturing organization is the competitive-sector small factory. These plants, generally involved in metalworking, woodworking, and garment production, represent the growing importance of subcontracting as a strategy allowing larger manufacturers to respond to changing demand. These enterprises are nonunion, pay piecework rates, and provide few benefits. Such firms are very important in the employment histories of Asian and Latino immigrants and of refugees from eastern Europe and Southeast Asia. Some of them are located in the older industrial areas of the city, while others are found in the suburbs (Petras, personal communication, 1990); some are owned by the families of turn-of-the-century immigrants, while others are owned by newcomer immigrant investors.

For example, a partially clandestine garment industry has developed, based on Korean and Chinese capital and newcomer Asian labor. Many Korean life histories include initial work in these firms in order to generate capital for shops. Often some family members remain in these jobs while others work in their own shops. An article by Edward Power in the *Philadelphia Inquirer*, "Asian Immigrants Lend New Life to City's Sewing Industry" (February 28, 1988), quotes the president of the Korean Businessman's Association as being aware of about thirty sewing businesses owned and operated by Koreans. Others are thought to be operating out of homes, basements, and garages and are described as employing from twenty to fifty workers of Korean, Chinese, Vietnamese, and Cambodian origin. They are engaged in subcontract work for Sears, Bloomingdales, the U.S. military, and New York garment firms.

Restructuring Social Space

As we have seen, the early-nineteenth-century immigrants were hardly clustered at all by nationality. Those of the 1880 to 1920 wave were more clustered but did not live in census tracts that were dominated by particular groups. Typical Italian or Jewish immigrants inhabited a tract with many people of their background, but not a majority (Hershberg 1981). This was even true of African Americans.

As workplace and residence became less connected in the commuter city, class and race came to dominate residential patterns. While African Americans were always more segregated than other groups, it is not until 1950 that census tracts appear that are more than 50 percent African American (Goldstein 1986). This segregation process was exacerbated by the racial polarization of suburbanization and the pivotal North Philadelphia riots in 1964, which accelerated the exodus of white residents and businesses.

Today the urban spatial structure is strongly affected by the racial dyad. Map 2 provides the location of the placenames in the following discussion. A map of the city (Map 3) reveals the increasingly stark division between African American Philadelphia in the northwest and west and white Philadelphia in the east. When the two maps are compared, the white (largely Catholic and industrial) areas can be seen in the river wards along the Delaware (Kensington, Port Richmond, Bridesburg, and Frankford) and in the former industrial areas along the Schulykill (Roxborough and Manayunk). The Northeast, an internal suburb built after World War II, retains an all-white, suburban character and houses many of those who have moved northward from the white river wards. African Americans moved into the western streetcar suburbs left by many suburban-bound whites in the postwar period.

MAP 2.   Neighborhoods in the study area.

While workplaces and schools have become increasingly integrated in the city and there is more social contact between whites, African Americans, Latinos, and Asians, there has been more resistance to integration in some residential areas. Some neighborhoods reinforce their boundaries through violence to keep outsiders from entering. Others have been rapidly depopulated and reconstituted. Disinvestment and nonmaintenance of low-income housing in North Philadelphia has created considerable pressure on the border between that African American district and the white industrial areas further

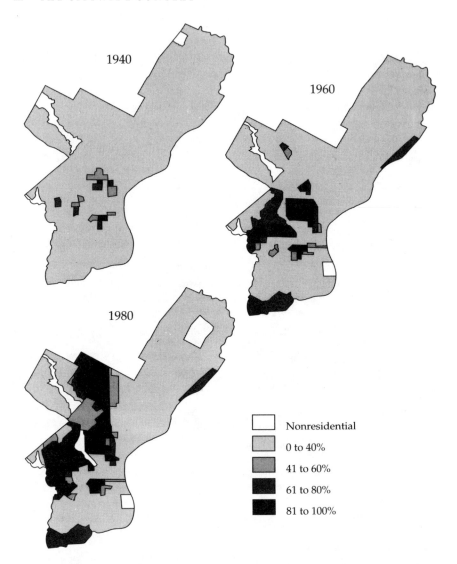

MAP 3.   The proportion of Blacks in Philadelphia neighborhoods, 1940, 1960, and 1980.
From Adams et al., *Philadelphia: Neighborhoods, Division, and Conflict in a
Postindustrial City* (Philadelphia: Temple University Press, 1991).

1990 census yielded the headline "Decades of Flight Turning North Philadelphia into a Ghost Town" in the *Philadelphia Inquirer* (April 12, 1991).

Overall, the index of segregation continues to increase in the city (Goldstein
1986, Adams et al 1991) as many all-white areas close ranks and protect their

The Political Economy of Philadelphia   43

borders through harassment of unwanted newcomers.[3] The census again showed an increase in segregation. Nearly three out of four African Americans in Philadelphia live in neighborhoods that are at least 90 percent African American. This 72 percent figure is up from 67 percent in 1980. It contrasts to a national figure of 30 percent, down from 34 percent in 1980 (*Philadelphia Inquirer*, April 11, 1991).

The city also has become more spatially polarized by class. The nature of the jobs in the restructuring economy increased the number of both high- and low-income workers, as well as the gap between them. The wealthy are increasingly isolated in the suburbs or in gentrifying areas adjacent to the city center. Meanwhile, a recent study of the growth of the very poor in the United States has indicated that Philadelphia has fared worst among the fifty largest cities in terms of the number of census tracts with high concentrations of the very poor (Hughes 1989).

Map 4 indicates the distribution of housing by cost. It reflects the division between old industrial housing, newer housing in the late nineteenth-century "streetcar suburbs," and the newest housing in the Northeast, Northwest, and the gentrified areas around the center. Except for pockets of gentrification, the older industrial housing close to the center is home to the poor. Housing becomes newer and more expensive as one moves north of the center. Thus, people in our neighborhoods associate moving "up" with moving steadily northward.

The extreme segregation of African Americans in North Philadelphia and of whites in the Northeast and along the river does not tell the entire story, however. Maps of the distribution of the population in Philadelphia by race and nationality show integration in many neighborhoods. Mount Airy and Germantown have been consciously integrated for years; in fact, the former was in the forefront of the national movement for integrated neighborhoods. While individual blocks are segregated in South Philadelphia, the entire neighborhood is a mix of whites, African Americans, and Asians, a multiracial pattern that has existed for decades. West Philadelphia is also a mixture African Americans, whites, and Southeast Asians. Our study looked closely at three neighborhoods in the eastern white Catholic zone (see Map 1); two are integrated, while the third is predominantly white. They are described in Chapter 4.

Class, Race, Power, and Development Strategies

In the 1990s, the city is trying to create political and economic strategies for development at a moment when few clear alliances between interest groups exist. As Warner (1968) points out, throughout its history as a port and an early, craft-based industrial center Philadelphia had local elites whose mercantile and industrial interests were tied to the locality and to each other. The

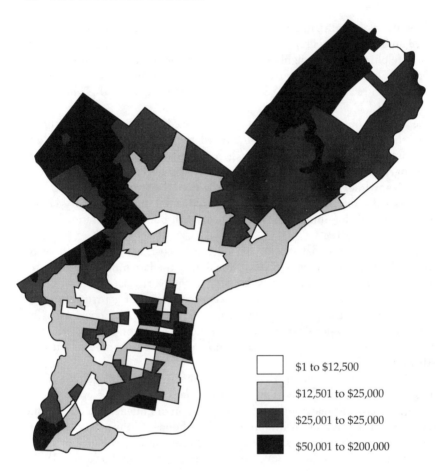

$1 to $12,500

$12,501 to $25,000

$25,001 to $25,000

$50,001 to $200,000

MAP 4.   Median housing values, Philadelphia SMSA, 1980. From Adams et al., *Philadelphia: Neighborhoods, Division, and Conflict in a Postindustrial City* (Philadelphia: Temple University Press, 1991).

history of the city is one dominated by private decisions and a lack of formal structures to link public and private interests, but the economic system of interdependencies provided a social glue creating multiple ties between workers and patrons, elites and neighborhood leaders.

Later, in the period of expanding industrial capitalism, the rampant pursuit of private interests was mitigated by the Republican machine, which brokered relations between elite owners and ethnic workers in the wards. Republican machine politics, punctuated by short-lived reform movements, dominated between 1850 and 1950. The machine mediated between the ethnic working-class wards and the business elite by providing jobs, services, and favors to the former while both allowing private interests to shape the growth of the city and sending a strong protective-tariff lobby to Congress.

The Reform Movement and Its Aftermath

Several shifts occurred after the end of World War II. First, public policy and planning emphasized the possibility of deliberately shaping cities. Second, the nature of economic change decreased the links between capital and local commitment. The reform movement of the 1950s was a watershed in Philadelphia, and it illustrates these shifts.

After the war a major break with industrialist/Republican machine domination occurred under the reformist Clark-Dilworth mayoral regimes. The reform movement, while partly a reaction to the excesses of the machine, can also be seen as the assumption of control by emerging forces produced by the shift from industrial capital to corporate services. The powerful "downtown" interests involved in reform were those corporate elites in the rising service sector: banking, insurance, large-scale retailing, and real-estate development. The Greater Philadelphia Movement, which represented them, did not speak for the formerly important manufacturers, who were organized through the chamber of commerce.

The reform administrations of 1950–62 held the postwar belief that technocracy could reverse the negative trends in the economy. Although aware of Philadelphia's declining economic position, they were optimistic that an end to graft and corruption and the replacement of the machine by technically sophisticated economists and professional planners could change the direction (Berson 1982).

Representing the new corporate bureaucracies, they espoused an architectural and planning approach to revitalizing the "city," which for them meant the downtown. Great plans were made to reconstruct the center as the site of corporate headquarters, financial institutions, business services, and retailing, which would bring people back to the city as workers, shoppers, and residents. The assumption was that benefits accruing from the enlarged pie would eventually reach everyone. The optimistic planners predicted continued growth for the city (Adams et al. 1991) in a time before the recognition of the depth of national and global economic shifts and their effects: capital flight and deindustrialization.

For a brief period, the progressive technocrats were joined by those segments of the traditional Democratic party, long out of power, that represented the white working class (ward leaders and labor), as well as by the emerging African American leadership. These new Democrats took over city government and strengthened the charter; a much-maligned machine was displaced by enlightened leaders who restructured the bureaucracies of government; and leadership of the moribund school district was taken over by an innovative progressive intent on change.

While Democrats have remained in control of city hall, the reform coalition is no longer functioning. Today, the nature of local elites and their ability to control local outcomes has changed. Very few local business elites have a serious investment stake in Philadelphia. As the economy of the city declines, major economic decisions are increasingly made by corporate leaders elsewhere, or by branch CEOs who view Philadelphia as just another step in a corporate career. More and more international money is invested in the city; at the same time, more and more Philadelphia money is invested outside the city for greater return.[4]

The once mighty Greater Philadelphia Movement, a tangible network of influential, locally committed business elites of the reform period, has given way to a sequence of similar groups.[5] Each successor, however, has contained fewer players with local interests, who come from increasingly limited sectors of the economy: leaders from the local real-estate sector, local law firms, and the few remaining companies headquartered in the city.[6] One journalist commented that only two of the twenty-two original members of the board of one such group formed in 1982 were still CEOs of the member companies. "That speaks volumes about the turmoil in executive suites here in recent years" (Binzen 1990).

The business elites who still have a stake in the city also exercise interest through proliferating nonprofit corporations (public/private partnership authorities). These operate outside the system of electoral accountability and continue to play a major role in program and policy development (Adams et al. 1991).

As absentee owners turn their backs on city concerns, they receive more and more attention from city government. In the past two decades, Philadelphia has increasingly used tax incentives to attract or retain large businesses. With increasing decline, the discourse on power relations in the city emphasizes oppositions between classes (popularly referred to as city versus suburbs, or downtown interests versus neighborhoods) or between racial groups.

Downtown versus the Neighborhoods

In the aftermath of the massive public and private capital investment in the center conceived in the 1950s and realized in the 1970s, a conflict between these "downtown" interests and the hard-hit working-class populations of the neighborhoods crystallized in public debate. Many saw the city as rebuilding itself by displacing the poor in order to build housing for the rich and lay the groundwork for further downtown gentrification. The attempts at reviving commerce in the center were seen as displacing jobs and entrepreneurs on the neighborhood strips. In the 1970s, a commuter tunnel was proposed that would link the two separate commuter rail lines to Amtrak and the airport. The plan was seen as providing benefits to suburban residents and downtown interests but diverting federal funds from the depressed neighborhoods. The same debate developed in the late 1980s around the construction of the convention center to abet the "tourism" strategy of development.

The neighborhoods movement in Philadelphia emerged in response to two forces. In the 1970s it was catalyzed by the pro-community, citizen-participation impetus of expanding federal antipoverty and community development funding, which emphasized citizen participation and community based organizations (CBOs). This pro-community impetus began in the Community Action Program of the War on Poverty; it was reinforced by the increasing mandate to award block grant funds through community based organizations defined by their community boards. Throughout the 1970s the city was divided into named communities with CDCs (community development corporations) and NACs (neighborhood action councils), many of which exist today.

The other force generating neighborhood empowerment organizations was the community empowerment activism of the 1960s associated with the work of Saul Alinsky in Chicago and its institutionalization in training programs and organizing manuals. These two forces working in concert engendered many local competing centers of power in neighborhoods, which related to the new city agencies that were replacing the traditional party structure as patrons. The conflict and accommodation between such empowerment groups and the traditional local civic groups is characteristic of white ethnic neighborhoods; it is discussed in Chapter 4.

Neighborhood activism grew as the expansion of business and legal services, health-care, and higher-education institutions accelerated gentrification in areas immediately north and south of the center of the city. Neighborhood groups in low-income areas organized to resist displacement and to seek control over their housing stock. Such nonprofits as the Philadelphia Council of Neighborhood Organizations and the Institute for the Study of Civic Values emerged to train local leaders and activists. Neighborhood groups formed alliances to fight redlining and downtown development. Today they ask for "linkage," a concept that, if implemented, would force those who benefit financially from development for the wealthier downtown constituencies to allocate a portion of their profits for the needs of the neighborhoods.[7]

The neighborhoods movement is symbolic of the fact that the old economic networks and links between owners and workers, firms and sectors no longer operate in Philadelphia. Those who remain in the city see themselves as unconnected by either patronage in the workplace, labor unions, or the ward structures of the political machine. They focus more and more on common residence as the source of "community."

Race and Politics

Religion, race, and ethnicity have always organized politics and conflict in Philadelphia. (Davis and Haller 1970). In the nineteenth century there were anti-Catholic riots in the industrial zones along the Delaware, as well as mob violence against African Americans. Nativist attacks occurred during the migration waves of 1880 to 1920. In the long run, however, the political machine, and later the reform movement, provided a mode for allocating public goods among the groups. African Americans have only been involved in this distribution since the civil-rights movement. Ironically, African Americans gained a political foothold in a declining civic order, just as they had gained an economic foothold in a declining manufacturing economy. Nevertheless, their movement into patronage jobs and positions of power has been much talked about by the inhabitants of white working class communities whose former political brokers have lost power.

During the reform movement, the races were linked in the coalition as the business elite, progressives, African Americans, and traditional white politicians of the working-class wards collaborated. However, in the 1970s, the policies of the combative administration of Mayor Frank Rizzo led to increased racial polarization in the city. The battle over the charter change that would have enabled Rizzo to run for a third term proved crucial in creating African American political consciousness and organization. It was this growing strength that undergirded the election of Wilson Goode as the city's first African American mayor in 1983. The victory was the result of a coalition between the new African American political structures and the technocrats and business elite; the white ethnic wards were often on the sidelines. In the 1980s African Americans demonstrated that they could rely on their own machine and be more independent in their dealings with downtown elites. Traditional party discipline weakened as the old coalition fractured (Morgan 1989; Adams et al. 1991).

The ascent of African Americans to power in city government has been very visible since the administration of Mayor William Green began in 1979. In addition to an African American mayor, the city council has had African American leadership during most of that time, and Constance Clayton, another African American, has acheived national prominence as the superintendent of the school district. Willie Williams, Philadelphia's first African American police commissioner, was succeeded by another African American when he was recruited to head the Los Angeles force after the 1992 riots. However, even while African Americans are becoming more visible in formerly white neighborhoods, in positions of power, in those sectors of the service economy where they come into contact with the public (public-sector jobs, transportation, retailing), and in large manufacturing and clerical bureaucracies, increasingly poorer, isolated census tracts that are almost completely African American are growing in number.

Moreover, much of the suburban population has little personal experience with African Americans. They represent only 6.5 percent of the four Philadelphia suburban counties (in Pennsylvania) in the 1990 census, an increase from 5.8 percent in 1980. Moreover, they are heavily concentrated in a few townships and boroughs (Fazllolah 1993). For many who work in the suburbs, African Americans are visible only in the media.

The communities we studies were chosen to represent places where different populations lived, shopped, worked, and learned together. They do not represent the experiences of those who live in very segregated areas of the city or the suburbs.

As we shall see throughout this book, the often perceived competition between established whites and African Americans for jobs in certain sectors of the economy, for political power and government programs, and for residential space creates a striking template that shapes views of and attitudes toward newcomers.

New Arrivals

It is into a city divided by the racial dyad and increasing class divergence that the new immigrant wave is entering. In Philadelphia, as in the United States in general after 1965, immigration is predominantly from Latin America, the Caribbean, and Asia.

The impact of this latest wave of immigrants has been relatively small in Philadelphia, largely because of the declining labor market and a poor opportunity structure. The city attracted an average of 7,117 newcomers each year between 1984 and 1986, as opposed to 92,345 for New York and 57,912 for Los Angeles (*Philadelphia Inquirer*, September 12, 1988). However, the number of newcomers who define themselves as different nationally and linguistically is considerably increased if Puerto Ricans (who are U.S. citizens) are included; they are the largest group of newcomers to the city.

Yet while relatively small when viewed against the numbers of whites and African Americans, without Asian and Latino newcomers the region would have lost population between 1980 and 1990 instead of gaining (Borowski 1991). In the city proper, the white population declined 14 percent and the number of African Americans fell by 1 percent; the Asians and Latino populations grew by 145 percent and 40 percent, respectively.

With the exception of the Puerto Rican newcomers and rural refugees from Southeast Asia, many immigrants are arriving in Philadelphia with much higher levels of education than earlier waves. Some are bringing in a considerable amount of capital. Accordingly, many of these immigrants are not entering the labor market in unskilled manufacturing jobs, as was the case with most earlier migrants and is still true for many other new immigrants. Similarly, the location of settlement is often newer suburban housing, rather than the poorest housing stock characteristic of earlier waves (Young 1989).

Puerto Ricans

The earliest wave of newcomers and that with the largest presence today are Puerto Ricans. This population began to enter Philadelphia before immigration reform. While significant Puerto Rican presence in New York City dates to the 1920s, just after the Jones Act granted citizenship, this community did not begin to form in Philadelphia until the 1950s, when agricultural workers were brought to the area to work on farms in southern New Jersey. Most of these newcomers came from the mountainous rural areas of the island (Koss 1965). The population as a whole remained small, localized, and generally invisible in the public life of the city for several decades, rising and falling in response to the relationship between economic conditions on the island and on the mainland. People moved back and forth in response to changing relative labor markets (Ericksen et al. 1985). As the island urbanized, newcomers were less frequently from rural areas, and many had urban and unskilled or semiskilled backgrounds.

The following figures are considered undercounts. Philadelphia's Latino population grew from less than 2,000 in 1950 to 7,000 in 1953, at least doubling each following decade; it reached 14,000 in 1960, 28,000 in 1970, and 64,000 in 1980 (Goode 1985). The 1990 figure showed a 39 percent increase to 89,193 (Carvajal and Borowski 1991). The community assessed the real population in 1980 to be more than 120,000, but experts on census undercounts feel that 80,000 is a more reasonable adjustment of the 1980 figure (Ericksen et al. 1985). Consequently, the 1990 figures are similarly contested and are probably closer to 100,000.

In 1970, Hispanics made up 2 percent of the population, in 1980, 4 percent, and in 1990 they have become 6 percent. One study of Puerto Ricans in Philadelphia based on 1980 figures indicated that at their present age and fertility rate the Puerto Rican component of the Hispanic population would account for more than 8 percent in 2000 based on natural increase alone (Ericksen et al. 1985). Moreover, the Latino population is clustered spatially to a very high degree. Fifteen contiguous census tracts account for 80 percent of the population (Map 5).

These figures are dominated by Puerto Ricans, who officially comprise at least 75 percent of the totals. However, the number of Colombian and Central American immigrants, both legal and undocumented, has also increased since 1980. The only Latin American nation represented in the top ten feeder countries in the INS figures for 1984–86 was Colombia, averaging 288 legal immigrants per year (*Philadelphia Inquirer*, September 12, 1988).

There are significant differences in the pattern of entry and experience among the Puerto Ricans in Philadelphia. Looking at differences in place of birth and the nature of social and economic ties to the island, three patterns predominate. First, there are homegrown "Philaricans," the offspring and grandchildren of those who took up permanent residence in Philadelphia in the

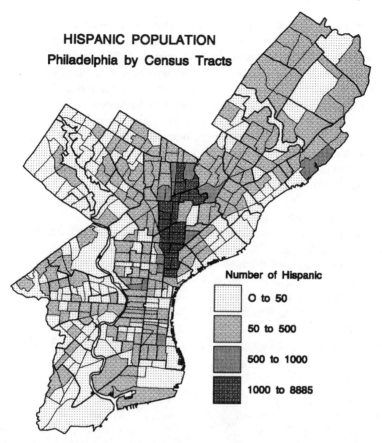

HISPANIC POPULATION
Philadelphia by Census Tracts

Number of Hispanic

	O to 50
	50 to 500
	500 to 1000
	1000 to 8885

MAP 5.   Distribution of Hispanic population in Philadelphia, 1990 census.

1950s and 1960s. This group largely contains those whose family networks have been relocated to the mainland and whose ties to the island are somewhat attenuated. The second group is made up of biresidential circular migrants, those who have maintained a pattern of movement back and forth to the island. For example, as we tried to locate "newcomers" in the communities we studied, we became aware that everyone who had come recently from the island had been here for some time before and had networks of friends and relatives in both locales. Finally, there are many Puerto Ricans who are secondary migrants from New York and New Jersey.

Koreans

When Puerto Ricans (who are citizens and not technically immigrants) are excluded, Koreans are the largest immigrant group in the Philadelphia. The INS study indicates that between 1984 and 1985 they were the largest entering group, averaging 1,082 newcomers per year. The next four highest nationality feeder countries were also Asian, with Indians averaging 738 individuals annually, Taiwan and Hong Kong 458, the Philippines 443, and Vietnam 437; Cambodia ranked seventh, with 380 (*Philadelphia Inquirer*, September 12, 1988).

The newcomer Korean population is hard to enumerate overall because individuals are not counted as Koreans but as part of the Asian category. The official number of Asians in the region listed for 1980 was 53,900; by 1990, this had more than doubled to 112,900. In the city proper, there was an even greater increase, making Asians account for 3 percent of Philadelphia's population (Borowski 1991).

The earliest wave of Korean newcomers in the 1970s were professionally educated people who entered through occupational preference. Many were professionals trained in the United States who entered the upper middle class (Young 1989). Since they brought their relatives in under the family-unification provisions of the law, the new migrants were somewhat different. While many such families had urban experience and were middle class (led by those with Korean university degrees or some university training), most professional and managerial jobs were not open to them. Accordingly, they established a route to mobility in many American cities through small business (Light and Bonacich 1988; Park 1990; Pyong Gap 1989; Young 1989).

Poles

Soviet Jews and Poles were the primary groups coming to Philadelphia from eastern Europe during the period of our study. Since most Soviet Jews settled in the city's Northeast, newcomer Poles who were first introduced to Philadelphia through Polish American neighborhoods like Port Richmond became a focus of this study. Map 6 shows the clustering of people who define themselves as Polish and includes several waves of immigration.

Unlike Latinos and Asians, the established ethnic community that Polish émigrés enter is itself the product of multiple waves of immigration, going back to the 1880–1920 period. Three major influxes of Poles to the United States occurred before the recent post-Solidarity migration: at the turn of the century, after World War II, and after 1968. For ease of reference, these four groups will be termed Polish Americans, DPs (displaced persons), the '68 Wave, and post-Solidarity. The class characteristics of each group of emigrants, as well as its economic and ethnic incorporation within the United States, has differed markedly.

Polish immigrants have been arriving in Philadelphia since the 1880s. Golab (1977, 146) reports that 31,112 people born in Poland lived in Philadelphia in 1920, approximately 8 percent of the population. The turn-of-the-century

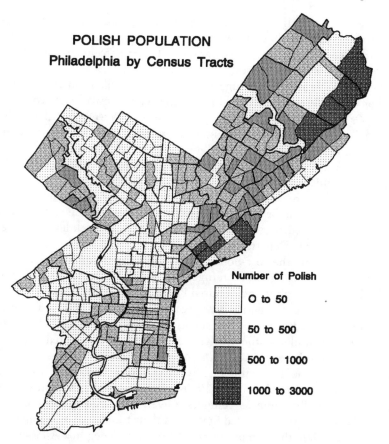

POLISH POPULATION
Philadelphia by Census Tracts

Number of Polish

0 to 50

50 to 500

500 to 1000

1000 to 3000

MAP 6.   Distribution of Polish population in Philadelphia, 1990 census.

migration of Poles to the United States consisted largely of a labor migration drawn from the peasant classes (Thomas and Znaniecki 1927; Golab 1977; Kleeman 1985; Lopata 1976; Radzialowski 1974). Once in the United States, these immigrants tended to find work in heavy industry. Most of the Polish immigrant population in Philadelphia settled in the industrial communities near the Delaware River. While the largest clusters of Polish immigrants were in Port Richmond and Bridesburg, they never completely dominated any of these neighborhoods (Golab 1977, 111–118).

The second wave of émigrés arrived in the wake of World War II and the installation of a communist government in Poland. The displaced persons included servicemen and others who refused to be repatriated to Poland after the war (Mostwin 1980, 63). This category also includes people who escaped from Poland during the early 1950s. The DP population fell into a different demographic pattern than the earlier "bread" immigration. While some of these refugees were from the peasantry, a larger percentage came from the middle and professional classes.

The '68 Wave includes refugees expelled from Poland in that year and a number of people who emigrated under the relaxed travel restrictions of the late 1960s and 1970s as Poland opened up to the West under the regime of Edward Gierek. Some of these émigrés intended to work to earn extra money to spend in Poland. These "visitors" on travelers' visas found employment in skilled, semiskilled, or unskilled positions within the working-class Polish ethnic community; some chose to stay in the United States.

This trend continues today as Poles come to the United States on visitors' visas and often extend or overstay them. During the political crises in Poland, visitors were allowed to stay in the United States and work legally under the Extended Voluntary Departure program.

The last wave are the post-Solidarity refugees. Approximately five hundred Poles came to Philadelphia as refugees between 1981 and 1985 (Schneider 1988a, 110), and roughly one hundred Polish refugees per year were resettled in the area before Solidarity was again legalized in 1989. The refugee population included a number of single men with skilled-craft backgrounds that were very similar to those of visitors coming to the United States at the same time. The refugee population also included young families in which the parents often came from the intelligentsia. Poles continued to enter the country as immigrants during the 1980s, often sponsored by family members who had originally come as refugees. Given the large number of visitors constantly coming to the United States and their transience, it is impossible at present to calculate the number of new Poles in Philadelphia. A large number of the refugees were originally settled in the Polish-dominant neighborhoods of Port Richmond and Bridesburg.

Economic Placement and Space

Given the economic decline and the spatial restructuring of Philadelphia, how are newcomers competing with established residents? While the former may compete with each other for some jobs, such as those in the informal economy, they tend to be clustered in different sectors than established residents. The new immigrants are overrepresented in some segments of the new economy and almost absent from others.

Chinese and Koreans are heavily involved as entrepreneurs in retail activities and the garment industry, using their own capital to leverage both public-sector and bank loans. They employ most of the Asians in the manufacturing and service-worker sectors. The voluminous Korean directory lists hundreds of such businesses (Goode 1994). There is also a significant

Asian presence (Indian, Filipino, Korean, and Chinese) in health care and higher education.

For Latinos, manufacturing is the largest employer of both men and women (Ericksen et al. 1985). Latinos work in both the primary and competitive sectors. In the former they rank third in seniority to whites and African Americans, a disadvantage as the multiethnic factories downsize. Latinos also work in monolingual small factories and construction crews in the competitive sector. University-educated Puerto Ricans are also concentrated in nonprofit service-delivery areas, where they tend to be segregated in jobs that serve Spanish speakers. They are underrepresented in public-sector service work and in corporate jobs.

New Poles find work as skilled craftspeople, in construction, in a variety of semiskilled service-sector jobs (such as cleaning offices), and sometimes in professional firms in the primary or secondary sectors. Many of the undocumented Poles and new refugees find work among their countrymen who emigrated to the United States after World War II or in the late 1960s.

Are there any serious issues of displacement specifically related to work? While the work of immigrants in the secondary sector has some economic impact on primary-sector jobs, we found little overt displacement in workplaces. Latino factory workers in primary-sector jobs were the last hired and first fired. It also appears that Asian retail businesses have not displaced former merchants but have instead bought stores that had been abandoned or put on the market by retiring established owners. Nonetheless, both established whites and African Americans see Asians as taking over important features of their local neighborhoods.

In Philadelphia there appear to be more overt problems with competition over residential space, shopping strips, and community control (as well as social services and minority-rights protection) than over jobs. In the 1960s, Latinos began to create a buffer zone between the white Catholic industrial areas and the African American communities further west, creating some tension between themselves and these groups. Latino clustering in this middle zone of eastern North Philadelphia is marked (see Map 5).

A majority of the predominantly middle class immigrants—Koreans and Asian Indians—are suburban bound. Those who live in the city initially settle in areas vacated because of earlier suburban flight. An example is Olney, one of the study neighborhoods that has the largest concentration of Korean (Map 7) and Asian Indian immigrants, as well as large numbers of Cambodians, Vietnamese and Chinese from Hong Kong, Taiwan, and Southeast Asia. In many cases, newcomer entrepreneurs—Koreans, Asian Indians, Chinese, and Palestinians—become significant in the revival of abandoned and declining shopping strips throughout the poorer areas of the city. However, while they continue to own shops there, they rarely live in these communities for long.[8]

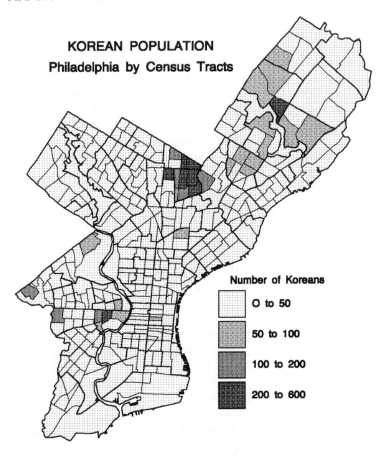

KOREAN POPULATION
Philadelphia by Census Tracts

Number of Koreans

O to 50

50 to 100

100 to 200

200 to 600

MAP 7.   Distribution of Korean population in Philadelphia, 1990 census.

Politics

So far, most newcomer groups have tried to enter into the pattern of racial and ethnic politics in Philadelphia, usually through organizations whose leaders develop patrons in city government. Recently, Puerto Ricans and Koreans have begun to use electoral politics to achieve power. New Poles are subordinate to the established Polish American community.

Since the 1950s, Puerto Ricans have moved from petitioning support from political patrons and corporations to attempts at playing coalition politics and electing their own. Recently they have also been more assertive in seeking a fair share of minority programs from mayors and governors and in making more militant demands for social change.

In the 1970s, a group of young professionals using civil-rights legislation sought to redraw political units to achieve electoral representation. A suit to revise state senate electoral boundaries signaled the beginning of an electoral strategy. Seeing possibilities in minority coalition politics, secondary migrants from New York and New Jersey who had experience in coalition politics tried to establish such alliances to elect their own representatives. By 1984 there were three Puerto Rican elected officials: a judge, a state senator, and a councilman at large. All of them had come from New York. Having elected officials has given the community official, authoritative spokesmen and provides a visibility that did not exist before.

While the state senator benefited from the new political boundaries, the at-large city councilman does not represent a specific district and was elected through coalition politics (an alliance with African American Democrats, having Mayor Goode's support).[9] Yet there are inherent weaknesses in this coalition strategy, since African Americans have already established their own independent voice within the party.

An example is the 1990 case of a Puerto Rican who ran unsuccessfully for office against a white incumbent in a district divided evenly among Hispanic, white, and African American voters. The latter groups had already accommodated each other in the local ward and committee structures, so the Puerto Rican could not appeal to African Americans as a common oppressed minority.

Over time, relations between Goode and the community became strained. The community sought a fairer share of "minority resources" through a task force on Puerto Rican affairs established by the mayor in 1983. The group commissioned a statistical analysis to establish the need for more antipoverty, social-service, and affirmative action programs. This forced specific comparisons to the social condition of African Americans. The report on the state of Puerto Ricans in Philadelphia (Ericksen et al. 1985) showed that they were worse off than either African Americans or whites on almost all social indicators (housing, employment, schooling, and health). The task force resigned en masse in 1988, citing the fact that the report had been passed off to low levels of government rather than to any policy-making level with teeth.[10]

Some Puerto Ricans argue that they provided the margin of victory for Goode in the close 1987 mayoral election and received nothing in return. They will no longer support candidates who do not speak directly to their specific issues. For example, in spite of the hostility toward the incumbent district attorney in the election of 1990 because of his actions related to two murders (see Chapter 6), Puerto Ricans threatened to "cut" his opponent by having street workers refuse to support him in their community because the opponent did not make an explicit public statement supporting their position on this issue.

The failure of the Goode administration and the African American power structure to be responsive to the community has diminished the African American–Puerto Rican coalition at the level of public collective action. Many Puerto Rican leaders feel that African Americans have reaped all the advantages of civil rights and affirmative action and are no longer in the same boat as they. They point to the social statistics that show their relatively poor position vis-à-vis both whites and African Americans.

While Koreans used their economic power to gain access to government on issues related to their small-business interests, unlike Puerto Ricans they were not already citizens and are still not a visible presence in city electoral politics. In 1991, the first Korean ran, unsuccessfully, for nomination to city council in the primaries. Like the Puerto Rican before him, and for similar reasons, he ran for the council at large rather than in a district. Control of council districts cannot be won without favorable demographics and party clout. The candidate had made citywide contacts through the major human-relations institutions. His English skills had given him a major role in conflict resolution, which led to major offices in the citywide Korean business association. This, in turn, resulted in his appointment to the Human Relations Commission and to the Mayor's Commission on Asian Affairs, where he made significant political contacts.

Paralleling the Puerto Rican case, the Korean candidate sought endorsements from African American leader through his associations with the mayor and city agencies. In his campaign, he often cited Koreans' common interests with African Americans as minorities who are victims of racism. Yet his financial base put him in a different position from Puerto Rican candidates. Well aware of the local and national media coverage of African American–Korean conflict, he downplayed the emphasis on tension and appeared everywhere with an African American entourage. He also often minimized his support from the Korean community, saying that while Koreans supported him morally they were not backing him "physically" (financially and electorally) since the community had little interest in politics.

This was a tricky strategy. Hearing stories about problems between Koreans and African Americans before they emigrate, many newcomer Koreans internalize aspects of U.S. racism early. This is reinforced by their experiences in low-income African American neighborhoods, where conflictual economic relationships are an important aspect of community life. Yet Koreans are aware of the importance of African Americans in the city power structure and of their mutual minority status. Thus, visible support of the African American community through ceremonies and scholarships is one response (see Chapter 3). Koreans have also considerably increased their politically oriented activity since it is crucial to improving their position vis-à-vis the police and other citywide agencies.

Thus, racial politics in Philadelphia has affected the electoral strategies of both Puerto Ricans and Koreans who seek African Americans as political allies. For Puerto Ricans, this involved recapitulating experiences in New York and New Jersey politics, with limited success. For Koreans, local political realities created a contradictory relationship between them and African Americans.

The interplay between the Polish American organizations and Philadelphia's power centers is also complex and contradictory. On the one hand, these white ethnics complained that the city's power structure catered to minorities rather than to established ethnic groups. When the city lent the Polish American umbrella organization money to buy a building, community members refused to cover the loans. The ethnic paper was filled with letters suggesting that since money is simply given to African Americans and Hispanics, why not the Poles, too? At the same time, leaders of these organizations have played the ethnic game as much as possible, using the voting clout of their community to garner funds from the city. The building loan itself is one example.

The emphasis on racial/ethnic politics limits the incorporation of newcomers into neighborhood-based structures, even though they tend to be clustered by neighborhoods. Neighborhood activists often see common problems and try to use them to link residents from disparate backgrounds. However, since federal programs also fund similar housing, community-development, or community-health programs through origin groups based on race, language, or nationality, these often compete with territorial groups for funding and loyalty. For example, much of the financial support in the clustered Latino geographical community in Philadelphia is received by groups defined as Spanish speaking rather than as territorial neighborhood organizations. Korean service centers have also emerged and are competing for the same public, foundation, and church funds. The fact that attempts to get funds for teaching English to new Poles have sometimes failed because of eligibility requirements exacerbates the conflict. These contending bases for categorizing population and channeling services compete for an increasingly limited pie and decrease the degree to which neighborhood groups can effectively incorporate newcomers into multicultural local structures.

The Future of the City

A recent analysis of the political economy of Philadelphia emphasizes the increasing fragmentation of the region. There are major cleavages between: (1) the declining city and the increasingly separatist suburbs; (2) the interests of the downtown service economy and the residential neighborhoods; (3) the professional, managerial upper middle class (inhabiting suburban and gentrifying zones) and the rowhouse dweller who has lost income level, job security, and career ladders; and (4) the established white and African American city dwellers (increasingly joined by new Asian and Latino populations) competing for work, space, and power within a context of decline.

At the same time, neither traditional economic nor political linkages remain to hold the disparate parts together. This analysis argues that the city cannot be saved by economic development alone. Increasing the pie will not work unless the fragmentation and lack of connectedness between classes, neighborhoods, racial and ethnic groups, and, above all, city and suburb is reversed. The new service economy creates wide disparities between rich and poor. Unless there are more structures of collaboration, cooperation, and linkage within the economy and polity, there is no bright future for Philadelphia (Adams et al. 1991).

The Effects of New Immigration on Social Categories and Human-Relations Institutions

In the 1970s, new immigrants arriving in Philadelphia entered a setting that defined social difference by experience with turn-of-the-century immigration from Europe and by relationships between African Americans and whites. As the effects of immigration reform brought more newcomers to the city, new possibilities for social differentiation, conflict, accommodation, and coalition emerged. This chapter describes the ways in which the racial dyad and the model of cultural pluralism affected the categorization of new immigrants and, in turn, how experience with new immigrants affected the perception of the racial dyad and the pluralist model.

Notions of difference are socially constructed on several levels from such particular attributes as race, nationality, or language. They are generated privately and locally, as well as in more formal institutional contexts. The development of citywide human-relations institutions leads to the construction of social categories that filter down into popular use. These groups, first created in the context of increasing racial division and the celebration of ethnicity, use racial and cultural categories developed for an earlier city. We look first at the categories and institutions of these citywide agencies and established residents. Next, we describe how new immigrant communities respond by creating organizations, alliances, and strategies to manipulate existing discourses about social difference.

Human-Relations Organizations

As an important seat of the Society of Friends and the Reconstructionist movement within Judaism, Philadelphia has long supported groups like the

Fellowship Commission and the Urban Coalition. Brotherly love was an expressed ideology of the Society of Friends at least since the time of the founding of the city by William Penn. The confluence of the Quakers and large, well-organized communities of Jews and African Americans created a significant focus on human relations for most of the twentieth century.

These institutions set the tone for the preferred pattern of racial and ethnic relations in the city. Most human-relations organizations rely on the model of cultural pluralism, often adding elements from the structural-racism model. All groups emphasize equality and the value of diversity, and most human-relations activities stress both group achievements and the importance of the individual. While they encourage a focus on group identity to establish pride, the organizations admonish everyone to avoid stereotyping groups and to judge individuals instead. As we will see in Chapter 7, this creates contradictions.

Christian models tend to emphasize the value of each individual, as exemplified in the Quaker tenet that the light of God is in every person. Jewish-centered programs, on the other hand, focus more on the value and contributions of groups and see society as made up of these autonomous groups or communities. This reflects the Jewish sense of peoplehood and concerns about historical oppression and the rights of groups. African American programs address the same issues: developing a sense of peoplehood, overcoming oppression, and protecting rights.

Even before the creation of public agencies like the Pennsylvania Human Relations Commission and the Philadelphia Human Relations Commission in the wake of the civil-rights movement, a private organization existed in the city to serve as a watchdog against discrimination. The Fellowship Commission, established in 1947, has long been instrumental in promoting equal justice and fair elections. It has also lobbied for the creation of commissions in Pennsylvania and in Philadelphia to enforce human rights.

The city's commission on human relations was founded in 1952 through regulations set out in the Philadelphia Home Rule Charter. Today it is divided into two sections: compliance investigates complaints and has broad investigatory and subpoena power; community services utilizes field operatives whose mission is broadly described as prevention (identifying potential trouble spots) and education on the street. This division is active in the aftermath of incidents as well.

With the advent of the civil-rights movement a large number of organizations developed to protect civil rights by preventing or intervening in situations of discrimination or abuse. They played three basic roles: enforcing new antidiscrimination laws in response to individual complaints, intervening in crises, and trying to prevent incidents by promoting tolerance through education. During this period of intense governmental focus on race, the North Philadelphia riots of 1964 and the movement of whites to the suburbs created a spatially divided city in which the world was seen as Black and White.

Other organizations in Philadelphia have recently broadened their activities to include intergroup-conflict resolution and a focus on education as a way of breaking down stereotypes and increasing intergroup awareness, understanding, and respect. For example, two groups that developed in the late 1960s to deal with African American gang problems have adapted their roles to contemporary intergroup disputes. There is also a Cardinal's Commission on Human Relations in the archdiocese.

Groups like the Urban League or the Anti-Defamation League of B'nai B'rith, often founded to protect one population, have broadened their mission to involve the new diversity of the city. The Jewish Community Relations Council, for example, developed programs mostly to maintain links between African Americans and Jews, but it sent a representative to speak at a meeting of Puerto Ricans reaching out to other groups for support.

The Human Relations Commission began to recognize the increased diversity in the city in the late 1970s. Latino field representatives were hired then; Asians were not taken on until 1988, after hearings on their community revealed the need. In 1990, out of seventeen community service operatives, there were five Latinos, one Russian speaker, and five Asians (one each Cambodian, Vietnamese, Laotian, Chinese, and Korean), as well as six established whites and African Americans.

New efforts by several citywide cultural institutions to encourage cross-group interaction emerged in the late 1980s. These included a citywide project by a consortium of a dozen museums, many training workshops for teachers by cultural organizations, and a citywide folklore project.

The activities of Philadelphia's human-relations practitioners created a dense network of people who work together and refer groups and clients to each other. Some have ties with the school district, and some work with other city agencies. A few practitioners have set up independent consulting firms to take advantage of the market for multicultural training in the private and public sectors.

Each new initiative brings together the close-knit network of human-relations specialists and the informally recognized spokespersons or brokers from the newcomer communities. In the same way, the accumulated repertoire of techniques for dealing with intergroup problems becomes widely shared and utilized.

Targeting Children

Programs to teach harmony and prevent conflict often concentrated on young people, who were seen as more flexible and open than adults. Specialists and the general population implicitly assumed that stereotypes were taught to children at a young age and, thus, that programs were needed to purge learned racist attitudes. One example is a group founded in 1957 by a member of the

Society of Friends; it developed programs for local schools and now aims to implement them in other states. Another local institution developed to provide a farm locale into which school or neighborhood children could be brought for several days to talk meaningfully to each other in an attempt to reduce conflict and increase understanding.

Most multicultural efforts for children were brief, involving assembly programs in school or workshops that lasted a few hours or, at most, a day. Very few programs created sustained intergroup relationships. One exception was an inner-city program, founded in the wake of some interracial violence fifteen years ago, that organized heterogeneous teen groups. Using staff members who were former participants, this program sustained the experience of intergroup relations longest within a context that encouraged both talking about difference and jointly pursuing goals. We will examine this latter strategy of bringing people together to deal with issues that are important in their everyday lives more fully in Chapter 8.

Working on the Mind

Developed largely to deal with relationships between African Americans and whites, human-relations organizations often use generic human-development practices to root out racism. These borrow from Gordon Allport's ideas about prejudice as a phenomenon of individual thought. The underlying goal of such programs emerged from the human-development groups of the 1960s, which emphasized strengthening egos and building self-esteem in the belief that making better people would facilitate the development of mutual understanding. The emphasis was on what was inside people, their ideas and feelings. The most important step was getting in touch with oneself.

Racism was assumed to be a latent element in the mind that needed to be purged. One citywide human-relations consultant is known for the phrase "Say UH-OH to the uh-oh"; it implies that everyone thinks biased thoughts, and that only by constant internal censorship (saying "UH-OH") can these dangerous thoughts be purged.

In order to make people sensitive to their racist feelings, human-relations organizations sponsored workshops to train public officials and neighborhood volunteers. One involved icebreaking games and making contact within a small, artificially constructed group, both literally (through touching) and figuratively (through self-revelatory games). Another workshop tried game techniques to build self-esteem and make people feel good about themselves. Others used techniques that encouraged people to explore their innermost feelings or to develop empathy by "putting yourselves into another group's shoes" through role playing and rapping. Here it was asserted that everyone was a victim of some kind of "ism"—sexism, ageism, classism, or racism—and could, in "touching base with their feelings," become empathetic to others. It was assumed that these brief experiences outside the context of everyday life would transform an individual's self-awareness and consequent behavior. While intense rituals can have a transforming effect on people's construction of reality, these experiences were too brief, too unrelated to issues of ordinary life, and lacked intensity. Such activities assumed that the causes and cures of racism were related to intrapsychic processes somehow isolated from ongoing social life, social structure, and external pressures.

Increasing Social Contact

Another central belief was that racism resulted from a lack of contact, knowledge, and experience of others. This could be remedied by satisfying person-to-person experiences, which would quickly translate into intergroup understanding. A common practice was to bring conflicting parties together and develop closeness between them by retiring to a neutral place and allowing them to develop some personal intimacy and to talk intensively about their feelings. While this can sometimes make a difference, the assumption that contact would lead to automatic solutions was overdrawn. For example, in commenting about a retreat picnic suggested to bridge the gap between whites and Latinos, someone said, "That's a good idea; they will eat each other's food and friendships will develop."

The Growing Significance of Cultural Differences

The skills and techniques developed in the 1960s were usually generic, designed to be applied across all groups. The advent of newcomers shifted the focus to cultural differences, which had negative as well as positive results. As immigrants and refugees entered Philadelphia, a new interest in multicultural- ism developed, generating contradictory ideas about what culture means.

Human-relations organizations responded to new immigrants with a strong endorsement of cultural pluralism. One group's slogan was Let Cultural Diversity Make a Positive Difference. Reflecting the postmodern romanticiz- ing of the exotic "other," one workshop leader urged the audience to approach multicultural situations "as if you are going into a museum looking for treasures." A teacher in a multicultural school said of herself and her fellow teachers, "We feel blessed to have so many cultures here." The implicit value in diversity was that it enriched the individual by broadening her or his world and enriched society through the cultural contributions of new, culturally exotic groups. These were often seen as more naturally and genuinely human than Americans living a soulless modern urban life.

In the official celebration of cultural difference, culture was limited to the same safe areas of group style (food, music, art, dance, and theater) that had become the public markers of third- and fourth-generation ethnic groups who lived predominantly "American" lives colored by occasional displays of ethnic culture. This limitation ignored the fact that immigrants were different in many other aspects of "values" and behavior that were seen as sources of problems.

Many programs assumed that the more one learned about the expressive content of the culture of conflicting groups the faster harmony would be induced. Underlying these performance events was the assumption that sensory experiential exposure would create understanding and respect. We call this approach the "culture at a distance" performance.

One coordinator of such programs expressed her belief in their power:

> . . . as people come together, meet each other . . . stereotypes will be done away with. [They] relieve tension and help people know how to interact with each other. [Other people] see them as human beings and concerns will be settled as people experience and enjoy diversity.

These performances occurred throughout Philadelphia for large citywide audiences; ethnic festivals, for example, were held weekly over the summer along the center city waterfront. They were also important in many local settings where tensions existed. While cultural performance can be a strong element in developing pride for the performing group and an emotional connection with the audience, much depends on who controls the event, how symbolic meaning is constructed, and who the audience is (see Chapter 6).

Established human-relations specialists often had certain romantic expectations of native culture. For example, at one event a Catholic Indian girl sang a hymn in English as she had indeed learned it in India. This reflected the cultural realities of a British influence in her homeland; the Catholic church in her state of Kerala operated partially in English, and her life was lived in a bilingual system. She chose the hymn because it was part of her heritage and had special meaning to her. Yet the organizers expressed dissatisfaction that she did not sing a song in her Indian language. At another event, a Puerto Rican group chose to sing an American popular song as part of their ethnic presentation. They were rebuked by the organizers for not providing a traditional Spanish song from "their culture," although the piece they sung was part of the actual popular culture of the island. At the next event they were asked to only sing songs in Spanish.

In addition, the ways of presenting these aspects of culture had evolved over time, so that they were often produced, packaged, and performed by professionals and semiprofessionals who circulated around the city. Ethnic museums and other citywide heritage institutions were ready to respond with material. Even locally developed resources soon became part of the citywide resources and grew semiprofessionalized. A teacher in one school created seven dance groups, representing both immigrant and established ethnic populations. She asked for help from adult volunteers from the groups, but she often had to rely on her own library research to re-create dances and costumes no longer part of people's lives. This was especially true for established ethnic groups. Her efforts were recognized by many citywide organizations, and she won a Spirit of Philadelphia award from a local television station. As her groups began to perform around the city, there was irony in the fact that these performances representing other cultures had been constructed by a middle-class African American. Throughout the city, as performances became more professionalized and packaged, fewer and fewer individuals participated in designing their own cultural expressions and most people were relegated to the audience.

The other major way in which culture was used was to reduce it to differences in communication styles—kinesics (body movement, eye contact) and proxemics (comfortable physical distance in interpersonal communication)—which were described through simple rules. As we talked to city officials and neighborhood leaders the influence of human-relations training was clear. Cross-cultural conflict was easily reduced to body-language miscues. For example, one community leader stated that Asian concepts of space were entirely different from those of the West and that this was the basis for almost all the problems between Asians and established white ethnics in his neighborhood.

There were two problems with this approach. First, it ignored all the structural bases for conflict. Second, even for understanding miscommunication, this oversimplified information did not deal with the importance of contextual variables of place, time, gender, and social hierarchy in communication. Providing a simple list of traits relating to distance between speakers or body language did not reveal accurate or useful specifics.

Creating Confusion about Culture

There are two fundamental problems with these cultural approaches. First, they are based on a view of culture as a static phenomenon practiced uniformly and transmitted without change from generation to generation rather than as dynamic and changing adaptations. The cultural-pluralism theme is based on the assumption that everyone is a member of "a culture," a way of life unchanged over time and clearly distinguished from other ways of life creating an essential, "natural," primordial identity. Cultures become reduced to a list of traits so that they can be easily taught to others. Such cultural traits frozen in time reinforce the notion of boundaries and division; culture is seen as ingrained and hard to change. Cultures become *essentially* and permanently different from one another, creating divisions that cannot be breached.

Anthropologists have abandoned such static, rigid notions. They define culture more as an outcome of process, with groups constructing a way of life in response to constantly changing conditions. Since each change necessitates new responses, national cultures are different at different historical moments. The English hymn and the U.S. pop song mentioned above are part of these immigrants' respective "cultures." Entering a new milieu as an immigrant also engenders modification and adaptation.

Moreover, individuals are situated differently within culture by such characteristics as gender, age, and place in the social hierarchy and the social geography. Their experiences and responses vary. Yet the need for quick generalizations for social-service workers about *the* Puerto Rican woman or *the* Korean family generate outdated or oversimplified cultural descriptions. Many human-relations workers who are aware of these complexities try to develop appropriate models but complain that clients want simple checklists that can be easily learned.

The newer view of culture as a process explains why current Polish refugees come from a very different background of experiences than their Polish American counterparts. The latter left Poland when it was a peasant society, and thus it is difficult to create a single "Polish culture" with which both groups would identify (see Chapter 6). Similarly, Puerto Ricans who grew up on the island and those who are secondary migrants from New York might have very different pictures of Puerto Rican "culture."

Cultural boundaries also shift through time. Italian migrants coming to the United States between 1880 and 1920, when Italy was only an incipient nation-state, had regionally based dialects, food patterns, and identities. For a Sicilian to marry a Calabrian was seen as crossing group lines. Yet over generations in the United States an ethnic identity based on nationality and language was forged, partly through dynamics inside the group and partly through external pressures (Goode, Curtis, and Theophano 1984). Ethnicity and ethnic identity are complex, dynamic phenomena.

Second, the concept of culture can be used as easily to point out similarities across groups as to point out differences. When one Puerto Rican woman remarks that her Black Caribbean friends also eat a dish like *mondongo* and her Italian friends also use *baccala* (dried, salted cod), she is employing similarities to feel a kinship with her different friends. Yet culture-at-a-distance performances often seek dissimilarities, as when Puerto Ricans are asked to emphasize their differences by singing songs in Spanish or Indians to avoid English hymns.

Macrocategories

In today's discourse on cultural pluralism, there are pressures to simplify the new cultural diversity even further by using the four major categories of difference that were politically emergent and legitimized by government after the civil-rights era: white, African American, Hispanic, and Asian. Three of these are based on race, and one on language. This kind of thinking among leaders and educators was what led to errors in a citywide teaching guide on the culture of Puerto Ricans.

The booklet had been prepared without any Puerto Rican advisers and obviously was constructed in terms of an outsider's notion of a pan-Latino culture rather than a Puerto Rican one. The booklet created a major incident:

> Rushing to fill a mandate to implement a multicultural curriculum . . . officials handed out a teaching guide about Puerto Rico that was filled by errors. It said tacos and tamales, Mexican foods, were from Puerto Rico. It misidentified the native Indians of Puerto Rico and said Dominican Republican baseball stars were from Puerto Rico. (Barrientos 1991)

However, even the use of native experts does not always ensure accuracy. At a conference to prepare social-service personnel to deal with diverse cultural groups, the authoritative "native" trainers often adopted the posture of the health-care institutions they worked in and depicted Puerto Rican or Asian behavior patterns negatively in contrast to dominant white patterns. "Puerto Ricans are very nervous and emotional," said a Puerto Rican workshop leader; "Asian women are too quiet and submissive," said a Vietnamese facilitator.

The official macrocategories also shape the views of established residents on the street. Such folk categories as "Spanish" for all Latinos or "Chinese" for all Asians are often used in everyday discourse by all groups, whether newcomer or established. For example, like their established neighbors, many Puerto Ricans refer to all Asians as "Chinos," and Koreans refer to all Spanish speakers as "Spanish."

The need to simplify underscored a strong resistance to more specific labels. One white ethnic, when asked whether she knew of different nationalities among Latinos, said, "I don't separate them that way. The Spaniards are Spaniards. I don't ask where they are from."

The official nature of macrocategories makes many people think they must reflect real social groupings and that when groups assert national identity they are just making trouble. One established leader suggested that it would be easier for both Asians and established residents if Asians would form a group. Speaking of Koreans in her neighborhood, she said:

> They're not the only Asians here. Why can't they have an Asian culture center instead of a Korean Center and Cambodian Center? They should all work together. We don't say Koreans, Cambodians—we say Asians when we have a problem with them. . . . I think the Asians should get together and form a group instead of being separate.

Yet an awareness of the historical conflicts and unequal power relations between many Asian nations, their different experiences with colonialism and the cold war, and the different patterns of entry of their peoples to the United States as refugees or immigrants would show that this grouping is not natural at all.

If nationality labels themselves are too inclusive—overlooking self-defined tribal and ethnic groups, as well as class and regional differences—

macrocategories further obliterate the importance of particular immigrant cultural identities.

Following the pluralism model, with its assumption of national or macro-category uniformity, it is easy for human-relations specialists to see new immigrant peoples as living in homogeneous and bounded entities based on either the four macrocategories, the language they spoke, or their nation of origin. Ignoring vast differences within these populations, they identify spokesmen or brokers within each presumed community. As indicated below, such assumptions overlook considerable differences (and often histories of enmity and conflict) within the macrocategories. They frequently generate resistance by groups who want to define themselves.

Unofficial Views of Cultural Difference

All of the accepted cultural programming is oriented to the safe areas of "customs", (i.e., expressive performances, or food and holiday celebrations) or to communication styles. It avoids the problem areas of behavior, where "values" and ideas of moral inferiority and superiority are implicitly evoked. Yet these are of central concern to those encountering different groups. Here the idea of culture is often used unofficially to give license to talk and think about difference in potentially dangerous ways.

Established residents often use the concept of culture when talking about social differences. However, unlike official cultural pluralism (which implies relativity, since all cultures are supposed to be equal), established residents often talk about cultural difference to place a veil of civility over moral judgments. When they wish to discuss negative behaviors of newcomers without sounding racist, established residents will talk about "cultural" dissimilarities. Culture can thus cover a multitude of sore spots and yet avoid race and class issues. Culture, not class, is used to explain problem behavior; this ultimately makes it easier to generate both positive and negative stereotypes without sanctions.

When one woman criticized Portuguese children for bringing junk food to school, she said, "I guess it is their culture." When two white working-class aides in preschool talked about two disruptive children from Latin America, one said, "That's the way the schools are in their country; they have no rules or discipline, that is just their culture." Thus, differences are explicitly discussed as value-neutral, in spite of an implicit message that many behavioral dissimilarities are not equally valid.

It is ironic that both newcomers and established residents assert an exclusive claim to stronger family values based on cultural difference. Immigrants often allege that their close-knit family ties make them different from and morally superior to other Americans. An example of this contrast occurred when an established Puerto Rican, translating in school for a newcomer Colombian, was incensed by a white teacher's failure to recognize the primacy of family obligations among "Hispanics."

> We are tight-knit in our families and we take our children to and from school every day. If another child is sick or someone is in the hospital or the mother is in the homeland taking care of a sick relative, the child may arrive at school late or not at all. However, unlike Americans, we are not laid-back and we protect our children and honor our family responsibilities; if the school does not understand, I will send my child elsewhere.

Similarly, a Korean college student contrasts Korean "deep love" to social relations in the United States:

> Americans are too individualistic. As we say, they have no "loving closeness" like the Korean way. For many years I have felt that Americans were less feeling people, not capable of caring for each other as deeply as we do. For a long time I did not believe that Americans were people just like me.

Thus all Americans are seen as individualistic and not family oriented (based on the model of professional, middle-class behavior), in spite of the very tightly knit kinship networks of most of the working-class or aspiring middle-class established families we encountered in all three neighborhoods.

In fact, established working-class women offered a similar discourse on the materialism and lack of family orientation among newcomers, based on their experience with immigrant women who used them as babysitters or who did not participate in schools and organizations. These were upwardly mobile professional women or those who worked in family enterprises. They were seen as too materialistic, working instead of nurturing their families, and buying their children's love with material things. Both groups confuse the exigencies of class-based mobility strategies with national or ethnic norms of family.

The emphasis on culture masks the importance of class differences among those with nationality or linguistic cultural backgrounds in common. Since many of the conflicts that human-relations programming was meant to prevent were based on class differences, identifying them as stemming from a lack of cultural understanding often missed the target.

"Minorities"

Like "culture," the word "minority" is also invoked to criticize others without talking about race. The term "minority" is officially intended to delineate nonwhite racial groups defined as historical victims of discrimination. However, it is often invoked to talk about any group of people who are socially different from the speaker, or it is used as a general term for the disadvantaged or the poor. The following statement about new immigrants in general uses "minority" to refer to outsiders who are considered lower in status and who do not know the rules.

> We expect them to learn to take care of their houses, to clean up the trash and keep the noise down. Just because they are minorities is no excuse. It is degrading to them to say that they don't have to learn the rules and behave like good neighbors.

This statement subtly connects the notion of "minority" to the view that different "others"—the underclass, other races, and foreigners—are being helped to avoid their social responsibilities by overprotective government programs that let them "get away with" inappropriate behavior instead of teaching them the rules.

Class

As is typical in the United States, class as an explicit social category is avoided in both official and popular discussions of social difference. This makes it very easy to focus on racial and cultural dissimiliarities in conflict situations. The cultural-pluralism theme is all about cultures as homogeneous; the structural-racism theme uses race as a category, with no attention to class difference.

The working-class, established residents we studied see themselves as middle class, but for them this means being squeezed in the middle, between rich and poor. For them, the rich are those in control—"downtowners," "suits," the professionals and managers in city government and the workplace. The poor are those who are dangerous, disreputable, and threatening. As one woman said,

> We're ordinary folks, not Society Hill [the first gentrified downtown area, a symbol of wealthy people with power] or Richard Allen Homes [a notorious public-housing project].

Another identified with her upwardly mobile immigrant neighbors when she said:

> They're just like us. They're not born rich or married rich. They have to work their butts off, scratch and claw just like the rest of us.

As we will see in later chapters, established residents subtly evoke class over race or cultural-pluralist categories when they talk about white trash and point out that their African American neighbors refer to some of their "own kind" who behave badly as "street niggers." For example, an upwardly mobile African American said he would leave the neighborhood if "niggers" moved in. One Puerto Rican woman was really talking about class in the following interview excerpt:

I don't like the Spanish—they're too loud and noisy.

Q.   But all of your close friends are Spanish, aren't they?

A.   Yeah, and they don't like the Spanish either.

She was using the label "Spanish" for a stereotype about poor Puerto Ricans that she accepted. She and her friends were all Puerto Ricans and proud of it, but they dissociated themselves from the stereotype of Puerto Ricans based on lower-class behavior.

Established residents also implicitly evoke class when they admiringly point out the respectability and professional standing of their African American and immigrant neighbors.

Dominant Media Images

The citywide media contribute to the views of newcomer groups. Group stereotypes emerge from the fact that most Puerto Rican coverage is generated by conflict situations and demands for equal justice, while Asians are often talked about in terms of success, educational achievement, and bringing back "American" values of family and hard work, which are disappearing.

As a favored "model immigrant" group, Asians are sometimes seen as the hope of the city by public spokespersons for downtown interests. An editorial about saving the city in *Philadelphia Magazine* (Lipson 1989, 1), which serves a professional and managerial population, stated:

> In practically every neighborhood of Philadelphia, you will now find thriving
> Asian small businesses. The men and women who spend 18-hour days in
> these storefronts are driven by the ethic of hard work; they sustain themselves
> through close family relationships. People . . . marvel at how well their
> children do in school, despite staggering problems of language, culture and
> economics.

Asians are then contrasted to the poor (implicitly, African Americans and Puerto Ricans) around them who perpetrate crime. The criminals are described as having limited education and employment and "hideously fractured families." The author then comments that these underclass groups complain that immigrants are being unfairly helped by the government and describes these complaints as "pathetic." The editorial ends by saying: "How do we save Philadelphia? Many Asian immigrants are doing just that."

This explicit contrast between the good immigrant and the bad minority is reflected in many people's statements. For example, a teacher of English as a second language (ESL) compared the hardworking immigrants who were attempting to learn English with the African Americans in her general-education-degree (GED) class by contrasting the "gratitude and spirituality" of the former with the "attitudes" of the latter.

Media coverage of the Puerto Rican community, on the other hand, is dominated by reports of drug activities and drug-related violence. Puerto Ricans received the most media visibility in Philadelphia during our two years of fieldwork as the result of two intergroup murders in the summer of 1989 followed by related Human Relations Commission hearings on discrimination against them (see Chapter 6). Coverage of these events appeared day after day; it emphasized poverty, antisocial behavior, civil rights, and fairness issues, confirming to established residents that this minority was part of the underclass.

Television coverage by the three local network affiliates of a meeting of Puerto Ricans with the Human Relations Commission emphasized the image of loud and angry protesters. One station played up the anger of the community and quoted one woman as saying, "Justice will be done? Ha! It makes me sick." Another station quoted a woman saying, "We have to be angry, it's the only thing which keeps us going." Both stations showed the Puerto Rican councilman criticizing the police. Only the third station gave any indication that the meetings had involved some listening, give-and-take, and small resolutions.

That these stereotypes shaped people's thoughts is demonstrated in the reflections of one established resident about the different newcomers in her neighborhood:

> It is very obvious that Asians are extremely hardworking and own a lot of business properties. You don't see in the papers every day that a multitude of Asians are on the welfare rolls like you do Hispanics.

Asian leaders, knowing that there are poor members of their community who need services, are also not happy with their image as uniformly successful.

Talk Radio

This medium has played a major role as a forum for the articulation of a citywide image of social difference. A recent study of the role of talk radio in New York, Chicago, and Philadelphia says that the motto of this format seems to be "If you can't say anything bad about a group, don't say anything at all" (*Philadelphia Inquirer*, November 8, 1990). While most of the comments heard in an analysis of ninety hours of radio programs (on both white and African American stations) were not overtly racist, the conclusion of the study was that this format "was far more an expression of racial divisiveness than of ethnic affirmation."

Philadelphia stations were characterized as having "the most racial characterizations [more give-and-take about race] of all the cities in the study." Commentators were acknowledged to be responsible hosts who did not incite their callers to make extreme statements. There was, however, a clear emphasis in African American programs on blaming structural racism (with some tendency toward self-blame, as well), while white callers clearly stressed resenting structural favoritism (along with affirming particular white ethnic heritages.)

One particular campaign was carried out by Georgie Woods, a popular disc jockey on WDAS, a local African American station. In 1986, he called on African Americans to boycott Korean-owned stores on the grounds that too much money was leaving the community and that African Americans should be running their own local stores. This campaign was still talked about later by Koreans and African Americans alike (see Chapter 7).

In 1990, former mayor Frank Rizzo hosted a call-in show just prior to and at the time of his entry into the 1991 mayoral campaign. The topic was frequently the "takeover" of city government by African Americans. One woman who listened regularly said:

> Blacks are the worst. Mayor Goode is the biggest racist. He does nothing for the whites and everything for the Blacks. The whole water department and everything is controlled by Blacks. Listen to Frank Rizzo, he tells it like it is.

In the unofficial media (talk shows) and the popular discourse on cultural difference that extends from pluralism, the discussion often shifts from a view of cultural difference as good to the dangerous zone of cultural (moral) difference as bad. The values of hard work, education, and strong families are seen as missing from some cultures, and this lack leads to group failure. Culture as morality becomes the natural, essential basis of difference.

Both the mainstream media and talk shows play an important role in people's knowledge of who lives in Philadelphia and what they are like. It has brought some groups to prominence, while ignoring others. Puerto Ricans and Koreans are increasingly visible. Recent coverage has seriously overemphasized Asian successes and Puerto Rican struggles. While the latter is partly a response to news events, the former emphasis serves a basic need to see immigrants as restoring traditional values. Many other groups are invisible. Very few people know that there are Spanish speakers other than Puerto Ricans in the city or know much about the new Polish refugees.

The open-access radio talk shows play an important role in shaping the citywide discourse about difference. On the street in all three of our study neighborhoods we frequently heard the same specific anecdotes, which originated with talk shows and then spread by word of mouth. Yet, mainstream media and talk shows are just two of the many sources of influence on people's ideas and actions. These distant ideas are filtered through more immediate and local experiences as people live their lives in neighborhoods among family, friends, and institutions that shape the frequency and quality of contact. They are also formed by the experience of intergroup conflicts that occur locally.

The View from Newcomer Communities

We have looked at how the human relations organizations and dominant media images define newcomers. At the same time, newcomer communities throughout Philadelphia are organizing themselves to participate in public life by adapting to the themes of structural inequality and cultural pluralism. In the following discussion, we will describe the ways in which the core immigrant communities of this study organize themselves to relate to the centers of power, attempt to control their images, and define who they are. Their responses are constrained by the established ideas and institutions of the city.

The most significant influence of the existing power structure (political parties, city agencies, media, and human-relations organizations) is its demand for "representatives" from newcomer communities. Consequently, a small group of individuals have become unofficial leaders and spokespersons, serving as middlemen in the ongoing established political order. There are two problems with this arrangement. One is the pressure it puts on the middlemen themselves. The other is the question of their ability to represent heterogeneous, often fragmented interests within the community.

The role of middleman is often burdensome, stressful, and frustrating. The visible representatives of all groups are overcommitted in their expenditure of time and energy and often feel pressured by both their constituents and the citywide elites who seek them out. One Korean leader remarked during an interview:

> Nothing has ever changed. It's always the same, the big officials ignore us. They come after us at election time, they just want to use us; they want the numbers, but when we go to them, they are ten thousand miles away. . . . Westerners just talk, talk, talk. They don't treat us like human beings. They treat us as an ethnic group. They use us to their purposes.

His sense of being used instrumentally was reinforced by the feeling that he was not treated in a one-on-one, personal way but as an impersonal representative of an arm's-length stereotyped group. The wife of another middleman said:

> My husband gives his whole life for the [immigrant-community] organization and he gets criticized by the members and tricked by the officials.

Another leader described at length the "burnout" he and his friends experienced as a result of being constantly called upon to represent Puerto Ricans. He said that he was exhausted from the constant demands on him by outsiders trying to get something from the community and by his clients, who always needed help.

Furthermore, many in the "grassroots" immigrant population are not linked to the leadership recognized by the city establishment. The internal variability within the immigrant communities, which are far from homogeneous, is based on immigrant wave, class, region of origin, and church membership.

Individuals within each group are here for different reasons, with particular resources and various ties to their homeland and the international political economy. They differ in their strategies of adaptation, as reflected in the existence of many, often competing, organizations and leaders. Moreover, much of the everyday lives of families is lived within the boundaries of the social network of family and friends and the church congregation, with little participation in the "community" as a whole or in its formal structures.

Nevertheless, linkages between newcomers and the city are increasing, especially for larger groups like Puerto Ricans and Koreans. There are several approaches to political linkage. In Chapter 2, we described such political strategies as seeking established patrons in the city through clientage ties or becoming players in political coalitions (and ultimately electing representatives from the group). More confrontational postures assert strong demands for a fair share of minority-oriented programs or participation in radical political-change movements. Still another strategy for those with economic resources is to make economic contributions to candidates and parties to protect the groups' interests.

Puerto Ricans

In 1990, Hispanics comprised 6 percent of Philadelphia's people, and at least three-quarters of this population were Puerto Ricans. Puerto Ricans are different from other newcomer groups in three ways. They make up the largest community, they have been in Philadelphia longest, and they are not technically immigrants but citizens of the United States. The changing strategies of the community have been tied to both citywide political shifts and island politics (Rodriguez 1989). Puerto Rican solidarity is reinforced by several factors. Sharing minority status ascribed by law, Puerto Ricans use the structural-inequality model of group relations to relate to the political system. Since the group's migration has largely involved unskilled and semiskilled workers looking for economic improvement (Ericksen et al. 1985), leaders argue that they are victims of historical colonialism (by Spain and then by the United States). Leaders often link the conditions on the mainland to those of the island and to five hundred years of colonial exploitation.

Second, island politics and the nationalism it invokes also provide a focus for group identity. Puerto Rico's unique political status as a commonwealth and the coming decisions on changing that status to statehood, independence, or an enhanced commonwealth have further linked political activity in Philadelphia to what is happening on the island.

Another reinforcement of Puerto Rican collectivity comes from the nature of residential clustering (see Map 5). Economic dispersion precludes work as such as a source of linkage. But since most educated Puerto Ricans work in nonprofit social services (housing counseling, job training, drug and alcohol counseling) or, less frequently, in public service (police, in prisons, as teachers and welfare caseworkers) filling the needs of other Spanish speakers, these services tie the upwardly mobile members of the community to the needy in mutual concern for the group as a whole.

Church affiliation both links and divides the community. While Puerto Ricans are increasingly Protestant, those who are active in the Catholic church as lay leaders participate in strong structures related to a citywide Hispanic mission. In 1989, there were more than thirty-one different Spanish-speaking Protestant congregations, some evangelical and some mainline. While the former tend to remain separate, an organization of Spanish Protestant clergy, Asociación de Ministerios Cristianos Latinamericanos de Filadelfia (AMCLAF), has developed in the city to focus on economic and community development with an eye to the role played by the organized African American churches in the development of that community's political power.

Organizations

While the Puerto Rican community has little access to economic sources of power, it has, through experience, developed political skills. Business leaders played an early leadership role in the community, but they have lost support to the activists of today. They originally sought patronage from governors and mayors (the Rizzo administration, for example), as well as from corporations; in turn, business people served as patrons to the poorer members of the Spanish-speaking community. The early leaders were island-born merchants whose organizations were built on the model of elitist charities concerned with maintaining a social-prestige hierarchy in the community. The major annual event of the first organization was the Puerto Rican Day parade, which began in 1963 and pulled together all of the then-existing small groups, such as baseball leagues and hometown organizations. In contrast to the Korean leadership, this mercantile group was very small.[1]

The influence of social-service programs funded by the government became the basis of community structures in the 1970s. With the advent of more public funding for social services, community leaders began to respond to the newly available programs. A conflict developed within the merchant-dominated organization, and another large social-service agency was created; it still provides publicly funded social-service programs. Today these organizations have been joined by several other localized programs, such as community development corporations funded by public economic-development agencies and private foundations. A schism between the established, mercantile faction backing the Puerto Rican Day parade and more activist organizations has existed since this time.

The cadre of young Puerto Ricans who sued for new electoral districts (Chapter 2) began to try to organize the community in the 1970s in a civil-rights fashion to use the legal system to challenge discrimination. Clustered in community legal services, they confronted the establishment in many ways, among them suing the school district over bilingual education and fighting for less discrimination in criminal justice. Such civil-rights-oriented groups as the Puerto Rican Rights Organization were developed. They engaged in struggle, *lucha*, against the system for more representation on the police force and in the school district.

Most Puerto Rican structures are tied together by links between staff members who participate in different movements and strategies. Yet in spite of these relationships, there is a split in the community linked both to local political movements and to island politics. These are well known and the subject of much discussion and self-critique.

Social-service organizations and civil-rights groups provide the major base for elected public figures.[2] They differ most from those clustered around the original merchant Parade sponsors on such issues as island independence and broader political ideology. Each group publishes a newspaper, and there are also community-based radio and television programs.

The shifting, unstable alliance with the city government (led by African Americans) described in Chapter 2 reflects an inherent competition for limited minority resources in a declining economy as Puerto Ricans use the structural-racism model to improve their position. One Puerto Rican stated boldly that African Americans recognize that "there is too much Asian and Puerto Rican competition for minority slots." At the Human Relations Commission hearings about discrimination against Puerto Ricans, one witness stated, "I don't like the word 'minority.' . . . Too many different people are put in the same pot." Yet often a kindred oppressed status is recognized. One Puerto Rican high-school student won a community prize with a paper lauding Malcolm X as her hero.

Many middle-class Puerto Ricans urge following African Americans in developing greater political consciousness of civil rights and electoral politics as American citizens in order to advance.

We are too content to take the leavings of the civil-rights actions.

Others march and stand up for their rights and protest, but Puerto Ricans don't do that and they should.

When African Americans demonstrated, they got their curriculum and history in the schools.

While they admire the strategies, they recognize the competition and envy African Americans their head start and numbers.

African American views of Puerto Ricans vary depending on where one is located in the class hierarchy. Many poor African Americans think that Latinos are less often victims of racism; they assume that most Puerto Ricans can ultimately cross the color line and assimilate. At the same time, some middle-class African Americans in positions of power share stereotypes of Puerto Ricans and dismiss them as unworthy. For example, one African American official of a mainline religious denomination made negative remarks about their behavior in an interview.

Nationalism

As alliance politics breaks down and island politics related to political status heats up, the links between the two are affirmed more strongly. Puerto Rican nationalism plays an increasing role in community politics. One Puerto Rican community leader and political hopeful who had grown up in Philadelphia with little experience on the island was asked whether support for independence was widespread in the community. He said:

> Most people are dealing with the everyday crisis of existence. The Puerto Rican community and the Puerto Rican people live under crisis, whether it's over there or over here. Here they live under very extreme poverty, drugs, poor housing, teenage pregnancy, and violence. Our high-school dropouts are probably the highest rates in the city. So it's difficult for one to concentrate on what's going on in Puerto Rico. People have to realize what we're dealing with in Puerto Rico. The kind of oppression. You're talking about a country that has never been free. . . . How do you expect the people to know about freedom? . . . We're talking about five hundred years of people owning Puerto Rico. We're talking about almost total control of our economy by foreigners. We're talking about nine military installations, but we have no army. We have no control over immigration, national currency, postal service. We have zip. On the other hand, if you look at that kind of oppression for five hundred years (four hundred under Spain and one hundred under the U.S.) and all their attempts to assimilate and swallow this nation we can still say we are Puerto Rican, and have a flag, and a tradition, and speak Spanish, we have a language, we have a country to identify with, so there are not many countries that can say that after five hundred years of war, domination, and control.

The focus on nationalism brings the Philadelphia community into contact with Puerto Rican political organizations throughout the country. It is also linked in more internationally oriented coalitions with those who are concerned about the dependency of third-world countries as victims of colonialism.

Cultural organizations in the community use both cultural pluralism and structural racism as they play an important role in maintaining this nationalist identity. A culture and arts center initially supported by heritage funding serves as a major center for disseminating Puerto Rican culture; it maintains an art gallery and a bookstore and hosts many performances, as well as presenting programs for children to develop cultural consciousness. The center also provides much of the Puerto Rican programming and cultural commodities for human-relations activities throughout Philadelphia and is active in the city-wide network.[3]

It is also central to the articulation of structural inequality and the effects of colonialism and racism on the community. At one fiesta, a Puerto Rican artist-in-residence presented a paper surveying the negative stereotypes about Puerto Ricans contained in ethnic humor in the dominant culture in the United States. Another segment featured high-school students presenting papers expressing anger about exploitation. In the words of one girl,

> The wealthy and powerful are using us to make profit for them. We did not bring drugs and guns with us when we came.

Identity

While there is great diversity among Puerto Ricans based on class, relation to the island, experience in New York, and other variables, many of the ways in which people express their identity depend on the ideologies of the local organizations. To the degree that individuals come into contact with and are affected by the activities and messages of an organization, they share points of view. For many Puerto Ricans, nationalism is an important part of identity. To them, the fact that they are already Americans has both cost and benefit. They acknowledge their official status as U.S. citizens and are thus insulted when they have the very common experience in banks and other places of being treated as foreigners—for example, being asked for passports and green cards or being told that their money needs to be exchanged.

Nonetheless, they regard their U.S. citizenship as distinct from their identity as Puerto Ricans. At an angry meeting in the aftermath of a crisis, one nationalist spokeswoman said,

> You forced your citizenship on us and now you have to respect our dignity.

Even for those who are indifferent to the nationalist cause and identify with the American dream of mobility, Puerto Rican identity supersedes everything else, such as U.S. or pan-Latino consciousness.

Often Puerto Ricans view U.S. nomenclature (lumping Hispanics and Latinos) as a sign of ignorance about the world. One young woman said, "You Americans are so parochial, so ignorant of geography and history." While preferring the label Puerto Rican, when a generic term is used more-nationalist Puerto Ricans prefer Latino to Hispanic, which they see as a U.S. government category or an overemphasis on the Spanish colonial part of their history. However, many of those less involved with Puerto Rican organizations accept the Hispanic label, or even the category "Spanish," without resistance. At mixed meetings, Puerto Rican representatives patiently explain their preference for Latino to whites. Ironically, one white established resident said she was always careful to call Puerto Ricans Hispanic because she thought Puerto Rican was derogatory, since whites often use "Ricans" as a derogatory term of reference.

Language and race also form an important part of identity. The persistence of language is an important mechanism in maintaining the boundary. Puerto Ricans will refer to established residents as English speakers even if they are bilingual, spend their whole day at work speaking English, and are losing the battle with their children to maintain their language at home. Alternatively they will refer to white people as white, even though they are often classified by Americans as white themselves and are often assumed to be Italian.

While some upwardly mobile Puerto Ricans agree with dominant negative stereotypes about their fellows on the mainland and want to disassociate themselves from them, they do not reject their cultural identity. In one woman's view,

> Eighty percent of the Puerto Ricans here are bad. You Americans are right. But they are not like those [real Puerto Ricans] on the island.

For the most part, Puerto Ricans identify strongly with "their country," as they call the island. Symbols of island identity abound, and references to the enchanted island, the climate, the cleanliness, salubrious countryside, and idyllic life are often made even by those whose ties are tenuous and who visit rarely if at all. Most people have social networks to resort to in both locations. In much discourse, the island is seen as an escape valve in times of trouble and as a nurturing environment, while the mainland is seen as a place to get educated and earn money. According to one newcomer who had also lived here as a child, "Puerto Rico is my mother [implying nurturance] and the United States is my father" [implying economic support].

There are many stories of people who have never lived on the island moving back, especially when careers or marriages go sour. One woman who was being threatened by a boyfriend moved to Puerto Rico immediately, although she had not been there for twenty years. Teenagers who have never seen the island are often sent there to finish high school in a safer environment and perhaps meet someone to marry.

Other Latinos

What about alliances with other newcomer Latinos who are not Puerto Rican? Given the need for more political strength, one possible source of allies would be other Spanish speakers. The Anglo population already sees "the Spanish" as an undifferentiated mass. Many structures created by the larger society to accommodate "the Spanish," such as English for Speakers of Other Languages (ESOL) bilingual programs and Spanish-language church services, bring them together. However, this kind of collaboration was problematic throughout the study period.

The visible Spanish-speaking organizations in Philadelphia are dominated by Puerto Ricans, who claim priority through long-term residence, numbers, and their unique political relationship to the United States. It is ironic that in the 1960s, when most Spanish speakers in the city were Puerto Ricans, the first organizations were given pan-Latino labels (e.g., Council of Spanish Speaking Organizations, Congress of United Latinos). Now, with the advent of Latinos from other countries, the organizations have increasingly emphasized their Puerto Rican orientation. For example, one group rejected the suggestion of a Central American that their organization be renamed Latino instead of Puerto Rican.

Many of the other Latinos want to distance themselves from Puerto Ricans, often explaining their attitude by difference in legal status and class. As noncitizens (and often illegal residents), they see themselves as not having a common interest. They resent both the rights of Puerto Ricans and what is seen as their arrogant "ownership" attitudes. One Guatemalan woman said, "They think they are the only ones who should be here."

Furthermore, new Latinos want to distance themselves from the underclass image of Puerto Ricans. They share established stereotypes. One Central American woman described Puerto Rican women as "too attractive," later modifying this to mean overtly sexual; another said it bothered her to be identified as Puerto Rican because "they do not know how to behave." A third woman combined the two themes, saying that Puerto Ricans were shamed by their commonwealth status (lack of national independence) and their immoral behavior.

As noted above, culture is a malleable concept that can be used to find similarities as well as differences. Yet often, in spite of many elements of mutually shared history and language, Colombians and Central Americans use cultural differences to separate themselves from Puerto Ricans. Many informants maintained that their "cultures" (i.e., food and music) are more similar to each other's than to Puerto Ricans'. A Nicaraguan woman notes that "we all eat rice and beans, but my food [and language] is more similar to that of Mexicans, Colombians, and Ecuadorans than to Puerto Ricans."

It would be very easy to make a case for cultural similarity or to find equal levels of difference between nations so easily grouped together. The actual bases for differences, however, are grounded more in class, citizenship, and the nature of immigration than in culture. Padilla (1985) documents similar fluctuations in developing a Latino consciousness among Mexican Americans and Puerto Ricans in Chicago.

Koreans

While the Puerto Rican leadership projects an image of an oppressed group linked to its homeland through the island's subordinate political relationship to the United States, the Korean community views itself as a transnational capitalist group. Koreans are linked to their homeland through business ties. These are maintained by frequent telephone and fax communication, as well as by newspapers and directories shared with other Korean communities in the United States and in the homeland. Many immigrants remain interested in Korean politics; in fact, two members of the local community were elected to the national legislature in 1988 and returned to South Korea.

Koreans have used all three models of difference in response to various conflicts. In one major incident (discussed in Chapter 6), they saw themselves as victims of structural racism. In their actions to modify a film about Korean–Black relations (described below), they emphasized their unique culture and how it fit into the pluralist mosaic. In another dispute, one of the leaders appealed to the story of earlier American immigration in his public response. He talked about the United States as the land of freedom and opportunity and asked whites to remember their own forebears' experiences in order to understand Koreans as good immigrants.

For Koreans, their shared mode of insertion into the economy and their relative economic power has been the primary factor in organizing the community.[4] Models of hierarchic organization, as well as transnational political and economic links, also influence their mode of adaptation to the local political economy. In spite of significant differences in their resources and strategies (compared to Puerto Ricans), the nature of race relations in the city, human-relations institutions, and the importance of African Americans in local politics have often generated similar minority postures and coalitions with African Americans.

The Korean community's major base, whether for internal or external group development, is its economic power. Yet as Light and Bonacich (1988) point out, while the economic power of the Korean community in Los Angeles may appear significant in contrast to that of other minority groups, it is still limited and localized when compared to the dominant power structures.

Koreans are the largest immigrant group in Philadelphia and come with high levels of education and often with some capital (see Chapter 2); they are seen as economically successful. While Korean merchants dominate some types of small-scale retail activity and some local shopping strips, however, they are not significant actors in the overall city economy. Nonetheless, their common economic niche does play a major role in linking them, much as space does in the Puerto Rican community.

Korean leaders often see themselves as providing important capital for rebuilding Philadelphia's economy. As one leader said, "We have come to make Philadelphia [the] number-one city again." By implying that they are benefactors, Koreans reverse the established residents' views of themselves as benefactors and hosts to the downtrodden. Instead, they see established residents as their beneficiaries. The Korean American business community is disappointed in the response of Philadelphia residents to what it sees as its sacrifices to save dying community shopping strips. Established residents often view this as arrogance.

Korean economic clout is also evident in how they influence public images of their group. The first public screening of a videotape about Korean–African American relations, *I'm Not Prejudiced, But . . .* (Ethnovision 1987), brought loud complaints from both communities, albeit for very different reasons. While African American verbal protests were noted by the producers, Koreans responded in a very different way. The filmmakers were invited to a dinner with the current Korean leadership. After discussing the videotape, leaders quietly asked how much it would cost to amend it. A second version has been created that incorporates some of the concerns.

Modeled after organizations in other Korean communities in the United States, Korean structures quickly proliferated. Such organizations are hierarchical; the official presidents of the associations are expected to be the spokespersons for the entire Korean population, and internal dissension is kept under wraps. This is quite different from the Puerto Rican community, where conflict is out in the open. Several figures who have recently been presidents are now on boards and commissions in Philadelphia. Once the networks of city influentials came to know these individuals, they become universal referrals for anyone who wanted to approach "the community." As we sat on the boards of programs for the arts, museums, and human-rights networks, it became apparent that this was the way things worked.

The community publishes an impressive, massive directory listing thousands of enterprises and individuals. There are two newspapers, one a local edition of a New York paper and the other a Philadelphia weekly. While their interests are less focused on social services than is true of the Puerto Rican community, there are two large social-service institutions that get their own funds for ESL, job training, and other federal programs. These two visible and connected organizations also provide significant contact persons to the public and private sectors. While many Latinos are served by generic (non-ethnic-based) ESL and Job Training Partnership Act (JTPA) programs, it is rare to find a Korean presence in any but a Korean agency.

This separateness is characteristic of the general posture of the community. It turns inward, attempting to insert itself into the larger society as a cohesive, hierarchically structured whole. There is a concerted effort to maintain a united front against the outside world and to control information about the community. Leaders are often inaccessible to the larger public and reluctant to provide information; invariably, they defer to those persons holding formal office. As one individual stated, "It is my duty to refer you to speak to our president about this." This appearance of inaccessibility is exacerbated by the fact that most of the brochures and information are in Korean, a language in which few outside the immigrant community are literate.

The citywide pattern is replicated in the neighborhoods. On each shopping strip, Korean entrepreneurs develop a separate local businessmen's group. One of the members then acts as the official spokesperson for the group, which usually includes established whites, African Americans, and Latinos, as well as other newcomers. The Korean spokesperson has regular contact with established leaders, goes to meetings, and brokers information. He also collects dues from his constituents for the group and solicits volunteers for local activities. Once again, hierarchy limits contact between individuals.

Organizations

Business is the major focus of organization, and two large groups dominate. The Korean Businessman's Association of Greater Philadelphia had more than five thousand dues-paying members in 1989 and was divided into seven specialty subgroups. The other citywide organization, the Korean Association of Greater Philadelphia, had fifteen hundred attendees at its annual dinner in the same year. This group is an umbrella for such others as the Lions Club, the Korean YMCA/YWCA, sports groups, Korean alumni clubs, and many of the seventy-plus Korean Christian congregations. Both these large groups hold well-attended picnics and other events during the year. There is some competition between them for the role of link to the city power structure.

There is also increasing competition for leadership within the two organizations beneath the tight-knit façade. Until 1989, elections to leadership were not contested, with slates being developed by sitting leaders. After the first contested election in one organization, one of the most respected early leaders was drafted again so that he could restore harmony.

This increasing competition reflects the fact that as the community has grown over time it has become more divided by interests. Our research showed that earlier arrivals who came from a poorer South Korea (before the economic "miracle") with a restriction on the capital they could bring often resented both their relatives who had stayed in the homeland and prospered and some recent immigrants who were arriving with large amounts of money and entering businesses set up by kin already here. Furthermore, today the large market of available, inexpensive stores that early migrants found as a consequence of the decline of local strips no longer exists—there are fewer "bargains" and more competition. This gap is reflected in the statements of merchants about the cooperation that was characteristic of their early days in Philadelphia and the increase in intragroup competition as more capital arrives to divide the haves and have-nots within a worsening economy. One Korean who is expert in legal and business affairs recalled:

> When I first worked on contracts between Koreans, they were only one page. They were not suspicious of each other. Now they are thirty pages long. Once they were willing to sacrifice to help less-experienced Koreans, now everyone is concerned with money.

Another gap is between persons tied to the citywide business community and those who own local small businesses. The first group includes business brokers, construction specialists and sign makers who rehabilitate businesses, and service providers like insurance agents, tax accountants, and the wholesale network (which serves local retailers and those from as far away as Pittsburgh and Baltimore). These are the people interested in maintaining strong, centralized Korean institutions. Small businessmen, on the other hand, very often find their interests to be increasingly located in the same community as their business and real-estate investments. These individuals have begun to participate in cross-ethnic local groups.

Citywide Linkages

The Korean citywide organizations participate in the life of Philadelphia through formal channels. They hold many ceremonial events at which guests recognized as important city figures receive awards. One group, the Korean American Friendship Society, has been created to improve relations. The organization has several non-Koreans (the African American city councilwoman from an area with major Korean presence, an African American judge, and a white police official) holding office. Their photos, along with those of many other leading politicians, are given prominence in the organization's brochure—the only such document in English that we have encountered.

In the aftermath of African American–Korean tension related to the radio-organized boycott, a program to give out food baskets in African American sections of North Philadelphia at Thanksgiving and several highly publicized scholarships for African American youth were developed.

While economic power allows the community to link to the political structure through contributions, gifts, and ceremonials, until the 1991 primary election (discussed in Chapter 2) political activity was largely limited to using this power to assure access to city government in matters that concerned citywide business interests. These relate to local shopping-strip policies and to heavily contested issues involving center-city street vending.

Racial politics in Philadelphia has created a contradictory relationship between Koreans and African Americans. Their experience as merchants creates conflict between the two groups. Yet, Koreans envy African American political power, and they have recently attempted to develop more politically oriented activity to improve their position vis-à-vis the police and other citywide agencies.

Identity

Koreans are similar to Puerto Ricans in their maintenance of a strong identity, although, as we will see below, this quality comes in different forms. The community uses the church to help children maintain language and identity, and membership captures much time and allegiance in the community. Almost all of the families we encountered belong to one of the more than seventy Korean Christian churches that are the basis of social life. All of Sunday is spent in church-related activities, divided by age.

Korea generates an ever-growing number of Christian ministers because this is considered a prestigious occupation. These aspiring middle-class individuals increasingly come to the United States to establish their congregations. They draw on a Korean community that has largely the same class background and goals; their churches become the focus of economic and social activity. Pressure to stay in the church and the community is great, as are obligations to support newcomers financially. Often, the emphasis of the Korean Christian church is evangelical, but with the assumption that Koreans alone are the target for community efforts.

Korean college students we interviewed made a major distinction between Koreanizing and Americanizing. Most who identify as Koreanized talk about the church as responsible for their maintenance of Korean values and language. As one student said, "It is easy for the second generation to fall into negative things, to forget who they are and what they must do."

As in the case of Puerto Ricans, nationalism is central to identity. Here, however, the focus of nationalism is not a history of oppression but a sense of cultural uniqueness often found in Asian nations that have recently expanded their economies and taken a larger role on a world stage long dominated by Western market economics. This attitude is reinforced by the U.S. view of Asians as model immigrants and by recent international comparisons of Asian and U.S. educational achievements.

Korean leaders, in this instance accepting the U.S. lumping of Asian cultures, allude to that continent as the source of all central religious values. Such pride was also asserted by a leader who said, "In Asian culture children are encouraged to be on top. Here failure is the mother of success."

An Americanized Korean woman who had rejected these views noted that

> Koreans are always talking about how great they are, better than anybody, including whites. . . . I really think if they had their way, they would pull themselves up here in the U.S. entirely by themselves, without interacting with anyone else. . . . [There is an] overweening racial pride and superiority.

Coupled with this and contributing to it, however, is an awareness of white dominance, a sense that Koreans can never become mainstream Americans because of racial difference. One parent, for example, reminded his children that "no matter how long you are here, your hair will not turn blond, your eyes will not turn blue. You've got to know where you belong."

In fact, this overweening pride and sense of superiority (like Puerto Rican nationalism and the assertions of moral superiority in family and personal relations by both groups) is in part a response to the feeling of being outside the mainstream, the reaction of outsiders facing barriers they cannot cross in spite of success.

Local party leaders report that Koreans are becoming citizens at a slower rate than other new immigrants, and informants often say that citizenship is mostly valuable for pragmatic reasons—to bring relatives over, for example. Certainly, the economic expansion in South Korea has created fluidity in migration as it becomes a viable and attractive option to return. As one Koreanized college student said: "We don't have to become citizens. We have our home. We can go back. If you are Americanized, you want to become a citizen."

However, more-Americanized Koreans are here to stay and seek permanent citizenship to symbolize the transition. Those whose future is here share a stake in the life of the city and the neighborhood. For them, the interest in electoral participation has awakened.

Poles and Polish Americans

The 1970s and 1980s also brought newcomers from the Soviet Union and elsewhere in Eastern Europe to Philadelphia. These émigrés differ from newcomer Koreans and Latinos because ethnic groups with ties to their countries were already established in the United States, as described in Chapter 2. Research within these communities highlights the dissimiliarities between new immigrant groups, which focus on the differences between their home country and the United States, and ethnic groups, which have combined aspects of the culture and class of their country of origin with conditions in the United States to create a unique entity (Schneider 1986). Polish American ethnics and new Polish refugees contest the meaning of Polish culture. Established Polish Americans emphasize the "good immigrant" model to judge their new Polish neighbors, who see themselves as more cosmopolitan than their "hosts."

Immigration Waves and Class Identity

In keeping with their peasant heritage, turn-of-the-century immigrants tended to be anti-intellectual and concerned about maintaining job security between generations. Only the third generation of Polish Americans is entering higher education in great numbers (Lopata 1976, 91–94); by occupation, until recently the majority of Polish Americans entered the same jobs as their parents (Lopata 1976, 94–96; Bodnar, Weber, and Simon 1979 and 1983). The current change reflects both additional education for the younger generation and the decline of the smokestack industries that employed previous generations of Polish Americans.

Polonia, as the Polish American community is called, has developed an ambivalent relationship with the home country over the years. This includes a debate between Poles and expatriates over whether Polonia even *has* a culture (Taras 1982; Symmons-Symonolwicz 1979 and 1983). Following World War I, Polonia began to focus inward. While generally supportive of the Polish nationalist cause, Polish American interpretation of events in the homeland is based on U.S. upbringing and received memories of the peasant past:

> The immigrant became a loyal American while his attachment to the Old
> Country was a sentimental image of a rural world that had been left behind.
> . . . America provided the immigrant with opportunity, and the immigrant
> responded by becoming a believer in America's mission and leadership. He
> was grateful and committed to America, while retaining a certain, hazy
> nostalgia for Poland. (Blejwas 1981, 60)

This understanding of Poland as a picturesque rural country was enhanced by the fact that it was largely closed to outsiders from the beginning of World War II until 1956. Combining the lack of experience with the modern country with childhood memories of stories of peasant Poland (and the general ideology of immigrant culture prevalent in the United States) gives an approximation of the Polish American's view of the overseas "other." Established residents have asked newcomers if they had heard of bananas or if there are bears on the streets of Warsaw, reflecting the third generation's view of Poland as a backward country.

Class differences became important in the community with the arrival of the displaced persons (DPs) after World War II. To quote Blejwas (1981, 76), "the new arrivals complained about the 'lack of respect for educated people' among Polish Americans, who remembered the Poland of low technology, poverty, and social injustice experienced by their parents or grandparents." The new immigrants struggled with the established Polish American elite over leadership of the ethnic community and the direction of its institutions. The DPs emphasized Polish high culture, instead of peasant-based traditions. In addition, while both factions were staunchly anticommunist, the DPs were more oriented toward attempting to change Poland. The majority of the educated DPs became successful enough to move out of the working-class Polish neighborhoods; a percentage of them regained the occupational positions they had held in Poland before the war.

The '68 Wave émigrés, unlike the first two groups, share with the post-Solidarity wave the experience of a rebuilt Poland. Largely born after World War II, these individuals have inherited the pride of experience of re-creating the Polish economy and society. Out of the destruction of the war, the Poles made every effort to rebuild the country. The social structure also underwent great changes, with the level of education being perhaps the most dramatic example. In 1960, 45 percent of the population over fifteen had not finished primary school, and only 17 percent had continued beyond. In 1970, only 24 percent had not completed primary school, and 31 percent had continued on (Majetco 1974, 40). The differences between waves in occupational and educational backgrounds create class-based splits in the community (Lopata 1976).

The DPs and the émigrés of the '68 Wave largely maintain a bicultural existence. While they often pass for established residents in the streets and in workplaces, schools, churches, and other community institutions, they frequently uphold the language and cultural styles of Poland at home. The children of these émigrés frequently become completely bicultural. Many '68 Wave and DP families send their children and grandchildren to Polish-language school and maintain Polish-language and culture at home. While in the English-speaking world, these children act like other established young people, using the same dress styles, dialect, and habits; but their class aspirations frequently mimic their parents' middle-class Polish background.

Organizations

Polish Americans have developed an ethnic culture widely regarded as unique to the United States (Obidinsky 1985; Blejwas 1981; Taras 1982). Centered on the Catholic church and highly patriotic, Polish Americans have claimed food items of peasant Poland (kielbasa and perogies) as ethnic symbols and have adopted a Czechoslovakian folk dance (the polka) as their own. A number of institutions, including newspapers and fraternal organizations, have developed within American Polonia. In Philadelphia, these organizations are currently run by Polish American and DP émigrés. The beneficials, fraternals, and political organizations in the city are all branches of larger entities headquartered in the more significant Polish communities of Chicago and New York.

Among local institutions, travel agencies become important centers for buying ethnic foods, translating documents, sending packages to Poland, and finding housing and jobs. They also serve as places to gossip, as well as performing the traditional functions of offering tickets to places inside the United States, travel to Poland, and bus trips to Atlantic City for the elderly. While the several travel agencies have their own clientele, most cater to portions of several immigration waves. There are also local restaurants, beauty parlors, shops, and sports clubs that are centers for community activity. In addition, a popular radio program sponsored by the Polish American political umbrella organization is hosted by a '68 wave émigré and is geared toward the more recent newcomer.

Philadelphia has its own Polish social-service agency. This organization was originally started to serve the elderly turn-of-the-century immigrants and remains largely devoted to their care. As the number of newcomers increased, the group has started English classes and other services, such as job counseling, in order to meet newcomers' needs.

The fact that most working age Poles and Polish Americans do not fit into federal and state poverty models because they frequently find work within the Polish-speaking community has hurt attempts to provide services to newcomers. Program administrators have applied for funding for ESL and social services with limited success. Initiatives for the Polish American elderly resemble other low-income programs: efforts for energy assistance and tax rebates are primary activities.

Most organizations are controlled by Polish Americans and established DPs and do not attempt to serve newcomers and longtime residents jointly. Examples of separateness abound. The Polish radio program run by the service organization has been defined as the information source for "Poles from Poland." Newcomer participants in the ethnic parade are put at the end of the line and referred to as outsiders (Schneider 1990a). In many cases, newcomer Poles and established Polish Americans use the same spaces for their activities, either ignoring the fact that multiple communities maintain activities side by side or exhibiting a shy coexistence. For example, the teenage group for one beneficial held meetings in the back room of a club frequented by newcomers. The Polish American girls would nervously pass the newcomers, who would ignore them or greet them in Polish.

Nascent newcomer groups include a social-service agency run by a priest on mission from Poland and a recently founded youth organization that attempts to develop cultural programs related to the homeland. The priest is considered an outsider because he advocates using the welfare system to support newcomers in the United States. His program clearly violates the rules for "good immigrants," which demand hard work and "paying your dues." As a result, he stays away from the larger Polish American organizations, drawing support from '68 Wave émigrés and more recent newcomers. The youth organization, on the other hand, uses space in one of the formal institutions and has the larger organization's blessing for its activities.

Identity

While knowledge of the Polish language and some other external markers of immigrant culture have declined through the generations, third- and fourth-generation Polish Americans are maintaining some ties to the ethnic community (Sandberg 1974; Obidinsky 1985). However, like most Catholic white ethnics, Polish Americans claim multiple ancestries, using the particular ethnic label that seems most appropriate at the moment. In many ways, the self-definition of the Polish American emphasizing patriotism about the United States has been reinforced by the presence of newcomers in their midst. Leaders of these organizations clearly see a difference between themselves and more recent émigrés. They signify their control over the institutional structure through programs geared toward their constituency, which feature a mix of transformed peasant cultural traditions and references to heroes of the American Revolution from Poland. Solidarity banners are also proudly displayed, but they are understood by Polish Americans as signifying Poland's love of democracy and freedom in the U.S. mold. English is the lingua franca of their activities, and all organizations stress that newcomers should learn English and become like them. As one Polish American informant said, "I don't mind my children learning a little Polish or whatever, but don't force it on them. This is America. They don't need it".

Recent newcomers, some DPs, and '68 Wave immigrants reject such transformed peasant traditions as the polka as inauthentic and do not share the understandings about the contributions of Polish heroes to the American Revolution. For them, Polish high culture should be more prominent, and their views of the Solidarity movement are quite different.

The content of the Polish cultural museum is an example of contested meaning. The museum is very Polish American in character. Some newcomers from the intelligentsia would much rather see Polish modern paintings adorn the walls. Again, resistance is most often passive, in the form of private complaints and simply staying away from the exhibits.

To some extent, a certain rapprochement between high-culture views and peasant ethnic symbols has occurred in more recent times. For example, Polish festivals regularly feature exhibits of important figures within Polish culture, such as Chopin, Pulaski, Paderewski, and Kosciuszko, while serving perogies and playing polkas.

Conclusions

In Philadelphia, human-relations organizations, established residents, and the popular media confront a new kind of city. The consciousness of a racial dyad is still there, along with well-honed white ethnic categories. Yet these assumptions are not sufficient to handle the new complexities introduced by the resumption of large-scale immigration. Overlapping and confusing categories of difference are emerging, and it is difficult to place everyone in a clear-cut cultural group, natural and primordial.

Underlying the older, clearer categories of race and ethnicity is a tangle of social and behavioral variations related to class, nationality, language, color, and time of arrival that makes it impossible for people to use any single dimension of difference in a consistent way. The basic four macrocategories are not even based on one criterion.

The old racial hierarchy dividing African Americans and whites still underscores ideas about difference. Yet, as we see in Chapter 5, in local institutions like stores on the shopping strip the influx of immigrants has created situations in which African Americans who are familiar with the rules of public life and competent in small talk are often seen as "more like us" than new immigrants of any background by their white counterparts. As such they are welcomed as allies.

When dating and marriage is the focus, physical markers are invoked. Latinos are often seen as white, not on the other side of the "color line," in spite of the fact that they are defined as minorities, see themselves as "others," and are often viewed as a major source of underclass problems. One white ethnic woman who was troubled by increasing flirtation by African American men said that catcalls from Puerto Rican men were not a problem. When her friend married a Puerto Rican, nobody objected. African Americans and Asians are often seen as "across the line" sexually. One teen reflects this view of the racial line when she says:

> My boyfriend is Spanish, but that's okay. If he was Black, they [her parents] wouldn't hate the person, but it would be awkward. . . . Spanish is the closest to white. If you are Spanish you don't have slanty eyes or whatever.

Yet when class is the focus, Asians, with their different racial features, are often grouped with whites as exemplars of middle-class life-styles. As one white teenager said,

> Whites are like Asians because their class and lifestyles are similar.

During the African American radio-inspired boycott of Korean merchants, likewise, Koreans were treated as an extension of the white power structure.

Yet these class similarities are again erased when "culture" is invoked, since conventional wisdom posits fundamental cultural differences between East and

West. This opposition has a long tradition in academic and popular culture. It leads to statements such as the following made by a community leader in Olney:

> Puerto Ricans are like us, they speak the language and they understand our ways. The Asians are working too hard to integrate. That is their culture. Asian culture is so far from Western culture, whereas Puerto Ricans are not really that different. It is still Western culture.

The several dimensions of difference lead to contradictory views of similarities and difference, resulting in different pairings and oppositions. These are often made by the same individuals at different times and under different circumstances. Both newcomer communities and established residents are confused by the way in which cross-cutting dimensions produce contradictions in categories.

Cultural Pluralism and Structural Racism

The experience of Americans with the civil-rights struggle and with the heritage movement that followed the 1960s continues to shape the ways in which newcomers are perceived and linked to the larger society. The cultural-pluralism model has created externally defined groups who are encouraged to forget internal differences and to create and participate in homogeneous cultural performances. Such presumably homogeneous communities are expected to be joined to the larger society by official representatives. The cultural-pluralism model is unthreatening. It states that the way to improve intergroup relations is to learn to understand and appreciate each other. It implies that problems emerge from lack of contact, lack of knowledge, and fear of strangers. It requires only that people experience each other's "cultures," learn more about each other, and censor racist thoughts. Much of what is presented about other cultures reflects a narrow range of safe domains like traditional foods and music, thus avoiding dangerous topics related to values and morality. The cultural-pluralism model ignores the socially constructed racial hierarchy in the United States. It permits painless, enjoyable exercises and is practiced by all organizations, regardless of their agendas.

However, in order for this model to work, the externally defined cultures must be natural, primordial, stable, and bounded—everyone must have a cultural identity. People of the same racial/ethnic categories, such as "Asians," "Spanish," or Latinos, should want to "stick to their own" through natural affinity. Yet people in these racial and ethnic categories vary, depending on when they came, why they came, the histories of their nations, the relationships between subgroups, regions, or classes in their homelands, and their class origins. Although gross categories of color or language are assumed to mark natural, "culturally" bounded entities, as we have seen throughout the history of Philadelphia, the very definitions of ethnic groups have been shifting and socially constructed. They emerge from pressures from official sources and internal community dynamics, both of which are colored by power relations and economic inequalities.

The structural-racism model also gives newcomers incentives to organize on the basis of ethnicity or nationality, to use race and ethnicity to lobby for a fair share of services, and to see racial discrimination and structural inequality as underlying factors in relationships.

Unlike cultural pluralism, the structural-racism model requires social change, rather than individual enlightenment, to end inequities. It is inherently threatening to other groups. Furthermore, while both Koreans and Puerto Ricans use structural racism as part of their political strategy, the game has been structured so that they must compete with each other and with African Americans for the limited "minority" slots. This precludes success in maintaining coalitions between minority groups. The overriding emphasis on race in this model has masked the importance of class differences; Puerto Ricans and Koreans, groups with different economic resources, are viewed and see themselves as similarly disadvantaged. At the same time, all whites—whether poor, working-class, or Polish refugee—are seen as part of the power structure.

Adding to the complexity of group identity and the process of transition from immigrant to U.S. ethnic is the fact that newcomer groups today are strongly tied to their homeland. Modern transportation and communications place the Philadelphia component in easy contact with communities in other cities, as well as the home country; frequent movement back and forth of people, capital, and information is facilitated. The expectation of one-way migration to "become" American, which fits the U.S. model of playing host to the huddled masses, is often not sustained. Both economic linkages of capital and strong nationalistic political concerns are often retained.

In Part I, we have looked at Philadelphia as a whole. We have explored the interrelations of political, economic, and population shifts in its history and how new immigrants fit into this process. Each wave of newcomers has helped to redefine the perceived social categories in the city. We have also examined the nature of shifting views of social categories within the context of human-relations organizations and media images. We have seen how newcomers develop political strategies based on the preexisting models of ethnic relations.

In Part II, we begin to explore life "on the ground" as it is lived in the three neighborhoods we have studied. Chapter 4 examines the ways in which each neighborhood was affected by shifts in population, politics, and the economy. Because of these differences, there are contrasts in the competition over work, residential and public space, and government services in each setting. We explore the changes in structures and organizations in each neighborhood and look at how these differences affect the dynamics of the discourse about difference and interrelations among groups in the public life of each community.

PART II

Life in the Neighborhoods

CHAPTER 4

Neighborhood Structures and Community Organizations

Chapters 4, 5, and 6 move our viewpoint from citywide structures to local settings, where much of life is experienced. This chapter describes the nature of neighborhood social structures and organizations as they developed in response to historical change and citywide pressures. Chapters 5 and 6 look at two aspects of local social process—everyday life and focus events. The latter include both celebrations and crises, which create a heightened consciousness of diversity. Local differences affect the nature of both everyday life and focus events.

Not all neighborhoods in Philadelphia felt the effects of macrostructural changes in the same way. These differences in trajectory affect who lives in the neighborhood in terms of ethnic diversity and class composition, the rate of turnover, and the ideas and actions of people toward each other. This overview examines the ways in which Kensington, Olney, and Port Richmond experienced effects of economic restructuring, as well as changes in the ways neighborhoods were linked to central power structures. The communities will be described in terms of their history and demography, including an in-depth view of their local organizations, leaders, and civic voices.

The three neighborhoods have been formed by different economic and demographic processes. The communities all see themselves as in decline, but only Kensington has really been starkly affected by economic shifts. Olney and Port Richmond see decline in areas near them and fear it. In their concerns about the quality of life and the future, many inhabitants resemble the Brooklynites described by Susser (1982) who fight to hold their communities together in situations in which the benefits of economic restructuring and urban development have passed them by.

Differences in turnover and in public and private investment generate differences in who lives in a neighborhood in terms of class composition and race/nationality. Patterns of social and geographical mobility create varying class compositions and class relationships, which play an important role. In all communities, the housing stock differs, the real-estate markets work differently, and segregation patterns vary. Consequently, the entry of newcomers, their accommodation to the community, and the public and private response of established residents to them are also very different.

The three communities in the study area are all located in the eastern part of Philadelphia, north of the center (see Map 1). They are in the historically white, predominantly Catholic working-class areas.[1] All three have reputations as tightly knit villages, the dominant Philadelphia image of neighborhoods. Each feels under threat from increasing blight (trash, graffiti, abandonment) and crime. To some extent they all respond by marking their boundaries in the face of a perceived "domino effect"—an inexorable social decay coming from outside their borders—but the interplay of differences in class composition affects these responses.

Kensington and Port Richmond, in the south, date back to the industrial mill areas that grew up along the Delaware River in the early days of the Republic. Olney, farther north, was a streetcar suburb built around the turn of the century, with bigger and higher quality housing. It was both more middle class than the areas farther south and more transient, as those with further middle-class aspirations continuously moved northward. Until recently, this area was white and predominantly Catholic.

While focusing on these three districts, the project also looked at the population movements between them and at their relationship to neighboring communities. Many Olney residents came from Kensington and still have relatives there. The changed nature of elective high-school programs means that Olney High School contains Kensington residents, while Kensington High School serves many students from Olney; the same relationship exists between Kensington and Port Richmond. All three communities once had similar institutional and organizational structures.

The social memory in these neighborhoods is based on their transformation during the 1880–1920 immigration waves. The popular view is to recall a past full of many nationalities ("We were always a little United Nations"), remembering the existence of nationality parishes and ethnic institutions. Yet the feeding of students from parish elementary schools to regional high schools often broke down nationality boundaries. Today, most of the established whites we encountered in fieldwork had multinational backgrounds.

Older residents remember when they were pressured to marry within the nationality group. "My mother-in-law never accepted me because I was not

German and she still doesn't," says a woman about sixty-five years old. Olney is remembered as a German and Irish neighborhood, and a few vestiges remain—a Sons of Killarney group, several Irish bars, occasional funeral services in German. While church membership rolls from the 1930s and 1940s are filled with German names, today's lists are not.[2]

Poles, specifically, clustered in Port Richmond. This remains the only neighborhood in the study area in which a single ethnic identity still dominates the reputation (but not the demographic reality) of a district. Port Richmond is also the largest, most institutionally complete Polish American area in the city.[3]

The North Philadelphia riot of 1964 was a major punctuating event in the historical memory and demography of the study area. It signaled the end of the white mercantile and residential presence in North Philadelphia (West of Kensington to Broad and west of Broad). It also accelerated migration of whites northward and eastward into Olney, Kensington, and Port Richmond and hardened the line between whites in the east and African Americans in the west on the Kensington border. In the 1970s' aftermath, Latinos began to move northward along a narrow band on both sides of 5th Street, forming a buffer between African Americans and whites.

Linking Civic Structures

In order to understand the local community groups, it is important to pinpoint changes after 1970 in the nature of civic organizations and in the way they link themselves to citywide structures. All three neighborhoods were once characterized by similar constellations of parish social structures, settlement houses (for immigrant services), nationality-based beneficials for mutual aid, sports leagues, home-and-school associations, male service clubs, businessmen's associations, and political-party clubs. These groups looked inward to the community and aimed for self-sufficiency. Many of them were linked to each other by overlapping leadership and to city government through the party patronage structure. Leaders were often committeepersons. As one leader said, "It used to be that if you wanted to contact city hall, you had to have an 'in' through the ward leaders and committeepeople."

Empowerment-oriented groups grew out of both the social change movements of the 1960s and 1970s, which emphasized community organization for local control and political change, and federal programs that emphasized citizen participation. These began to take on new significance in shaping city–locality relationships. Today, staff members of such city agencies as the Office of Housing and Community Development (which administers the Community Development Block Grant program) and the Philadelphia Citywide Development Corporation (which develops local strips and malls) have become important patrons for the neighborhood-based organizations as they vie for limited funds.

The old structures now exist beside the new, and some have adopted features from other groups. Yet there are distinctions in how these different types of civic groups define expectations for the neighborhood, recruit leaders and staff, seek funding, view newcomers and intergroup relations, and relate to citywide power structures. The types are not mutually exclusive: one organization may include several orientations, and neighborhood groups that began as one kind of organization have developed in other directions.

The first category, established community groups, includes entities like the parish societies, beneficials, service clubs, political clubs, and home-and-school associations, which have existed for decades. The leaders and most of the active members of these institutions in all three neighborhoods tend to be white established residents. These groups draw their mostly volunteer leadership from within the community, funding themselves through dues and such local events and activities as bakesales, raffles, and door-to-door solicitation. City-wide organizations generally ignore them unless there is a crisis in the neighborhood. Tied to the city in the past through the old party structures, these links weakened as the parties lost ground. Yet the links of these groups to the post-1970s' federal housing and antipoverty programs are also tenuous or nonexistent. They relate to the city when necessary through leaders who develop close working relationships with individuals in citywide institutions that service specific concerns, such as the police, recreation department, zoning board, or Licenses and Inspections.

The relationship between these organizations and newcomers varies, but all established groups share an expectation that newcomers should be brought into an existing community rather than a notion that the community should adapt to the needs of newcomers.

Established organizations make clear distinctions between insiders, people who are "of the neighborhood," safe and reliable, and those who are outsiders, threatening and dangerous. It is not race or nationality that distinguishes between the two; often, it is not even length of residence. It is, rather, whether one participates in neighborhood institutions and is articulated into neighborhood-based networks of communication and social relationships.

The second category, community empowerment organizations, includes groups that are by-products of increasing policy focus on neighborhoods, as well as grassroots political-mobilization movements. While the leadership of these organizations may be either homegrown or come from outside the neighborhood, the groups share a notion that they are developing resources within distressed communities. Furthermore, they use Alinsky organizing methods to perform their tasks, emphasizing social change. This category includes a variety of institutions created in response to antipoverty programs, such as neighborhood action councils (NACs) and community development corporations (CDCs), as well as mission-oriented projects that have emerged in long-established settlement houses and antigang programs.

All of these organizations are more likely to have paid staff and to rely on an array of private foundation, church, and government grants to fund their programs. Because of their funding sources and orientation, they are much more tied to new citywide power structures than are the established groups.

While organizing for collective empowerment, community control of housing stock, and other social changes is a primary goal, available funding sources create ongoing programs of social-service provision. Many have similar programs in housing, energy assistance, education (ESL/GED), human relations, and job development, as much because grants are available in these categories as because community members need these services.

Programs are frequently oriented toward the most impoverished members of the community, and in many cases staff members are much more comfortable working with newcomers and people of color than with white established residents. Since the white working class often views people with college education as outsiders who look down on them, and since staff are often more liberal than most residents, the tendency to downplay white working-class needs is reciprocated by established-white trepidation.

Whereas traditional groups respond to citywide forces by turning inward, empowerment groups are approached by citywide institutions whenever there is a perceived problem in the neighborhood. The relationship between these organizations and larger institutions is often contradictory. On the one hand, staffs of local organizations and citywide agencies work together closely on many projects. On the other hand, grassroots groups are much more likely to confront the powers that be than are established community organizations.

The difference between the two in relating to larger power structures reflects different modes of resistance. Members of established community groups use more passive methods of resistance (such as simply not involving themselves in citywide issues), while empowerment groups will stage sit-ins at city hall. When really pushed, established groups will resort to tactics like blocking a major intersection in their neighborhood, thus disrupting the flow of outsiders through the community, rather than going downtown and confronting city leadership. The key difference here involves the perceived relationship of the organization to the rest of the city.

Established community residents tend to view their neighborhood as a cohesive whole that is affected by hostile outsiders. The point of resistance then becomes limiting outsider access to the neighborhoods. Empowerment organizations also frequently view the city power structure as hostile, but they do not see the neighborhood as an isolate in relation to the rest of the city or, for that matter, the world—they often tie neighborhood conditions to global patterns. People in both types of organizations work with the existing power structure. However, while leaders in established groups more frequently develop strategies to work within the parameters of the existing system, leaders in empowerment groups expect to change the social and economic hierarchy.

In our description of community organizations and their activities, we do not mean to imply that one type of group is "better" or "more authentic" than the other. Nor do we mean to suggest that one type of organization should turn into the other. Both types serve constituencies within these neighborhoods effectively. Both are equally important and necessary. However, each type of organization operates in a different way and is likely to respond to different program initiatives to facilitate the interaction among newcomers and established residents.

Neighborhoods

Olney

Olney is the most diverse area in the city. One newspaper article describes it as follows: "Olney, with its *Casablanca* of cultures and people, symbolizes the massive population shifts that have given the city Spanish, Korean, Chinese, Vietnamese, and Cambodian accents" (Carvajal and Borowski 1991). In comparison to a decline in the city's overall population, Olney census tracts increased by 6.2 percent, including a 961 percent increase in Asians and a 360 percent increase in Latinos.

Since it first housed the new middle class in its early days as a streetcar suburb, its housing stock has attracted upwardly mobile people who often moved on to still better housing. The 5th Street corridor traverses residential neighborhoods from center city to the suburbs. It has long carried aspiring middle-class whites, followed by aspiring middle-class Latinos, northward. They cite the same pathway from parish to parish in their trip up this corridor to find better housing, regardless of whether they came five, fifteen, or thirty years ago.

Yet the neighborhood is also the center of remarkably stable institutions and many intergenerational families. A major campus of health-care institutions that exists nearby serves as a place of employment for both established and newcomer residents; a few scattered industrial sites are also nearby. Olney thinks of itself as a village and feels like a small town. A pattern of one-way streets and railroad obstructions forces all traffic onto 5th Street, a veritable main street that is the site of convenient shopping, several schools and service institutions, and many churches. A dense network of venerable neighborhood organizations also exists.

In a play developed by the community as part of an arts project and based on interviews by the playwright, Olney was frequently described as "a pass-through place" where seeking people stop for a while among the stable on their way to something better. Among the metaphors for describing the dialectic between the oldtimers and the newcomers was a sketch about Cain and Abel:

My name is Cain. The name "Cain" comes from the Hebrew word
kanah, to acquire or get. I have land. I own property. I have put down
roots. Here.
My name is Abel. My name comes from the word *hebel*, meaning breath,
vapor, anything moving, anything transient. I wander through these dry
hills and valleys.

Analysis of the data in Table 1 indicates that among the three neighborhoods Olney has the highest income, occupational, and educational levels, as
well as a high rate of home ownership, especially in contrast to Kensington.
This conforms with its role as a community of upwardly mobile middle-class
and aspiring middle-class residents. In Olney, the housing stock tends to be
larger than the rowhouses in Kensington and Port Richmond, although some
parallel housing exists. Front porches, backyards, and shade trees are found
more frequently. One Olneyite says,

> I could never live in Port Richmond, although the houses are sometimes
> more expensive than here [because of upkeep and remodeling]. Just
> think, the houses are built right up to the sidewalks and there are no
> lawns at all.

In contrast to Kensington, homes and lots in Olney are not only larger but
significantly different in condition. There is very little abandonment and
deferred maintenance in Olney. Moreover, there is little presence of government housing programs in the area. The first placement of a homeless family
in a house under a new nonprofit program for the homeless in 1988 generated
considerable community debate. While the housing pattern here has involved
largely single-family owner–occupants, there have always been some multifamily (low-rise) units. Today there is some negative comment by oldtimers
about increasing transiency in these units, largely attributed to newcomers.
One community leader told of a multifamily dwelling on her block that housed
a series of recently arrived Latinos as a way station.

> Every fifteenth of the month like clockwork, a moving van comes and
> one of the families moves out to be replaced by another.

This concern, however, was not raised as a public issue at any of the meetings
attended in two years.

At the time of the study, Olney was experiencing an even more rapid rate
of turnover. In 1980, census figures indicated that this neighborhood had a
high turnover rate; since 1984, when mortgage rates were lowered, the process
has accelerated. A recent report indicated that Olney had one of the highest
numbers of housing transactions (during a period in which the housing market
was stalled) of any area in Philadelphia. There were 921 sales in the Olney zip
code, with 212 in a comparable Kensington zip code (Stains 1991). One

Table 1. Community Socioeconomic Characteristics (Based on 1990 Census)

	Kensington	Olney	Port Richmond
Population	25,211	17,706	21,448
Median Age	33.2	27.5	35.4
(All numbers below are percentages.)			
White	49.5	28.9	96.7
Black	7.1	45.2*	1.9
Asian	1.2	8.6	0.9
Hispanic	51.8	31.8	1.3
Other	42.2	17.3	.5
Ancestry of Whites			
Multiple	19.8	11.3	35.2
Polish	2.3	0.7	31.2
Irish	15	6.4	23.7
German	10	4.2	14.3
Education			
High School Grad.	32.7	49	46.4
Some Coll. and Grads.	8.3	19.3	13.9
White—HS Grad.	38.8	57	54.1
College	9.7	21	15.7
Black—HS Grad.	36.5	72.2	40.3
College	3.8	30.3	20.4
Asians—HS Grad.	56.3	39.9	39.7
College	44.6	22.7	25
Hispanic—HS Grad.	29.1	49.5	—
College	8.3	16.5	—
Occupation			
Prof. and Managerial	11.7	18.3	15.3
Tech., Sales and Admin.	34.2	33.6	38
Blue-Collar	54.1	48.1	46.7
Household Income			
Less than $15K	58.6	34.2	36.4
White—<$15K	49.2	38.1	36.6
Black—<$15K	76.9	32.8	46.7
Asian—<$15K	54.9	30.7	27.5
Hispanic—<$15K	70.5	39.2	17.1
In Poverty	49.6	26.3	14.7
Not in Poverty	50.4	73.7	85.3
Asians in Poverty	8.8	25.5	71.9
Hispanics in Poverty	66.7	34.3	10.7
Ratio of Owners to Renters	1.5:1	2.5:1	4.6:1
Percentage of Vacant Housing Abandoned	72.2	53.6	63.9

Note: The census tracts used to depict Kensington, Olney, and Port Richmond are those indicated on Map 1. The population totals add to more than 100 percent because the Hispanic data are from another census file.

*The Black population is concentrated in one census tract with 79 percent Black population; the remaining three tracts contain an average Black population of 27 percent.

informant commented that after the winter of 1988 she came out of hibernation to find that her block had turned over more than half. Almost twenty new real-estate firms are operating in Olney, and several are resorting to such illegal practices as steering and phone solicitation. Multiple For Sale signs are visible on every street.

Residents and leaders bemoaned the decline in the quality of life. One school principal, who had been in the area for six years, remarked:

> You can see the decline around you. When I came, the streets were clean as a whistle. Today, we have regular patrols to pick up the trash that litters the sidewalks around the school. There was no graffiti. Today, the walls are covered.

Nevertheless, the community is considered a garden spot by the city agencies that serve this region (police, schools, etc.) compared to the neighborhoods to the south and west, particularly because there is little drug activity and housing abandonment. Nonetheless, there is an anticipation of decline from the south. In the words of one community leader:

> . . . They don't feel threatened yet. . . . I try to tell people that it's a domino effect. What happens in Feltonville [the next community to the south] is eventually going to happen here.

A Puerto Rican woman who moved from a drug zone farther south says, "It's coming. It's not bad yet, but it's coming."

Many continue to invoke the historic view of the area as "always a little United Nations," alluding to the days of the nationality parishes and underscoring their tradition of welcome and tolerance. Given that the influx of both immigrants and African Americans coincided with a decline in services, school overcrowding, turnover of business strips, and concern over drugs, there has been remarkably little blame placed on newcomers. Instead of serving as scapegoats, they are often viewed as fellow victims of city government, the media, and impersonal external forces (Goode 1990).[4]

Few of the incidents of harassment and violence that have occurred elsewhere in the city happen here. While there are reports of vandalism perpetrated on some African American and immigrant families, such events are uniformly blamed on immature teenagers and outside gangs and are publicly deplored.

Diversity Seekers

People are moving to Olney for very different reasons. These differences affect the public discourses and the underpinnings of intergroup communication. Inflation, recession, and the rising cost of new home construction have created a housing gap in Philadelphia for the white middle class since the mid-1970s. Fewer and fewer young families earn enough to afford a median-priced home in the region, and more and more middle-class people are looking to the older areas of the city for affordable housing. This factor has also contributed to the real-estate boom in Olney. The established white population in the neighborhood in 1980 was similar economically to that of Port Richmond in income and occupation. However, the recent changes have created what appears to some to be a very diverse white population. As one teacher says:

> You know, the white population here is very mixed. Most are middle class, but we also have upper middle class, blue-collar workers, and even outright "rednecks."

Whites who are younger and more middle-class than the majority of established residents are an important presence in the new public life. Not all of them are new to Olney; some are returning to the neighborhood where they grew up, and others have never left. These latter two groups have higher levels of education and often distance themselves socially from their parents:

> I like the diversity, but if you asked my parents they would say they hate it.

> I have decided to stay, but my parents are old fashioned and don't like change. They gave up and left.

The response of Olney families, especially the younger ones, to newcomers has been more than welcoming. Their model is Mount Airy, one of the few neighborhoods that resisted white flight in the 1970s and that remains integrated. Diversity is a sought-after neighborhood attribute, expressed in terms of broadening experience and increasing knowledge about and connectedness with the world. One new empowerment-oriented leader described Olney as

> a very diverse neighborhood that has some great potential. . . . It's got things that everybody wants. Good, affordable housing. . . . First-time home buyers can find a place in Olney. We have excellent schools. Integrated schools. Schools that are really committed to the neighborhood . . . with the . . . bonus that we're integrated and can learn from each other and encounter the world in a really unique setting of our everyday life.

Established People of Color

Aspiring middle-class African Americans and Puerto Ricans also come looking for better housing. Whites see these individuals as critical to creating the atmosphere desired by diversity seekers. Established people of color also speak positively of diversity. A Puerto Rican professional whose friends all live downtown observes:

> I like the neighborhood . . . because of the cultural flavoring. You know, the ethnic neighborhoods . . . have everybody, all kinds of people, all kinds of things going on, people speaking all kinds of languages, all varieties of stores. . . . In my neighborhood you can walk out and see movement going on, people going in and out, people hanging on the corner; . . . it's sort of like a mini-U.N. area.

Yet because the institutional and church lives of African Americans and Puerto Ricans lie further west and south they are not very active in the neighborhood. Most of the Latinos in Olney have moved there from further down the 5th Street corridor, and their institutional focus remains further south. Latinos we met as store owners, ministers, and social-service professionals active in the life of Kensington often lived in Olney for their family's housing and schooling needs.

Intermarried couples are visible in the public spaces of Olney. Many of the families we knew well had experience with intergroup marriage, whether their own, their siblings', or their children's. One such couple told of selecting the area because they had heard of its tolerance. A local white resident commented:

> There are so many interracial couples here that it has made Black men bold. I have lived in Philadelphia all of my life, and Black men have never bothered me in the street. Now they say suggestive things when I walk by. It is too acceptable here, and I do not like it.

New Immigrants

Newcomers find Olney attractive because there are ethnic real-estate submarkets; core institutions like churches, social-service centers, and retail stores that use native languages; and kin and landsman networks. The neighborhood is today a major institutional focus for several immigrant communities—Koreans, Asian Indians, Portuguese, Colombians, Central Americans, and, most recently, Cambodians. Each group has a different relation to the real-estate market. Several Indian and Portuguese agents and developers supposedly have been heard declaring various blocks to be "theirs." Suburban-bound Koreans (those who reside in Olney view their stay as temporary) do not play an active role in residential real estate but are central to business turnover. Cambodian refugees are initially placed by volunteer agencies and are not players in the real-estate game. The head of their association often helps clients find housing in the area by maintaining contact with several real-estate agents.

The immigrant populations in this area seem generally better off than many of their established neighbors. Those who were interviewed held jobs of equal or higher level, and they were often better educated than many of the long-term established whites, who either inherited their homes or bought them at very low prices. In general, members of newcomer households who were interviewed had very different material-consumption patterns and home-presentation styles than did established residents—they were both more cosmopolitan and had newer material possessions.

Newcomers are often suburban bound, using Olney as a temporary stop on the way to something better, as did their white predecessors. Both their material-consumption patterns and their lack of commitment to the area are sources of tension that raise concerns among established residents about their materialism, cheating, and failure to participate.

In spite of incipient submarkets (North Olney has a larger concentration of Asians and higher-income families, and South Olney has a higher concentration of Spanish speakers and lower-income families), the neighborhood is not characterized by significant residential segregation or clustering by group. It provides the greatest opportunity for interaction between newcomers and established residents—on the block, in schools, in stores, and in neighborhood organizations and other institutions.

Politics and Organizations

Traditional established organizations dominate the public life of Olney. There are four civic structures, some of which have existed for more than forty years.[5] The local strip-business association works closely with all these civic structures and also sponsors annual events.

All groups have overlapping leadership. In the first year of the study, the head of the businessmen's organization ran a major civic. The leaders' group consists of individuals who have run the organization for years or a group that rotates the leadership. Together they create a dense network of linkages and information channels in the neighborhood, set up to handle outsiders and to relate to citywide structures. We saw representatives of city organizations being passed along the same chain of contacts that we were sent to as we entered the community. While overlapping somewhat in function and territory and experiencing periods of competitive feuding, the leaders have increasingly worked together as the neighborhood transition accelerates.

Political party lines have become less significant in recent years in Olney and no longer organize relationships. One person who has been active in politics and has run for ward leader recalls:

> [We used to operate through party connections] but now my vice
> presidents are of different parties. We go to every hearing and visit every

elected representative regardless of party affiliation. Today, committeemen from both parties collaborate actively in the civics.

The election of an African American councilperson in the 1980s required some adjustments in interaction. One leader said, "When I went to her first meeting, I was the only white person in the room." Initially viewed with hostility in Olney as an extension of the generally distrusted mayor, she has proved to be hardworking and effective, sends helpful staff members to all local meetings, and is no longer seen as favoring her African American wards farther west. Part of Olney is also represented by an African American state legislator, who also enjoys an excellent reputation among all the leaders of the community. The staffs of these leaders regularly attend civic meetings and events. Organizations headed by Republicans also work well with the African American Democratic elected officials who are necessary brokers to the administration.

The civics touch most oldtimers in the community. Although attendance at meetings has declined as population changes, most people hear about what goes on at meetings, and this contributes to shaping the public consensus on difference and change. The main activities of Olney civics have traditionally been annual celebratory events and regular public forums. As the neighborhood is increasingly seen as threatened by decline, these organizations focus largely on issues relating to local quality of life, acting as clearinghouses for reports of crime, abandoned cars, zoning irregularities, and other transgressions related to parking, garbage, odor, and noise.

The relationship between the leaders of these groups and community residents is that of brokerage. One leader said, "I am a middleman. People bring me their problems and I refer them to the right people." In many ways they resemble the old machine. Leaders are intermediaries with city agencies and often invite public officials to meetings to allow residents to air complaints. Expressing frustration and making attempts at timely problem solving are the core of these meetings. Rather than being adversarial, the relationship of leaders to the city is frequently one of seeking patrons for protection. Besides serving on the boards of the local police-advisory and recreation commissions, leaders find friends in the power structure who they can call to alleviate problems. They frequently told us about friends and contacts in certain agencies who fulfill this role.

Civil Public Discourse

At public meetings, the community presents an image of itself as caught between the rich and the poor. Residents project a self-image of responsible taxpayers who are getting less and less in return. "Where are our taxes going?" is a constant refrain in discussions about declines in city services. Often, meetings consist of a litany of complaints and expressions of frustration.

Oldtimers want to enclose the community, protecting its traditions and keeping out what they see as inexorable decline. Military metaphors imply siege conditions—"standing our ground"; making "a last stand in the city"; "I was pushed out of North Philadelphia [by the threat of lowering real-estate values]. Never again!"; "If you love your community, stay here and fight for it."

Yet newcomer people of color are not the enemy. The subject of group difference is avoided by talking about the deterioration of the neighborhoods as the result of impersonal forces and of Philadelphia's power structure. Rank-and-file residents often express hostility toward the city government and what is happening to the city. Newcomers are not seen as culprits but as fellow victims. They are welcomed as allies in the fight.

Allusions to city agencies that will not respond in a timely fashion and policies that will be harmful occur at every meeting. One committee chair in a traditional civic begins his report every month with, "Look what *they* have done to us now." Some of the alleged violations of Korean merchants are even blamed on the city. In this argument, the lack of city enforcement of codes is at fault. If done properly, code enforcement would educate the newcomers. The media are also frequently blamed for generating a negative image of Olney.

To avoid accusations of group bias, discourse in Olney involves complaints about rule infractions and implies that rules can be learned and behaviors can be changed. In constant references to "they have to learn," any problem situation is viewed as temporary. People recount tales of "teaching" newcomer neighbors "the way we do it here." Finally, legal transgressions are tied to building codes and noise ordinances to underscore the legitimacy of the complaint and avoid the appearance of intolerance.

In one case of censorship of complaints against groups, a member criticized Koreans for seeming not to participate in the community. Immediately, three members jumped to their defense. Two used the "model immigrant" image: one said that Koreans cannot participate because they are family oriented and have to be home for family dinners (which, incidentally, rarely occur in this mercantile group as a result of time pressure); another said that they worked long hours in their businesses. The third speaker made some chiding remarks about racial stereotypes and cited the hard times that immigrants have.

The posture of established leaders in both public and private conversations is that all people are welcome so long as they behave properly. One leader, whose organization's motto is Good Neighbors Make Good Neighborhoods, said of accepting new racial and nationality groups:

> We just asked the neighbors to treat them as neighbors. If they're good neighbors, fine; if they're bad neighbors, we'll let them know. . . . If they live in this neighborhood, they're neighbors. We accept them and act like it.

At one particularly angry meeting someone said, "The ones who move in [unlabeled] are not keeping the place clean. They blast their TVs and radios. They put trash on the sidewalk." Another resident replied, "It's not that they're not clean. They just do it wrong. They push leaves into sewers and stuff up the culverts." They have to learn.

Even though much of the explicit conversation at regular meetings is directed at blaming city government, to some degree outsiders and newcomers are covertly blamed in coded talk about changes in the quality of life. Overall, the coding of this discourse reflects larger societal norms. These white working- and middle-class people have learned not to utter remarks that might be interpreted as racist.

While perpetrators of the many transgressions are *never* labeled in public settings as coming from a particular country, resentment of newcomers is frequently stated in private. Everyone "knows," for example, that Koreans ignore trash-day rules and park their mini-vans on the sidewalks, that Puerto Ricans work on their incapacitated cars on the street, and that people from various Asian groups create "funny" cooking smells.

The stereotypes that fuel the complaints come from actual experience in the daily lives of these community residents. Some foreign-born and nonwhite newcomers do not play by community rules. When pressed, established residents assure outsiders that problems stem from people not knowing the rules, not from skin color. This is, in fact, largely the case. People are well aware that some of their major problems are with "low-life" or "trashy" whites. "The white families are the worst," said one white informant who was having a serious feud with her next-door neighbor involving constant vandalism and harassment. Another established woman on a block with almost complete turnover in the past three years said, "The only problems we have had were with a new white-trash family." Many were quick to point out that the graffiti problem in the neighborhood was started by a white gang.[6] We frequently heard a common human-relations message, "There are good and bad in every group."

Empowerment Network

As change accelerated, established leaders saw that the broker system was no longer sufficient and exhorted members to become more active in self-help. The message is that we can only solve our problems if we all get involved, work together, and volunteer for self-help cleanups, town watch, and systems for reporting trash and zoning violations. In recent years an empowerment-oriented network has developed in Olney, especially among the younger established residents who seek diversity. One organization in the neighborhood that clearly fit into the empowerment model was the creation of an activist minister.[7] It is involved in a number of programs, such as block organizing, ESL, and neighborhood human-relations projects. A satellite office of a settlement house, it is also the center of a network of progressive clergy and others developing empowerment activities throughout the neighborhood. Among these is a coalition group trying to stop questionable real-estate practices that accelerate turnover (see Chapter 8).

In its efforts, the group has imported training in community organization from Kensington; manuals based on the Saul Alinsky principles of community organizing were used in these sessions.[8] For empowerment leaders, there were two dominant images of the powerless newcomer minority. Since the African American/white dyad was uppermost in people's consciousness, African American leaders were often recruited from nearby communities to integrate organizations. The other image was of the political or economic refugee; newcomers were viewed as oppressed and needy, established residents as potentially racist, regardless of relative class status or economic power.

In explaining why established residents feel threatened by newcomers, an empowerment leader demonstrates his view of undifferentiated newcomer powerlessness:

> Oldtimers experience a feeling of powerlessness when they hear other languages being spoken . . . but that's okay because many of the new residents of Olney have to endure that every day. And the conversations they hear are decisions of power, decisions that are influencing the direction of the neighborhood for them. And because of the language barrier, they are not able to participate.

This statement fails to take into account that newcomers are in fact exerting a lot of influence on the neighborhood through their enterprises and the carving out of real-estate submarkets. It also assumes that newcomers have a long-term commitment to the neighborhood; in fact, like the upwardly mobile whites who preceded them, they often have more choices than established residents and quickly move to the suburbs.

The empowerment group found racism to be a critical problem in the neighborhood and consequently fostered many human-relations activities. Over the two years of fieldwork, the diversity seekers tried to broaden group representation in leadership positions in one of the traditional civics. During this time, the organization was often a battleground between those who saw change as positive and the old guard, who felt threatened. When a diversity seeker chided people at a meeting for complaining about newcomer nonpartici-pation, one older regular asked loudly, "And where do you live, Ms. X?" This reminded everyone that even though she was an officer, the chastiser was an outsider, a staff member of an empowerment group who did not live in the neighborhood.

As those from the empowerment network became active in the civic, they brought in more "outsiders," like an African American nonresident teacher from a local school, to make the board diverse. The teacher accepted the post as a favor to her friend in the empowerment group; but she was sometimes absent and not interested in many local issues, thus inviting private critiques. These moves were never publicly contested by the established members, whose commitment to nonracist civility and need for volunteers was preeminent. Several established leaders, moreover, were deeply committed to a multicultural community and worked exceptionally hard as brokers between the empowerment and traditional factions. Mutual hostility dissipated gradually. By the time fieldwork was complete, an empowerment figure had become president of the group, and representation from the empowerment organization on the board had become part of the expected leadership structure.

Participation of Newcomers

In attending monthly meetings of two traditional civics for two years, we found that only a handful of newcomers was ever present and that each came only once. Each was brought personally by a different central figure who wished to increase representation. Over the same time, until a nonresident was brought in as an officer, the only regularly attending African American was the representative from the city councilperson's office. When a Latina known to empowerment leaders moved into the neighborhood, she was immediately tapped for leadership. In both cases, prior working relationships between organization leaders and persons from non-European backgrounds in citywide human-relations activities was the salient factor in involvement, rather than interest in or knowledge of local issues. When a nonresident Korean field-worker began to attend regularly, he was approached eagerly by the leadership of several organizations as a possible "representative." He came to be used as a contact and broker to a community of which he was not really a member.

Ordinarily, newcomers are not part of regular community channels among organization leaders; both sides distance themselves from one another. One individual in the local established network was seen as the key person in contacting members of "other groups." At one meeting, a leader looked at him and said,

> You contact the Hispanics and the Asians. You seem to know what to do and who to call.

In fact, the "experts" just relied on the standard brokers, the visible business-persons, social-service agents, and heads of ethnic associations, whose identities were shared by the human-relations institutions in the city.

Leaders are clearly aware of their dependence on newcomers' participation and capital if local groups are to remain viable. The head of a business organization points to Korean capital as preventing the demise of the local shopping strip and the organization's annual round of activities. The town watch actively (but unsuccessfully) tries to incorporate Asians. A community leader exhorts Latinos to "bring your people. Let me sign you right up for committees." At another meeting, a leader asked everyone to bring an Asian or Latino with them to the next session—"You know, one of the people you know on your block."

Established residents express a desire for newcomers to join in helping to protect the community in its struggles. They want newcomers who will participate in structures and who see the value of long-standing traditions and institutions. Becoming an insider in Olney can be achieved by "paying dues"—learning how to fit in, volunteering, and participating in established community systems. This is contrasted to the perceived behavior of newcomers—being aloof and standoffish, "taking care of their own," or "sticking together too much."

Established residents complain about low newcomer participation and blame them for not being community oriented. Complaints are rampant in all the home-and-school associations about the nonparticipation of newcomer families—Koreans in one school, Puerto Ricans and other Spanish speakers in two others. At one community organization meeting an established white resident angrily complained that while everyone on her block got fliers she was the only one who came to the meeting. The resident listed the others on her block: nine African Americans, five Latinos, and four Asians.

It is often assumed that newcomers are participating in their own parallel, U.S.-type local organizations. At a meeting of an empowerment group that was embarrassed about its almost totally white regulars, one participant said, "We should send someone to the Latino and Asian meetings and explain ourselves to them."

This low level of participation is no doubt partly attributable to lack of time and interest on the part of the newcomers; as we have indicated, many are suburban bound, with Olney being merely an entry settlement. It is also due to the pull of competing citywide ethnic organizations. Many people say they do not come because of concerns about language and their ability to (mis)understand and be (mis)understood.

Yet there is also a palpable boundary around the mutually known group of established insiders that is difficult to penetrate. Meetings often begin with greetings between old friends and take on a tone that often implies cliquishness and disdain of newcomers who do not know the rules. While leaders reach out, the rank and file cluster in closed groups. A Portuguese real-estate agent was once persuaded to come to a meeting to talk about a problem. By drinking coffee during the proceedings he violated the rule of waiting for the meeting to end before drinking and being sociable. Oldtimers talked about his having broken the rules; he never returned.

These kinds of problems were also significant in the Home and School (Parent–Teacher) Associations we observed in two Olney schools (Goode,

Schneider, and Blanc 1992). In one school, newcomer parents stood around the periphery at a luncheon cookout watching a group of established white and African American teachers and parents joke loudly together around the barbecues. Only one teacher approached the five new-immigrant parents to talk.

The formality of most meetings exacerbated this distance. The presence of officers seated up front, the podium format, and the adherence to formal procedural rules were intimidating. While established officers complained that new families did not participate, at the first meeting of the parents' group at one school we observed that new-immigrant Latino parents outnumbered oldtimers. The meeting was a formal presentation of the planned events for the year and assumed much prior understanding of the nature of these activities. The only informal communication was the collection of dues. The Latino parents did not return for subsequent meetings.

Newcomers may also choose not to participate in these events because of their often correct interpretation of the coded discourse—that they are frequently seen, covertly and privately, as the cause of local problems. At one public meeting in a community just south of Olney called to deal with the aftermath of a Puerto Rican death at the hands of a white youth, there was no explicit mention of race or ethnicity except for a negative remark about one Hispanic spokesperson. The usual litany of complaints about no parking spaces, increased crime, and trash on the sidewalk occurred without mentioning race or ethnicity. The meeting was called for city officials (mostly African American) to explain to the community what was being done; as usual, there were negative remarks about city government. Yet at the end of the meeting a young African American woman got up to say:

> I'm leaving. I've sucked in what you do to me. You judge one and all. It's not fair. I get accused of bringing rats. You have done nothing but talk racism. Against Spanish. Against African Americans. [Loud shout of denial from the audience].

It was not clear whether she identified with the Latinos and resented the coded and implicit hostility toward them or whether she did not like the subtle hostility to the African American city officials and interpreted that as racist.[9] Her reaction does show the fear and trepidation that is felt by minorities when they come to meetings so dominated by established residents. The outburst was greeted by a plea for the woman to come to the human-relations committee and "bring your people."

Coming together can sometimes cut through problems. A Greek couple had bought a building near the high school and wanted to set up a food/video game shop. Fearing the congregation of high school students because of their antisocial behavior, the community had stopped zoning changes for similar (but oldtimer-owned) pizza parlors and other hangouts in the past. A petition campaign had already collected signatures protesting this zoning change as well. However, the couple developed the strategy of doing their own petition, explaining to neighbors that they would close the store during dismissal time at the high school. The door-to-door, personal approach had worked, even with their limited language skills. They presented their petition to the organization at a session where the husband's appeals in halting, accented English were seen as brave and charming and won the support of the members.

Empowerment groups, in spite of their mission to reach out, have the same problem with participation, often finding it necessary to import African Americans from nearby communities. They also actively recruit Latinos who show interest, as in the case of a Puerto Rican from New York who moved in, became involved in an arts program, and was recruited for several political activities.

Port Richmond

In contrast, Port Richmond retains the flavor of Philadelphia's classic working-class white ethnic neighborhoods. It sees itself as a bounded entity apart from the rest of the city. Community residents clearly feel an allegiance to their neighborhood instead of to the city as a whole. For example, during a lunchtime conversation at the Polish nationalities parish school about holiday vacations in Florida, New Jersey, and even Poland, one child said that the family was going to Bridesburg, where her mother was born. Bridesburg is the next neighborhood north, less than two miles away. While it, too, is predominantly Polish, both children and adults in Port Richmond recognize Bridesburg as a different place, as separate as a town in another state or country. They often speak of the various neighborhoods in the city as separate entities and, like established Olney residents, want to protect their village from encroaching crime and drugs brought by outsiders.

Port Richmond is part of an eastern promontory or bulge along the Delaware River, and it does not follow the grid pattern of the city. The streets are not contiguous and often are attached at an angle to the main thoroughfares. It does not easily articulate with the transportation routes and traffic of the rest of Philadelphia. This helps the community to maintain its boundary and sense of separateness.

Most of the housing stock consists of late nineteenth-century rowhouses that either front directly on the sidewalk or have small porches. Port Richmond residents take great pride in their homes, most of which, over the years, have been renovated inside and out. Neighbors know each other here, and maintenance standards are reinforced by informal community pressure. Housing values in Port Richmond are generally double those of adjacent Kensington, even though the housing stock is identical, and prices often rival the larger houses in Olney. Residents are also fiercely proud of their relative degree of safety, and they fear that the decline of Kensington, specifically crime and abandoned housing, will encroach on their neighborhood. The housing market operates largely on an informal basis. There are rarely For Sale signs, and many buyers and sellers are brought together by word of mouth. Intergenerational inheritance is still common. Table 1 indicates the highest ratio of home ownership here.

Both the physical space and social dynamics of Port Richmond are dominated by four Catholic parishes and several large Protestant congregations. In this predominantly white Catholic neighborhood, the parish is the basis of social life. In the heart of Port Richmond, this is visually symbolized by the presence of the large spires of four major Catholic churches: three nationality parishes (Polish, German, Italian) and the territorial parish, recognized as Irish. Many residents claim Polish descent. However, as in other working-class communities formed at the turn of the century, many families have intermarried with other people of European descent, and people transfer membership between the ethnic parishes frequently, depending on family allegiances, feelings toward other parishioners or the priest, or expectations of the parish schools.

Polish national ancestry is dominant here, in contrast to Olney and Kensington. The Polish presence in the neighborhood is symbolized by a number of institutions and businesses. The largest Polish nationalities parish is in Port Richmond. Several of the beneficials and several Polish travel agencies are located close to the parish; a bank started by Polish immigrants is also nearby. Although the bank maintains a Polish-speaking teller to serve new émigrés and has kept a Polish name to attract business in the community, it is now a branch of a larger regional banking conglomerate. Polish bakeries, restaurants, and other businesses are also located in Port Richmond. Polish émigrés and Polish Americans from throughout the Philadelphia area regularly return to this neighborhood to buy special foods and other items for holidays.

Residents remember Port Richmond as a tight-knit immigrant community where people took care of their homes and each other. In the first half of the twentieth century, foreign languages (particularly Polish) were often heard in the neighborhood. Women would wash the stairways and sidewalks, and residents would look out for their neighbors. For example, some of the small stores on the community shopping strip were owned by Jews. One teacher at the Polish nationalities parish school reports that her grandmother would look after the store for one Jewish shopkeeper during her Sabbath.

The neighborhood experienced a number of changes in the intervening years. As workers gained more income after World War II, some families moved to newer sections of the city and to suburban New Jersey. This trend continues today. However, families maintain ties in both sections of Philadelphia, and a number of households have moved back to Port Richmond.

As in the rest of the city, most of the larger industries have now relocated; however, a number of small factories, such as machine shops, still exist in the area. Since some small factories and some service industries are owned by Polish Americans, by established Polish immigrants, or have Polish-speaking employees, newcomers frequently find jobs in these secondary-sector businesses where Polish is spoken.

Changes in the economic base brought several concurrent trends in local mobility patterns for established residents. Some local people remain in blue-collar occupations, while others have moved up into supervisory jobs within manufacturing firms or into white-collar managerial positions in the service sector (see Table 1). Increasing numbers of third- and fourth-generation community residents go to college. On the other hand, some people in the neighborhood have become increasingly impoverished as the economy restructures.

Despite movement both to and from the neighborhood, Port Richmond maintains an aura of cohesion. Whole families remain nearby, and neighbors keep track of each other. This community has the largest proportion of nuclear-family households, and Table 1 indicates the highest median age of the three study neighborhoods. In fact, there are many three-generational families living near each other in close interaction. A nun who teaches at the Polish nationalities parish school commented that her students know that "if Babci [grandmother] lives on Edgemont street and if I get in trouble at school at 11, she's going to know about it by 12:15."

The community also maintains its European immigrant flavor. A large percentage of Polish émigrés settle initially in either Port Richmond or Bridesburg. Some people from each of the immigration waves described in Chapter 3 stay in the neighborhood permanently. Polish is spoken openly on the streets, and newcomers are visible throughout the area.

While Port Richmond generally maintains an aura of relative prosperity and safety, crime and drug use do exist there. One park is considered dangerous because drug users frequent it. People report that friends and family members are addicted to drugs. Unlike the situation in some sections of Philadelphia, most drug dealing and use in Port Richmond takes place within homes or local bars instead of on the streets. Since residents seldom see drug use or drug-related crime, it is not perceived as a crushing problem. Teenagers hang out on corners and at the playground late at night drinking and causing trouble. The community is aware of these problems, but they are often blamed on outsiders or a few bad residents. Other community members note that they hung out on corners when they were growing up and see problems with teenagers as a familiar transitional generational issue. Newcomer Poles are seldom blamed for community problems.

Port Richmond sustains a number of small businesses on the major thoroughfares of Allegheny Avenue and Richmond Street. Several other businesses (corner groceries, neighborhood bars, and other local service businesses) are located throughout the neighborhood. Unlike Olney and Kensington, the majority of the businesses located in Port Richmond are owned by longtime Port Richmond residents or by people with long associations with the community.

The Aramingo shopping strip (a series of malls with supermarkets, fast-food outlets, and stores representing large national retail chains) forms one boundary of the neighborhood. It replaced some of the closed factories and warehouses in this community. Most residents shop on this strip and frequent the restaurants there, which have become favorite hangouts for neighborhood teens.

As one of the few large mall-like areas in the city, the Aramingo strip is frequented by many groups from the Kensington area and is one of the few settings in which African Americans and Latinos come into regular and frequent contact with people from the white-dominated areas of Port Richmond.

Port Richmond presents itself as all white, and Table 1 indicates a striking dominance of whites here, compared to Olney and Kensington. A pocket of African Americans, however, has been there for generations. A few Puerto Ricans also live in the neighborhood. The community is portrayed as extremely racist throughout Philadelphia. Puerto Ricans say that when they arrive in the city, they are warned to stay out of Port Richmond at night to avoid trouble. This perception is based in part on historical fact and present-day realities. One middle-aged resident reported that people would lock their doors and close their shutters when African American salespeople came into the neighborhood when she was growing up.

While Port Richmond residents now include people with a range of occupations, few are affluent, and most retain a working-class sense of insecurity. Their well-maintained homes are their primary assets. Many residents connect the decline in Kensington with the time when people of color moved into that neighborhood. They also note that city services declined when the African American mayor took power. They fear that the city administration will forcibly integrate their neighborhood, bringing on the white flight and decline they ascribe to Kensington and North Philadelphia.

Despite the image and reality of racism in Port Richmond, residents maintain contradictory attitudes toward people of color. Long-term African American and Puerto Rican residents are taken for granted within the community. People in Port Richmond often work in integrated workplaces and the older children mostly attend integrated schools. Many residents have friends from different races and express openness about people of other backgrounds. They are curious about Polish newcomers and some of the people of color they meet on the Aramingo strip. As discussed in detail in later chapters, in many ways racism in this community implies fear of unknown outsiders moving into the neighborhood.

Politics and Organizations

Traditional ward politics is still strong here. Most residents seem to go directly to ward leaders and committeepeople for help. While leaders in Kensington claim that neighborhoods like Port Richmond receive more attention because they are closely looked after by their city councilpersons, average residents of Port Richmond seem as frustrated with the decline of city services as do residents of other neighborhoods. In the tradition of ward politics, local people clearly see city neighborhoods and politics as based on ethnicity and race. For example, residents at a town watch meeting complained about lack of police response. The town watch leader explained that he would get a police car to guard a Puerto Rican–owned business that had been threatened after racial incidents. Residents grumbled that it was up to the Puerto Rican (at-large) councilman to send a car down from "their" neighborhood to protect "their" business, rather than having this community use "its" resources to protect something of "theirs."

The neighborhood has become more oriented toward the Republican party in both national and local affairs. Part of this comes from the "Rizzocrat" Republicans who shifted party allegiance when former mayor Frank Rizzo switched parties. His move was taken by white ethnic communities to be an unspoken declaration that the Democratic city government was too African American and too liberal. Generally conservative sentiments about welfare and mistrust of government also led many Port Richmond residents to support Ronald Reagan. The endorsed Republican mayoral candidate for the 1991 election kicked off his campaign with an appearance here. Leaders of Polish American organizations have become visibly Republican in recent years, inviting then-candidate George Bush to open their cultural center and including a Republican registration table at the Polish weekend at Penn's Landing, a center city festival location.

Port Richmond is very different from the other two neighborhoods in the way public linkages are articulated, relying more on informal communication than on formal structures. Although Port Richmond is dotted with sports leagues, parish structures, and other groups, there are no large civic umbrella organizations, empowerment groups, or community development corporations in the community. Groups here rely more on personal communication between people known to each other. Port Richmond was just organizing its first town watch in the summer of 1989, and there were very few of the formal block organizations found in the other neighborhoods. This was not surprising in an area that both resists such citywide organizing and is bypassed by most of it.

The four parishes are important centers in Port Richmond. Each well-kept parish reveals a committed congregation. All maintain separate schools that, in turn, receive substantial financial and volunteer support from the community. During the school year, the public spaces in the neighborhood are dominated by children in uniforms from the various schools. Like the residents, the clergy, teachers, and church secretaries are interested mostly in events and activities within the community, an attitude typical of established groups.

Longtime community residents put as much effort into city-sponsored local facilities as they put into the parishes. For example, the playground advisory group at the local recreation facility runs a full range of programs.

Many of the citywide human-relations organizations consider Port Richmond exclusively white territory that is beyond the pale of their activities. In the past, the informally enforced boundary inhibited the regular occurrence of crises that drew attention to other parts of the city. Moreover, the perceived racism of neighborhood residents is seen as too formidable for human-relations activity to be effective.

As in Olney, people become insiders by working for the community. But it is harder for new immigrants than for established residents from other neighborhoods to become insiders here. Most of our work in Port Richmond focused on Polish organizations. The parish activities cater primarily to the Polish American established residents. While Polish masses are offered as a community service for the elderly who did not learn English and for newcomers who have not yet mastered the language, the parish makes no attempt to bring newcomers and established residents together on an equal footing. All parishwide events respond to established tastes. While Polish-language classes and new-comer-oriented events take place in the parish hall, they are kept separate from other activities. For example, a dance class that included both newcomers and established residents took place on the same night as an ESL class for newcomers; the events were held in adjacent rooms. While children danced and played together, newcomer and established parents sat at different tables talking about similar topics in different languages. As newcomers came into the hall looking for the ESL class, established residents would give them directions in Polish, then resume their conversations in English.

Much of the distancing that occurs between newcomers and established residents in Polish ethnic organizations centers on different expectations held by the two populations. This is particularly true of the church—established residents expect newcomers to conform to the "good immigrant" model, being grateful for church charity and eager to Americanize.

Newcomers, on the other hand, expect another kind of church and a different attitude toward Poland from Polish Americans. The Catholic Church in Poland has always served as a primary social-service agency and has been in the forefront of the battle for democracy. Newcomers expect full support from the church. Although accustomed to supporting the church financially, they are surprised at the level of volunteer effort expected of them. Since many work long hours to establish themselves here, they do not have as much time to give to the church as do established residents. They also expect Polish Americans to know about modern Poland and to show an active commitment to improving its political and economic situation. They are frustrated that Polish Americans think of the homeland as a backward country and are more concerned with events in the United States than events there.

Newcomers from the intelligentsia are particularly chagrined to find that the church and the Catholic relief agencies often offer them "secondhand clothes that anyone would be ashamed to wear" and low-skilled jobs. They expect much more help from the parish. Occasionally they look down on working-class Polish Americans and their Americanized Polish. Established residents, in turn, consider these newcomers pushy foreigners. Working-class newcomers fit in much better than members of the intelligentsia; they expect less from the church and are more successful in meeting established expectations.

Like Olney oldtimers, established residents in Port Richmond resent the fact that newcomers do not participate in parish activities and see them as too materialistic. Yet here there is no pressure to keep resentment out of public discourse, since race is not involved. Primary critical models applied to new Poles revolve around materialism, arrogance, and expecting more than turn-of-the-century immigrants received. For example:

> They are materialistic, they want everything in a year's time. They think we owe them.

> When I came, nobody helped me make my way. How do they get all this welfare and stuff when we Americans can't?

> When we came to America you went to Ellis Island, and if you had one scab on your finger you were sent back.

> We could pack the church every Sunday, but they don't support or go to church, they worship the almighty buck.

> We sell coffee and cake at the masses, but [at] the [Polish] mass no one ever comes. If it was free they would all be down there, but to pay a quarter for a cup of coffee to support the church, they won't show up.

Yet the lines between newcomers and established residents can be crossed, and each group is genuinely interested in the other. Established residents within the Polish ethnic community maintain concern for Poland. Children try to make newcomers welcome and sometimes attempt to learn Polish. Both adults and children are curious about aspects of Polish culture. Newcomers enjoy the abundance of material goods in the United States. Most are in the country by choice and intend to make a life here. The majority expect to learn English. Newcomers who participate in established organizations are incorporated over time.

Kensington

Unlike Olney and Port Richmond, Kensington has been directly and massively affected by deindustrialization.[10] It has long been described as a stable white Catholic community in which families sent generation after generation to work in the local factories (Seder 1990; Binzen 1970). The small rowhouses were built for the industrial work force in the late nineteenth and early twentieth centuries. As the plants closed and jobs disappeared, depopulation followed. Abandonment was viewed as a serious problem as early as twenty years ago, when people began to organize at the grass roots to control the housing stock.[11]

In Kensington, much of the abandonment was not attributable to slumlords, since the rate of owner occupancy was high. Instead, as the real-estate market became depressed and the population aged, many people died or left to join families who had departed before. With bank redlining, people could not afford to maintain their houses and when they could not sell them they walked away from tax encumbrances (Bartelt and Leon 1986).

Kensington overlaps and adjoins the official North Philadelphia planning area, the poorest in the city. Although North Philadelphia is largely African American, West Kensington, on the boundary, is where very poor African Americans, Puerto Ricans, and whites share space. Today, it is also one of the most infamous "drug supermarkets" in the city. It most resembles the situation Susser (1982, 206) found in Brooklyn, with poor whites living on the border of a ghetto. For them, it was easy to equate the deterioration of quality of life with race and to see racial competition as a ready explanation for the problems they faced.

Kensington is the poorest of the three neighborhoods we studied in income and in the number of households in poverty (Table 1). Levels of education, occupation, and homeownership are markedly lower than those of Olney and Port Richmond. The dynamics of white and Puerto Rican—African American Kensington are different from each other, with Puerto Ricans and African Americans less well off and more transient than whites. Yet, some of the poorest whites in Philadelphia live here. The neighborhood holds the most families on public assistance and has the highest proportion of blue-collar workers across groups. Kensington has more abandoned housing than the other two communities, as well.[12]

As the housing stock emptied, Latino migration to the area increased; African Americans moved eastward after the North Philadelphia riots. Other sources of diversity in Kensington include many non–Puerto Rican Latinos, Koreans (who mostly live above their stores until they can afford to move away), some Asian refugees, and a large community of Palestinians. Neighborhood leaders have noticed the increase in Asians and are beginning to recognize the need to incorporate them in programs.

Some of the whites who remained had all their equity in their homes and could not find affordable housing elsewhere, nor a good price if they wanted to sell. One informant said:

> We can't sell our house. L and I [Licenses and Inspection] says we have to put $11,000 in it to bring it to code before we sell. We can't afford this so it will just fall down around us.

The real-estate submarkets here are diverse. A new Latino housing market developed on the western end of Kensington for both owner–occupiers and landlords and tenants. Several established real-estate firms still operate a for-profit market. In addition, the community development movement, helped along by CDBG legislation, has created locally controlled corporations and coalitions whose goal is to take control of the empty housing stock, rehabilitate it, and sell it. This is the central activity of six local organizations. Two groups have started land trusts, which will accumulate vacant properties until they can be developed. Finally, Kensington is a major location for scattered-site public housing units.

The name "Kensington" refers to a large block of territory that includes a number of distinct neighborhoods. While decline has occurred throughout the area, different sections have had different experiences. This study concentrated on Norris Square (which is predominantly Puerto Rican) and on another area near Kensington and Allegheny, the major intersection, which was occupied mostly by poor whites (see Map 1). Our work with organizations provided some information on areas that resemble Port Richmond and on others with widely divergent demographic profiles.

Two decades of transition in Kensington have led to contested lines and a striking, checkerboard population distribution. Today, the community is spatially divided into white-dominated areas (largely in the east) and sections dominated by Puerto Ricans (along with some African American areas) in West Kensington. Both English and Spanish speakers are found throughout the neighborhood. There are clusters of blocks in the western zone where Spanish is the dominant language on the street and Spanish speakers control local institutions. Further east, there are all-white clusters of blocks where "people would fight like hell if Blacks and Spanish tried to move in" and others that are accommodating to newcomer Latinos, although still English dominant. One informant in a neighborhood that has recently become Spanish dominant remarks:

> If there [are] just one or two Puerto Rican families on the block they make an effort to get along. But in this neighborhood, they are the majority and they make no effort.

In mixed areas, while locals of either group are comfortable in their immediate setting, African Americans, Latinos, and whites who are out of their locale and not known locally are concerned about their safety in an area reputedly "belonging" to another group. For example, one white family will not let their children go to a community program because they would have to walk through a Puerto Rican area and would get "rushed."[13]

Front Street is perceived as a racial line between whites and people of color, even though the areas on either side are now mixed. Crossing the line is still contested by violence or prolonged campaigns of harassment. A house sold by a community development corporation to an Asian/Latino couple was the subject of a nasty letter campaign and threats, a situation that the CDC was able to mediate. Street violence on the basis of race is constantly reported, and teens know which group controls which space.

In Norris Square, in West Kensington, devastated blocks are often cheek by jowl with organized blocks, the latter physically symbolized by the colonial-style streetlamps bought for safety and beautification. Block parties are another major activity for organized blocks.

Rachel, an African American woman in Kensington, has been block captain for ten years. She recalls vandalism when she was the first African American to move in twenty years ago, but she took a tough stance with teen vandals and they soon left her alone. Today, her block is almost half white and half Puerto Rican, with a few African American households. She often goes door to door to organize cleanups and to raise funds for the annual block party.

Since West Kensington is considered the heart of the "barrio," Latino (particularly Puerto Rican) identity is strong. While Hispanics in Olney tend to identify themselves to census takers as white (51 percent), in Kensington 80 percent define themselves as "other," signifying a separate identity.

Gentrification and competition for space and housing is feared from two white middle-class sources in the Norris Square area of West Kensington. One is an enterprise zone developed by a city–state partnership for midlevel manufacturers and distributors. The zone business association has mounted cleanup programs in the area closer to center city, leading some activist groups to worry about approaching gentrification. Meanwhile, they are angry that the zone association has excluded Latino small businesses from its activities (Ninivaggi 1994). Since most of the enterprises here are not labor intensive and hire from a citywide pool, they have had little positive impact on the neighborhood.

The other feared source of gentrification involves some middle-class people who have moved from center city as part of a socially committed religious community. This church includes white and Latino members from a range of class and professional backgrounds. Committed to work in the neighborhood, church members have set up programs like a health-care clinic focused on Latinos. Some of the younger white members moved into the neighborhood several years ago and have been careful to blend their life-style into the framework of the community. For example, afraid that exhibiting middle-class taste in renovating their homes would bring in speculators and separate them from the community they intended to serve, they carefully limited the outside renovations of their homes to the style used by others there. Many Latino leaders, nevertheless, saw them as appropriating valuable housing.

Politics and Organizations

Since Kensington is perceived as a blighted area by the citywide groups, it has become the center of numerous efforts at rehabilitation. Greater Kensington now includes dozens of active CDCs and NACs, supplemented by a number of church programs and other organizations with a variety of goals. Many Puerto Rican groups have branches in the community; however, many traditional organizations have faltered as established businesspeople and residents leave the area. In the white-dominant district we studied around one school, an Olney-style civic, with its monthly luncheon meetings, still operates. Its participants are limited to older established residents; leadership has been assumed by professionals from the nearby school, who aim to activate and inform the neighborhood. This group is totally isolated from the dominant Kensington community-action milieu.

Other established organizations have changed as the area has changed. Since Kensington was originally an immigrant community, several settlement houses have been located there since the turn of the century. As the neighborhood evolved, each of the programs chose different strategies to work with the community. One group developed a seniors' program for the remaining elderly residents and a women's program based on an empowerment model. Another settlement house has changed strategies over time. During the 1970s, concentration on empowerment models led to its creating and spinning off one of the most active empowerment groups in the city. It currently runs a variety of social-service programs and works with the controversial enterprise zone.

The core of Kensington relates to the city power structure through neighborhood empowerment groups. Using a variety of confrontational and collaborative strategies, they bypass elected officials and deal with city agencies, banks, and other "downtown" corporate centers of power directly.

Ties to the party structure are gone. The white-dominated area in the part of Kensington where Latinos, whites, and African Americans were just beginning to live together was ignored by the white ethnic councilman. He concentrated, instead, on the still all-white easternmost river wards in his district, which he saw as his base.[14] In 1989, the councilman angered Latinos and white activists by calling a meeting attended only by his white constituents. Those in attendance made overtly racist and largely anti-Latino comments, as did, reportedly, the councilman himself.

On the other hand, Norris Square, a clearly bounded area defined as Latino (the barrio), has drawn sustained attention from many activist-oriented funding sources and city government, but not from the city council. It is officially represented on the city council by one of the new powerful African Americans who, it is said, "has never even come into this part of his district." It is known that he sees his base as farther west in North Philadelphia.

Another white Kensington community activist, whose organization incorporates all groups, commented that her constituency is "neither African American enough, white enough, [nor] Hispanic enough" to get any attention from city hall. These sentiments attest to the strength of the division of the world into race groups in structuring political interactions in Philadelphia.

Most community organizations in Kensington fit the empowerment model to a large degree. Part of this focus comes from the perception of the neighborhood as a distressed area. For example, one college-educated, white established resident started an organization along the established model. She soon became aware that her group was eligible for public funds because of the poverty in the area; she also was eligible, since she had nine children. While her organization is run like established groups in Olney, relying on community insiders for staff and lots of volunteer effort, it does draw funds from the city, which treats it like an empowerment group. Its boundaries were restructured to fit the CDC and NAC structure of the area.

Many CDCs have similar programs, both because housing and employment are pressing issues in the community and because federal funding only allots money for such specific programs as housing reconstruction, employment services, weatherization, ESL or GED, and low-income heating assistance. The same organizations often find themselves competing for funding from the city and from local foundations.

In Olney, the major community shift took place between the traditional and empowerment components of the neighborhood. Attempts to recruit new immigrants were relatively unsuccessful and communication with them was limited to brokers and spokespersons. In contrast, Kensington empowerment groups have been more successful in linking Latinos, African Americans, and whites in a strong activist network in spite of their competition for funds and constituents. However, there has been little collaboration, and often hostility, between the residents involved in empowerment activities and the large number of unaffiliated established residents who see the empowerment message as blaming them for racism.

Today, the empowerment groups get their funding from a variety of sources, including federal programs, mainline church urban mission programs, foundation social programs, and private-sector consortia designed to deal with inner-city problems.[15] While competition for clients and funding creates tension, cooperation results from linkages between leaders in issue-based coalitions. Jobs in one organization are very often filled through referrals from others, sometimes involving relatives or friends. As one leader said, "We are an incestuous bunch down here." As we attended meetings for different events, the group representatives would often refer to having spoken to each other a few hours before about another issue or would check the dates of a set of meetings for another activity.

Some of these groups were affiliated in a coalition that deals with banks and housing agencies. It has successfully pressured banks on mortgage lending policy in the wake of the Community Reinvestment Act. A similar coalition fought for city "linkage" legislation, which would mandate that a proportion of moneys for each downtown project (e.g., the current convention center) would be set aside for neighborhood development. A number of effective coalitions run campaigns against drugs.

Whose Group Is It?

Established whites clearly "own" the neighborhood organizations in Olney. This is not the case in Kensington, where public life, like residential space, is divided between whites and Latinos.[16] While most Kensington organizations make a conscious and consistent effort to reach out to the broader community—through multilanguage literature, recruiting efforts, programs designed specifically for all segments of the population, and having both Spanish speakers and whites on staff and in leadership positions—they are usually perceived as belonging to one group or another. For example, one organization thought to be white dominated in fact runs a block organization program in which all the block captains are Puerto Rican. While the leaders are white established residents, they are careful to include elements in their program that appeal to their largely Puerto Rican constituency. In each of these cases, the structure of the institutional environment (in terms of the ethnic makeup of leadership and staff cliques) is a powerful device shaping the community's perception of the institution.

Here many organizations share an ideology that emphasizes the structural underpinnings of oppression, often linking local problems of the inner city to those of third-world countries in a model overtly based on class and world systems. This helps maintain linkages among organizations and between progressive white and Latino leaders. While there are differences between leaders in their explanatory models, the idea is to empower the powerless through awareness of the effects of external systems. In several organizations, this message is part of the ESL and GED training, and such programs have had important successes in the neighborhood. However, this message of empowerment is often resisted by many established residents. As a result, some organizations are frustrated in their efforts to include the white ethnic population as equal participants in their programs. Sometimes different programs in one structure are "owned" by different groups, as in the case of one organization whose senior center is totally white and whose day-care center is totally Latino.

One local empowerment organization dominated by Puerto Ricans saw the white mission group in Norris Square as competing for the housing stock. Distrust was exacerbated by the fact that several middle-class Latino members of this church group are tied to the entrepreneurial faction that is linked to the Puerto Rico Day parade. The entrepreneurial faction, in turn, is distanced from the progressive nationalists who are most active in local empowerment groups. Despite the fact that both groups included Latinos and whites, the Puerto Rican group labeled the mission group as white gentrifiers bent on pushing Puerto Ricans out of the community.

Interactions between a local Polish immigrant organization and other Norris Square empowerment groups are also fraught with distrust. The Polish group was actually a long-standing mission project run by a priest from Poland. For more than ten years, he had worked in the United States to provide guidance to Polish émigrés in this country, to solicit donations for the poor in Poland, and to serve the population in the neighborhoods where he settled. He had been given a burned-out German community center in the neighborhood by a Polish-American real-estate agent in the early 1980s. Much of his work focused on slowly refurbishing this building, for which he relied largely on reclaimed materials and the volunteer labor and design expertise supplied by new Poles—people visiting from the homeland and émigrés. He had also created a community garden, but quickly discovered that he had to lock it to prevent vandalism by local children. His long-term goals included providing social services for émigrés at this location, creating a housing complex for the largely white and African American elderly population, and serving local Puerto Ricans through ESL classes and after-school programs.

One local community development corporation and the priest had struggled over territory for years. He wanted a building controlled by the CDC for his social-service and elderly-housing projects, and he interpreted the agency's refusal of use as "They only want to serve Puerto Ricans." The CDC, in turn, thought that the priest represented gentrification and wanted to replace the Puerto Rican population with Polish émigrés and white elderly. Not understanding how he could restore the building without major external support, they guessed that he was funded by the CIA. The locked garden communicated that he viewed the Puerto Rican population as a threat. The last straw came when the CDC asked the priest to lend the artisans who worked on his building to help train its fledgling housing rehab crew. He refused, saying his men were skilled artisans and not laborers.

One group seen by everyone as Puerto Rican was originally formed by Puerto Ricans to deal with housing and quality-of-life issues. Accused by whites and African Americans of being too Latino, new leadership has taken over. A board including African Americans and whites was formed and an effort was made to be redefined as inclusive and neighborhood based. However, tension over "who owned" the organization continued. One non-Latino board member who gave the leadership credit for hard work in an understaffed situation still complained that many good African American members had left.

Much of the perception of the group as Latino stems from the fact that 80 percent of the population in the area it serves is Latino. Depending on the context, the dynamic bilingual leader sometimes presents the organization as Spanish dominant and at other times emphasizes its mixed nature. As the assertiveness of the Puerto Rican community in citywide media accelerated in 1989 and 1990, the group presented itself more and more as Spanish dominant.

The activities of the organization represent its contradictory nature. While all public meetings are bilingual, and every statement in Spanish is translated into English and vice versa, the office is often staffed by individuals who are primarily Spanish speakers. This often makes telephone as well as in-person communication frustrating for monolingual English speakers. Nevertheless, the programs offered there do serve all low-income residents of the neighborhood, who are often seen in the waiting room.

Yet in spite of the structural opposition between Latinos and whites maintained in housing and individual organizations, there are many more links and contacts between racial and ethnic groups in organizations in Kensington than in Olney. Regardless of tension, many governing boards are integrated. The activities of the empowerment leadership in coalition activities brings them into frequent contact. In this way, leaders also help to create ties between the rank and file as they pull them into coalition activities. The Olney pattern of restricting contact between subcommunities to one-on-one links between brokers is less common here. Social distance shrinks as collaborators work in informal and easy relationships rather than the more formal communications in Olney.

For the many local residents who are not tied to any organization, however, relationships between groups are more tense. Occasional public meetings like the one called by the white councilman are allowed to engender uncivil discourse unlike anything heard in Olney. Furthermore, the major expressions of hostility are the more frequent acts of public violence. The outside perception of the community as racist further exacerbates this tendency. For example, the Ku Klux Klan wanted to hold a rally at Kensington and Allegheny, the heart of the community. The effort was stopped when local empowerment groups were contacted by the Klan in the mistaken belief that any local Kensington organization would likely be a white-dominated potential ally.

Many empowerment leaders include concepts based on the structural-racism model in their work. This was clear in the contradictory treatment of the role of a growing number of Palestinians around Norris Square. Leaders knew that the Palestinians owned fifty-two houses in a ten-square-block area of one community association, as well as several groceries that were viewed as economically exploitative. Nevertheless, the Palestinians were not publicly viewed as impinging on neighborhood control (gentrifying) in the same way as were the white middle-class church activists and the Polish priest, even though the latter two owned little property. Instead, attempts were made to appeal to the Palestinians through a third-world coalition group and to represent them as common victims of U.S. oppression.

The following statement by one progressive white neighborhood activist shows understanding and support for nonwhite domination of organizations as a compensatory move:

> The way I understand it is that in every part of society you participate in Anglos run it and call the shots and Anglos are the bosses. You ought to have your own organization. . . . I can respect that and I don't harbor any resentment. Sure [one wants] to belong, [one wants] to participate in the neighborhood. . . . Maybe there's some sadness there. . . . I don't begrudge them. I really don't.

Summary

All three neighborhoods were shaped by the history of European immigrants and their descendants. Yet they have had different experiences in the postwar context of deindustrialization and suburbanization. This has affected the nature of their organizations. In Olney, established groups have been joined by empowerment groups. After a period of tension, they have come together on certain issues. Empowerment groups have added elements of the structural-racism model to the more palatable models of cultural pluralism and the "good immigrant" shared by oldtimers. This occasionally creates tension. However, the dynamic has been between these two components of established residents who dominate the organizational structures and are socially distant from the newcomers. In spite of an expressed ideology of diversity seeking, communication between newcomers and established residents is limited, formal, and carried out through brokers. The positive views of diversity do not reflect much contact in public life.

In Kensington, educated, progressive white activists oriented toward a third-world model share a strong structural-racist model with their Latino and African American counterparts. Facing more immediate threats to the quality of life, they work in many coalitions that often involve ordinary residents in interaction across groups. However, their activities fail to incorporate many of the white poor and working-class residents, who resist an ideology that emphasizes the structural oppression of peoples of color by those of European descent. Nonetheless, these organizations, in trying to create inclusive coalitions to handle their many problems, actually generate more contact across groups than is the case in Olney. Nonetheless, a polarized oppositional structure of whites and Latinos, which is seen clearly in the checkerboard segregation of the residential and institutional space in much of Kensington, engenders continuing conflict.

In Port Richmond, established groups work to maintain community in the face of perceived onslaughts from other neighborhoods and the city government. The lack of interaction between citywide structures and the community involves negative stereotypes from both sides. The central model of oldtimers in this community is that of the "good immigrant." Newcomer Poles are judged by the kind of commitment they make to becoming American by contributing to community structures through volunteer time and financial assistance.

In all communities, tensions exist between "insiders" with long-term links to each other and those who have just arrived, regardless of race or nationality. The common experience of overworked volunteers, the need to actively court some constituencies and use personal ties to get people involved, and the tendency to view activities as belonging to "cliquish" groups of "others" plague voluntary organizational structures across the communities. Although these pressures are common to such organizations in general, they become even more problematic when fragile intergroup alliances are being created in tense situations.

The structures and dynamics of each neighborhood frame ongoing local life. In the next two chapters, we will explore life "on the ground" by analyzing two different aspects of it. In Chapter 5 we look at how social relationships are shaped by the flow of everyday experiences in informal personal settings, as well as in more structured public space. In Chapter 6, we explore the sporadic events in which racial, national, or ethnic difference is the focus. These include both celebrations of difference and episodes of intergroup conflict. These two kinds of localized experiences often contradict each other. Everyday activities and focus events interact in the ongoing production of social constructions of difference.

CHAPTER 5

Everyday Activities: Personal Ties and Structured Institutions

Within each neighborhood, everyday activities bring people into varied situations that play a role in structuring contact and forming ideas about social differences. The daily lives of adults take them into many different settings where they sometimes intimately and sometimes impersonally interact with people from other groups. They also observe interactions between others, as well as participating in conversations about individuals and groups. This chapter describes two aspects of everyday social reality: the intimate, trusting personal relationships of individuals and the structure of public institutions that channel their contacts. Our observations of the personal social networks and daily activities of community residents help to illustrate how the structure of these networks and institutions influences the nature and frequency of social interaction and help to shape definitions of likeness and similarity contributing to the various models of difference.

Often there are major discontinuities between the ideas people express and their behavior toward others in different settings. Entering discontinuous social frameworks as they shop, deal with their children's school day, go to work, see neighbors on the block, and spend leisure time with friends and relatives, individuals experience social difference in a wide variety of ways. Many of the structures that frame daily life have been shaped by political and economic changes in Philadelphia. Some have been affected by broad citywide policies and processes. Others reflect more local influence, where the experience of turnover and change, crisis events, and memories of the past affect perceptions of social categories in the present. Self-identities form and reform,

alliances are forged between individuals and groups. We explore these discontinuities in the following discussion, moving from the most personal, intimate
relationships and interactions to the more impersonal.

Personal Relationships

Individuals and families are embedded in networks of personal, intimate, and
trusting relationships. For some individuals we knew, both established and
new immigrant, important friends and relatives were limited to those who
shared the same background, had common experiences, and had known each
other a long time. These kinds of social links characterized "tight knit" social
networks in the classic work of Bott (1957).

However, given the nature of change in work and neighborhoods in
Philadelphia in recent years, most of the people we encountered in fieldwork
described growing up in such networks but no longer having such tightly
bounded social circles. They often had intimate ties with people from very
different backgrounds who had very different experiences and opinions. These
close ties between people with many with different perspectives created
discontinuities as the individual moved from one social context to another.

Isolating Forces

There were still some pressures that reduced the diversity of social networks.
Many established residents and new immigrants had social networks in which
the sheer density of mutual obligations did not provide people with much
social space for close ties to "others."

Lifelong Kin and Friends

For established residents, relatives and friends from childhood were often
those with whom weekends were spent and close emotional bonds developed.
Life revolved around a long series of celebrations of calendrical holidays and
life-cycle events within a small network. Most of the adults in these neighborhoods had lived in the city all their lives, as had their many siblings. Regular
visiting within the extended family was expected, and the year consisted of
sequential seasons of celebration. The Thanksgiving through Christmas cycle
was followed by Easter events, and then came the intense spring life-cycle
season. First Communion, showers, weddings, anniversaries, prom nights, and
graduations, as well as Mother's Day and Father's Day, filled April, May, and
June. In between were birthdays and patriotic holidays. Unscheduled events
related to birth and death required time as well. One established white Olney
woman reported:

I do not have any time the next few weekends. Father X wants me to work on Polish Day [a parish celebration], but I told him there is only one weekend this month when I can do it so he better schedule it then. One weekend is my sister's anniversary, the next is my mother's birthday, and the other is my nephew's confirmation. My mother-in-law is sick and I have to cook and clean for her every day, too.

In addition, growing up in Philadelphia created a large network of long-term friendships based on school and work relationships. Candy, a white woman who had grown up in Olney, said:

> I have a sister and three brothers. They are all married and have children, and we like to get together with some of them every weekend. In addition, there are three girls I went to school with who live in the Northeast today. I see a lot of them. They know what I am thinking and feeling, and I do not have to explain anything to them.

Immigration

The dominant pattern of immigration to the United States has always been what is called chain migration, involving people following relatives and covillagers who help them to find housing and work (Macdonald and Macdonald 1964). The preference for family unification in post-1965 immigration policies and the need for sponsorship reinforces this pattern. Networks of people who have past ties or who are connected to others through mutual friends are used to provide sources of information, mutual aid, and the re-creation of familiar aspects of life.

Many immigrants arriving illegally without kin ties relied on bonds begun in the homeland and/or ties formed through the kinds of monolingual workplaces that employed them. Lucy, a Colombian woman with a Nicaraguan boyfriend, talked about spending her leisure time within a network of South and Central American immigrants. They worked together in Spanish-speaking sewing shops (female) and construction gangs (male), and spent their weekends at "house parties" at each other's homes or in the three "Colombian" discos that served the needs of all these nationalities who were new to the city and were not served by Puerto Rican institutions.

Most Puerto Rican families had chosen Philadelphia as a destination because of kin and friendship ties. For example, Lorena's mother had brought her to Philadelphia as a child when she separated from her husband in Puerto Rico. Lorena's mother's sister was already here. After a few years in the city, Lorena went back to her father's mother on the island.[1] More than a decade later, after several years of college on the island, Lorena returned to the mainland seeking better opportunities. Her social contacts were limited to her mother and her mother's kin network.

Since the recent wave of Korean immigration was based on family reunification, family-based patterns were also typical. Young Sun's family had been "invited" by his mother's brother in what was a typical family "master plan" to bring over all his siblings and eventually his parents. The uncle set them up in a house. "He did everything, we didn't have to do the lease or anything."[2] Several recently arriving Koreans entered businesses that were already arranged for them by kin who were here. For other groups as well, often houses and businesses were transferred between immigrants through kinship links.[3]

Among the new Poles in Port Richmond there were several families whose social life was limited to other recent arrivals. Most of the new Polish families knew each other. Visitors came with the sponsorship of kin or friends, and refugees quickly found other newcomers here. Both newcomer and '68 Wave families spend much of their leisure time with others from similar backgrounds.

Immigrant organizations also circumscribed the relationships of newcomers. Hometown ties formed the basis of sports leagues and social clubs for some Puerto Ricans, and regional social clubs exist among the Indians. There is a Portuguese club with day care and a language school. Among Poles, DP, '68 Wave, and some post-Solidarity parents send their children to a Polish class that is held in the basement of the parish but includes only the children of émigrés.

Diverse Networks

However, most people we met did not have such homogeneous networks. Instead, they had close friends and relatives from different backgrounds who did not share common life experiences. This was especially true in Olney and Kensington. While in Port Richmond localized networks of kin and neighbors focused on church activities, the presence of new Poles and workplaces outside the neighborhood brought people into close contact with diversity.

In moving through a variety of conversations and activities with friends from different backgrounds, individuals experience discontinuous influences on their ideas and behavior, as illustrated in the following descriptions of the networks and social relations of particular individuals. Several factors stand out as shaping these diverse relationships. The nature of the block people live on, their experience with intermarriage, the role of church-related organizations, the nature of their workplace, and the role their children play as brokers are consistently important.

Inez Gutierrez and Ester Ramos

Two of the Puerto Rican women we came to know well lived in complex social circles that affected their views of others and themselves. Inez and Ester were both born in Puerto Rico and were brought to the United States as preteens. They are upwardly mobile residents of Olney who are single parents. Both spent time with whites from work and church. Ester says, "I do things with Claire [white friend from church] I never did before, like go to concerts." Inez spends long periods of vacation time with her best friend, a white woman she has worked with for ten years, who is godparent to her children. These patterns reflect their expanding relationships beyond their ethnic group.

At the same time, their Puerto Rican family and friendship links remain central to their lives in terms of time spent and the exchange of favors, loans, and services. Both constantly referred to themselves in opposition to whites. They refer to whites in general as English speakers, although their entire workday takes place in English. Coworkers are also referred to as whites, although both women are considered white by their fellow workers. When focusing on identity, they reflected their national pride and fear of racism. Yet they both criticized Puerto Ricans for being too cliquish and separatist and often blamed the attitudes of Puerto Ricans for the group's problems.

Inez and Ester have intimate white friends whom they see outside work. In both instances, these women have been incorporated on the white side of a strong racial dyad in their workplace. There was no significant Spanish-speaking presence in their unit, forcing them to ally with one side of a racially split office. Both women have worked in their jobs for more than ten years and have long-term ties with several coworkers. Each was first identified as Italian by coworkers who encouraged friendship. At the same time, Ester and Inez are more distant from their African American coworkers.

In Ester's office, that of a city agency in which African Americans control all the supervisory and professional positions, the "upside down" power relations between groups exacerbates normal worker–boss tensions. She has little to do with her African American coworkers. She speaks of socializing after work with several white friends, as well as having intimate talks with them about problems with men and raising children. She remarks:

> They talk about Italian men and raising Italian children and it is just the same as Puerto Rican. We are just the same. Irish and German, too. There are no differences. I can tell them anything.

Inez's workplace is also polarized, and she describes her African American coworkers as "having attitudes," a phrase often used to refer to those who are constantly making accusations of racism. Inez is close to her white coworkers, especially the one who is her children's godmother, whom she thinks of like family. Her children often stay at their godmother's home in New Jersey during their school vacations.

Nonetheless, most of these women's key social relationships are based on kin and church-related Latino groups. Ester had been active in several Spanish-speaking parish groups for ten years. As a single parent with no close relatives in the city, she considers four of the families she knows from Latino-oriented church activities as her surrogate family:

> They are always there for me. I know if I ever need help they will give it. I turn to them [and to the priests and nuns she knows well] in every crisis.

In fact, the group of four families had loaned her money to help her make the downpayment for her house.[4] Inez relies on her sister and mother, who live with her, and on her other sister nearby for routine support and help.

In the neighborhood parish that forms their major everyday social world, there are strong pressures on both women to identify as Latinos. They have been incorporated into the Spanish component of their parish, a group whose separatism is reinforced by the enthusiasm of the pastors for their Spanish mission. Through the parish, both had participated as Puerto Rican representatives in the meetings that surrounded the interracial conflicts of the summer of 1989 (see Chapter 6); they both often simultaneously bemoaned white racism and Puerto Rican behavior patterns. While they trusted their own white friends, they feared racism from whites as a group.

Yet Inez has developed some resistance to being identified as Puerto Rican by the parish Puerto Rican group. She says,

> they think I'm Ecuadoran or Central American because I do not try to get friendly with them. They clique too much.

Because of their familiarity with established residents at work, both Ester and Inez were able to crash through the barrier of the established women's circle of the parish in the preparations for a parishwide event (see Chapter 6).

Often the two women shared the Anglo critique of Puerto Ricans (read: lower class) as having the wrong values and behaviors. This was not unusual among the aspiring middle-class Puerto Ricans we met in Olney, a number of whom are tempted to distance themselves from their group. Conflation of class and nationality is central to this process. While they see Puerto Ricans as tight-knit and caring in contrast to whites, they also see them as boisterous, loud, immoral, and lazy. An example of this attitude is the Puerto Rican woman with Puerto Rican friends (described in Chapter 3) who does not like "the Spanish."

In the same way, Inez and Ester also distanced themselves from African Americans, seeing them as lazy troublemakers. One of the "cultural" similarities often mentioned between African Americans and Latinos is their sensuality, their "love of life," or knowing how to enjoy themselves. However, this is also seen as leading to profligacy and danger. Both women have African American siblings-in-law, but their experience with them has been problematic. Ester has little contact with her in-laws, while Inez's sister's marital problems have made her distance herself more from African Americans.

For Inez and Ester, both the workplace and the church shape their social relationships with other Latinos, as well as with African Americans and white ethnics. Long-term job tenure and residential stability are important here. They also have been influenced by direct experience with intermarriage in their families.

The Bakers

The Bakers are a white ethnic family that demonstrates much ambivalence. Jim works for city government in a municipal blue-collar service that is mostly African American and white, with some Puerto Ricans. Their union is often a target for media criticism. In this context, Jim admires the strength and hard work of his African American and Latino coworkers. He shows tremendous camaraderie when defending them against public accusations of laziness and featherbedding. "Those guys really work hard."

The sisters of his wife, Jenny, are married to African Americans and Puerto Ricans, and there have been some marital conflicts that color her views of intermarriage. Jim often articulates an opinion of minorities as irresponsible, describing them as fathering too many illegitimate children and not being good family men. In addition, his job has exposed him directly to affirmative action, giving him a sense of competition over work. He shares anecdotes with white fellow workers about what they see as favoritism on exam grading.

For a school family-tree project, the Baker child made a complex presentation. When complimented on it, Jim explained that his aunt had recently investigated the family's old-world roots. While the couple represents three European ethnic heritages, only one is publicly claimed. In fact, a framed family herald and genealogy for that line hangs on the living room wall. He complains that the Black and "Spanish" children cannot trace their family trees as his family can. Jim says, "Those minorities, they don't know who their fathers were," implying unstable families and promiscuity, a common stereotype in the United States.

At the same time, Jenny singlehandedly acts as an ambassador to newcomers in her neighborhood. She works both for a religious organization and for a political party, which involves going door to door to hundreds of households in her area. Through these activities she does a lot of one-on-one service—recommending schools, churches, and professional services to newcomers, keeping lists of prescriptions for "my families"—because she feels that this is her calling.

She has daily, personal contact with her immediate neighbors on the block, who include Indians, Puerto Ricans, Portuguese, and Koreans. Her children's best friends come from all groups, and she is proud of this. All sorts of kids come to the house frequently, often as a consequence of her former babysitting activities for neighbors. This work brought her into close contact with her diverse neighbors. She tells of being invited to birthday parties and other life-cycle rituals for the children in several of these families and being the only American there. Jenny has tried to learn Spanish to talk to her new neighbors. Her husband, however, will not allow "any language but ours" (referring to English and the European-heritage language he has chosen as their ethnicity) to be spoken in the house, and she affirms his allegiance to this ethnic identity.

Her experiences in her neighborhood, particularly on the block, and her church activities have brought her into intimate contact with a variety of people. As in the case of Inez, intermarriage has created negative and positive relationships. Jenny says, "Don't call me racist, I have Blacks and Hispanics in my family"—a twist on the usual "Some of my best friends are . . . "

The Baker family represents the result of the different daily experiences of the two adults. It also represents a common pattern of gender dissimilarity in regard to attitudes and behaviors toward difference. Several blocks away, Sally, a lifetime Olney resident in her twenties, describes herself as a "culture fanatic." She is trying to learn recipes from her diverse neighbors and is proud to describe her son's three best friends as Taiwanese, Korean, and Indian. She and the children are active in a mixed Protestant church with a majority Puerto Rican and West Indian congregation. Yet on weekends she and her husband socialize only with other working-class whites, her husband's work buddies. "He has a harder time adjusting," she says. "I don't understand why. Perhaps it was the way he was brought up." In Port Richmond, Carol speaks fondly of the four close African American friends she had from her former hospital job. She has lost touch with them since she left work, because "my husband would not let them in the house."

Marisol Minh

Marisol is a Nicaraguan woman married to a Vietnamese man. She met him in Philadelphia after she came illegally with an invitation of help from one of her sister's workmates in Nicaragua. When Marisol arrived, her contact's daughter found her a job as a domestic, and she later found a job for her own sister. Today, she is at the center of an ever-expanding network involving persons each of them has helped. Through such referrals, families become "instant friends," often asking each other on short acquaintance to help celebrate birthdays and to serve as godparents, since they are "vouched for" by someone in the network. They also provide information about jobs as domestics or in sewing factories. The intensity of sharing and mutual aid engendered by the immigration experience often creates strong, durable ties.

Marisol has become the center of a large network of Spanish speakers because of her excellent English skills. She is often called upon to help others. At one typical visit to her home, she was called by a Colombian domestic who needed help translating a note from her employer, visited by a Colombian friend who came to tell her of hiring at a suburban sewing factory, and visited later by two Guatemalans who were bringing her children home after taking them to a nearby playground.

But intermarriage and relationships through her children's friends and on the block have extended her ties beyond the community of Spanish-speaking immigrants. Marisol also visits her husband's Vietnamese friends for weekend activities, although she misses a lot of the conversation, which takes place in Vietnamese. (She and her husband have always communicated in English, which she feels has helped her learn faster.) She has also been drawn into a close relationship with a Korean neighbor through her children and their friends. They visit back and forth and feel they have a lot in common. She has been "adopted" by a white neighbor who calls and visits frequently to tell her about events in the neighborhood and sales in the stores. They often go shopping together and spend time together during school hours.

Ruth Olanski

Ruth is an example of someone whose life is circumscribed by the immediate neighborhood. At seventy, she is in poor health and has a disabled husband. Ruth has lived on her block for thirty years. Since most of her neighbors have died or gone to facilities for long-term care, she relies on many old ties for frequently needed assistance. The daughter of her deceased former best friend still lives around the corner and does much shopping and errand running for her. She also relies on Alice, an elderly widow who goes to the doctor with her, and on a next-door neighbor, whose husband, "in maintenance," helps fix things. In spite of turnover, the grapevine still operates on Ruth's block. When she was mugged recently on the shopping strip, many neighbors who work and are rarely seen came over when they heard the news. With these longtime friends, she shares memories of the old days of a clean, tight-knit neighborhood and expresses wariness about the ways of newcomers and the increase in blight.

However, one of her closest friends is Elena, a Costa Rican who used to sit with her on the steps when she arrived twelve years ago. Ruth helped her to practice her English. Elena drives Ruth to her relatives in another neighborhood and stays for parties there. She also watches Ruth's husband when she goes out. Her son takes care of Ruth's trash for a nominal fee. According to Ruth, "She loves me and would do anything for me."

Ruth knows many other newcomers, too. One is the Indian landlord who owns the apartment building next door, one of four houses that he maintains as his basic source of income. She often talks to him when he comes. When a young Indian woman living on the next block whom Ruth had talked to many times came to look at an apartment, Ruth interceded on her behalf in asking for cheaper rent. She remarked:

> She's a nice little girl, give it to her for a few dollars cheaper a month.
> She'll be reliable. It will be worth it.

While both the potential landlord and tenant were of the same nationality, Ruth did not see them as members of another group, more like each other than like her. In fact, she viewed herself as a broker between two of her fond acquaintances who were strangers to each other.

Ruth's reaction to newcomers shows her greater concern with their respectability than with their race or nationality. Her neighbor across the street, Nancy, was the first African American on the block and a victim of tire slashing and broken windows when she came seven years ago. Ruth proudly described her first and foremost as a department head at a hospital. The other African American household head is quickly identified as a policeman. She knows that the Korean family who moved in across the street are quiet and clean, sweeping their front and hosing down the street regularly, but she has not talked to them yet. She also knows about the Cambodian couple who have fixed up their house beautifully. "Where did they get the money?" she asks her friend Alice, who knows them better; "He works two jobs," Alice replies. Ruth describes the house of the Filipino professional couple who had a wonderful housewarming party and invited the whole block.

Mary Hanson

Mary Hanson has lived all her married life on a stable, tight-knit, all-white block in Kensington. Her neighbors often sit on the steps together, go to the store for each other when someone is not feeling well, and look in on sick spouses and children. Couples go on outings to the Atlantic City casinos together, and women frequently crochet as a group. Mary's neighbors often speak about defending the block if African Americans or Hispanics try to move in. Mary loves the area and her neighbors.

Yet she also has a daughter who is married to an African American and a son whose best friends at school are African American. He participates in an integrated Kensington teen leadership organization; as a result, she works as a volunteer for the group. This has brought her into contact with an integrated antiracist coalition that includes many Puerto Ricans and that also works against drugs. She has become an active member. About these activities that bring her into settings dominated by minorities, she says:

> If you don't like the idea of working or associating with colored or Puerto
> Ricans, then you have no business being involved in them, because that's
> what it is all about. I mean like united neighbors, you know, we are all
> neighbors, United Nations. . . . We're all from different neighborhoods.
> There's your Hispanic neighborhoods, your white neighborhoods, and

your colored neighborhoods. Now we unite our neighbors against drug addicts [and] to get our kids to understand one another. You know, that we're all here and that we can get to work and play—how should I put it, [the teen program] is mainly to get the children to know that we can get them to work and play and have fun as a united [group], which we can do without having battles or fights or something. You know, as one, as one family.

Mary reconciles the notion of residential segregation (Hispanic neighborhoods, colored neighborhoods, white neighborhoods) by assuming that ethnic neighborhoods are the result of natural affinity. Differences are analogous to nations, and "international" collaboration on common goals is desirable.
She says about her daughter's marriage:

Della married a colored guy. I didn't like the idea at first. I'm still not crazy [about it], I think; I still say that they should stick to their own kind, because if they have children then it's the children that get hurt, 'cause they're not colored and they're not white. They are half-and-half. They're zebras or something, you know, they're a mixture. But I love Frank [her son-in-law], I mean Frank's great. I mean he is fantastic with Della. . . . I couldn't ask for anyone better. Al [Mary's husband] gets along great with Frank. Frank and I are close.

She takes care of her granddaughter every other weekend at her home in an area where she acknowledges that people "would fight like hell if Blacks or Puerto Ricans moved in." While originally concerned that her son-in-law would have trouble coming into her white-dominated neighborhood and that their house might be vandalized, there have been no problems. He is not seen as a dangerous stranger but a vouched-for extension of her family.

She also comments positively on their relationship with Frank's family and the frequent family gatherings. She contrasts this to a friend's case. Her daughter had a baby with a Puerto Rican, which was followed by difficulties between the two families because of culture and language. This is one of many examples of situations in which African Americans are seen as sharing more common cultural understandings than new immigrants.

Mary Hanson's social relationships are strongly influenced by the nature of population shifts in Kensington brought on by the impact of deindustrialization. In particular, her neighbors on the block have created a tight-knit network in an attempt to keep out outsiders. She often participates in conversations that laud the good old days and stereotype those groups who are feared as outsiders pressing on the border. Yet, through her children's intimate relationships, she has also come to know African Americans intimately, to like them, and to become involved in an intergroup organization whose message of harmony she shares.

In Port Richmond, the nature of residence patterns and the nationality parish schools did not provide the same opportunities for contact, and there was more community pressure to keep outsiders out. We saw in Carol's case that it was difficult to bring racially different workplace friends home. Her neighborhood is one where the presence of minorities set off social alarms.

Bridging Forces

We see from the above examples that in spite of the density of personal and intimate networks based on lifelong local ties or having undergone intense struggles to adjust, there are many examples of adults who have developed very close and sustained cross-group friendships. Ruth, Jenny, Marisol, Inez, Ester, and Mary come to mind. In fact, these mixed networks were more common than isolated ones. Most of the close ties across groups can be traced to the role of children as brokers, neighboring on the block, experience with intermarriage, church, and workplaces. These intimate ties often lead to a search for cultural commonalities rather than difference. However, experience with such close ties can also lead to conflict. In the following discussion we will deal with each factor in greater depth.

Children as Brokers of Intimacy

Different mechanisms shape the development of children's relationships. These will be discussed later. Yet because children form intimate ties across boundaries and because a common interest in children brings women together in sustained relationships, they often serve as the brokers in key adult dealings. Such is the case for Mary Hanson. Her involvement in her son's intergroup program has led her to further intergroup community activity, and her daughter's intermarriage has brought satisfying relationships with African Americans. Jenny Baker's children and her babysitting activities have led to strong mutual concerns with immigrant and African American women. Marisol Minh frequently visited and was visited by a nearby Korean woman whose son played with hers.

Like Jenny Baker, established women who are not employed outside their homes often babysit for newcomer professional women in Olney. Babies are innocent and easy to love and nurture. They bring the adult women together in common concern. One woman who babysits says:

> We have everyone on our block. I babysit for them all. I love the children and I get along with all the mothers just great. My mother came the other day and saw them—six babies—three Indian, one Spanish, one Turkish, and mine. I said, "Doesn't it look like a real United Nations?"

Everyday Activities   147

After the mother commented that there were no "Chinese" (Asians), her daughter told her that there would be soon. Her Korean neighbor had just had a baby. In fact, she had been called to assist in the emergency home delivery, but was not home at the time.

Celia, another established resident, included the parents of her son's Korean best friend in all family celebrations. Yet children's behavior can also be a source of conflict, as set forth below.

Life on the Block

Children often brought the block together around concerns that were often related to their safety. One established woman who had organized her multiethnic block said specifically:

What we all have in common, what brings us together, is that we all want to make a good life for our children. They are our number-one priority.

In this case, a successful block organization in Olney arose informally in response to a local problem and has continued to operate as an example of successful relations between newcomers and established residents. The conflict arose when a newly resident white household with a troublemaking young adult was seen as a source of vandalism and drug traffic. The block organized to achieve a legal remedy to the situation. This was followed by an organized cleanup of a trash-ridden lot to make it safe for children to play on.

Now almost all the families on the block meet monthly in the established leader's home. They include a Vietnamese family who have been taught to monitor license plates of suspicious cars, two Puerto Rican families, a family from India, and one Middle Eastern family. Only one household does not participate. Visits to the block found everyone outdoors sitting on their stoops. Children move regularly between households, and adults often bring home extra food or toys from their businesses to distribute among the residents.

Most established individuals interviewed could identify the people on their block by group, by facial recognition, and frequently by name. They greet immediate neighbors regularly and often have brief conversations. Yet for those who spend much time at home, like Mary, Jenny, Ruth, and Marisol, many neighbors are turned into friends. Blocks are most important to those who are there all day: older residents and mothers with young children who do not work outside the home. Both newcomers and established residents report examples of friendship ties between neighbors on the block that involve mutual child care, significant time spent together, and exchanges of food and other goods and services.

Relationships between neighbors are strongly affected by the rate of turnover on the block, the degree of formal organizing of block structures, and such features as whether it is a cul-de-sac or has heavy traffic and whether there are lawns and gardens in which people encounter their neighbors. For example, on one street a woman commented on knowing the names of all those people who gardened or watered their lawns as she did.

While many established residents reach out to immigrants paternalistically, with a sense of teaching rules, relationships often become reciprocal. Ruth extended a helping hand to Elena as an American to a newcomer, but she receives lots of concrete help in exchange. Carmen, a Colombian, is very close to her established next-door neighbor, who welcomed her when she moved in two years ago and provided useful help and information. Carmen is now arranging to get her sister to give the neighbor a sofa she no longer wants to show her gratitude and friendship.

Neighbors from different backgrounds who have known each other a long time easily form links across groups. Marge Randall is a white in a Spanish-dominated area of Kensington. She describes how her family, especially the five children, has come to be protected by all the Puerto Rican and African American families on the block, who form a tight-knit communication system.

> If my girls were in trouble they would help my girls. . . . Mostly all of them, some of them would walk 'em to school in the morning if they thought somebody was suspicious, some of the guys around here would just escort them to the El, make sure they got there, and come back home. I mean, I know what they do. If [the girls] walk two blocks away and they're doin' something they're not supposed to, I know before they come back. 'Cause everybody knows.

However, the process of adjustment takes time. In Olney, Peggy and Joe have become close to their "Hispanic" neighbors. Joe describes how they gave his wife the most help "sending down stuff, and taking my kids out and buying them stuff," when he had major surgery. "I did not know them. I used to leave the house at 5:30 and I don't get back till 5:30 and then I did odd jobs on the weekend." His statement demonstrates that women do the "social" work of neighboring and that work outside the neighborhood limits male contacts, just as we saw with the Bakers. But this neighbor relationship did not start off well. Peggy, his wife, added:

> When they first moved in, they were up till 3 o'clock in the morning making all kinds of noise, parties. But I found out later that she hated the parties, she could not wait till they left. Now they have parties once in a while but not like when they first moved in. They are great people.

This illustrates to Joe and Peggy that their neighbors "learned community rules."

On the other hand, blocks are often the site of major conflicts. Over the fieldwork period, we encountered a number of serious problems on blocks where we knew families. Several patterns existed. First, like the problem that led to the block organization described above, many involved new white neighbors, described as "poor white trash" or "lowlifes." Incidents often concern children's behavior. Fay, a white ethnic woman with five children, recalls:

> Our one neighbor who is seventy [white lowlife] picked our tires. All four of them. Because she could not boss [the children] around she just came out and did the tires. And there's the nut [also white] across the street who calls and harasses me.

The crux of most intergroup conflicts is not racial antagonism but quality-of-life concerns. However, they often lead to using racial epithets as the parties involved seek to maximize their distance through emphasizing social difference. Any basis of social difference becomes consciously called to attention in the process.

Two conflicts that were related to the nature of row houses (which share median walls and driveways) led to the use of epithets in the heat of argument. One new Pole in Port Richmond told of a dispute with an Irish American neighbor during a rehabilitation job. The neighbor said, "You stupid Polacks! Go back to where you belong!" The police called the Human Relations Commission, which sent a letter saying that it would take action if something like this happened again. While today there is no longer tension between established Americans of Irish, Italian, and Polish descent in Port Richmond, foreigners in general were resented in the neighborhood for being too demanding (see Chapter 4), and the new Pole was a foreigner. While it is unlikely that the difference between a Polish American and an Irish American neighbor might be similarly brought out, given the rate of intermarriage and multiple ancestry, serious conflict often heightens awareness of any basis of dissimilarity.

On one mixed Olney block, one family singles out Indians as the only problem newcomer group. They are seen as "pushy" because they put chairs and garbage cans out to protect parking places all day. Once again, a scarce quality-of-life resource, commonly contested, underlies the stereotype. Ironically, while this behavior is seen as rude and unfair in Olney, where it is not common practice, it was probably learned in one of several Philadelphia neighborhoods where it has long been considered appropriate. Yet here it is blamed on a stereotypical view of Indian "culture."

In Olney, a dispute raged for months between a Colombian and a Puerto Rican family who lived in adjacent homes. It centered on conflicts over shared space and accusations of Puerto Rican drug dealing. Here again, however, shouts of cultural disparagement about Colombians and Puerto Ricans occurred on both sides. Mediation was necessary. To the established neighbors, this was a confusing conflict, since "Hispanics" were supposed to stick together.

Intermarriage

All of the social networks described above except for Ruth's were affected by intermarriage. Marriage across racial boundary lines is very common in both Olney and Kensington. It is ironic that in these communities, which are stereotyped as racist by the media and human-relations officials, a large proportion of families we knew well had nieces and nephews who belonged to "other groups." This has been so in Kensington for a long time, and Olney has been attracting more and more mixed couples as its diversity is recognized. For example, two such couples, one white/African American and the other African American/Latino, cited this as a major reason for choosing the neighborhood. At each successive community event we observed, more and more interracial families were present.[5]

Milly, a white woman married to an African American, talked about the possible need to move since the city was condemning some houses on her Olney block for structural defects.

> I have to think about the kids. I couldn't take them to an area where they would be ridiculed. . . . That wouldn't be fair to them either, to have them put up with all the name calling. Nor would I want to take them to an all-Black area either. They are just as bad. That's why I would want them to stay here. There is nothing they have to feel out of place about. There's other children of interracial marriages.

Experience with intermarried families does not necessarily make individuals more tolerant. Inez Gutierrez and Jim Baker spoke disparagingly about their siblings-in-law and said that, overall, their siblings' experience had increased their desire for their children to marry someone more like them. Celia described the problems her parents had bringing up her "half and half" nephew in a Polish neighborhood after her sister left her African American boyfriend and sent her son to live with them. He was having adjustment problems now.

People who have experience with intergroup dating and intermarriage have very concrete concerns. They usually involve difficulties that the children of the marriage will face and the possibility of strained relationships between both sets of in-laws. Candy, a white ethnic woman, says about marrying outside one's group:

> Religion and nationality don't mean a thing to me. The color line is something else. I dated Black men. Thankfully, I came from an open household. But I never engaged the idea of marriage. If my children wanted to cross the color line, I would be supportive. It's very hard. It's a hard road to go. . . . Your children will be stigmatized. . . . It's hard to function in daily society.

Most people we encountered make the best of such situations, especially after children are born. Both Mary Hanson and Celia's parents loved their grandchildren and went out of their way to protect them from harm in hostile neighborhoods. Celia, Inez, Ester, and Jenny Baker love and take care of their nieces and nephews. Milly's mother, while at first cutting herself off from Milly, became very close to her daughter and son-in-law after the children were born. Once again, the interests of children bring people together.

The nature of relations with the spouse and the in-laws tend to be related the amount of conflict between the couple. In the cases of Inez, Ester, and Jenny's siblings there are marital problems, and the sisters side with each other (as is often true in racially homogeneous families as well). On the other hand, Mary Hanson has adapted well to her son-in-law and his family, and she talks about the good quality of their marriage.

Church

Church activities can be both isolating and bridging. For both newcomers and established residents, church-based activities were also central to creating intimate relationships; whether they brought different people together depended on the nature of the church structure. The sodalities and musical groups organized on the basis of language and nationality within Catholic parishes often tended to bring Spanish speakers together but to separate them from others. This was particularly true for Ester, whose surrogate family was made up of church-based Latinos. However, as a leader of her group, she also developed close ties to Claire, a white ethnic, and to the pastors and nuns.

Korean churches tended to strengthen intragroup bonds and did not extend them to outsiders. They engaged all family members in age-graded activities throughout each Sunday; while the children attended classes, the adults studied the Bible together. Business connections and rotating-credit groups also sometimes emerge from such relationships. Church-based activities also played a major role in the friendships of established white ethnic women, as in the case of Jenny Baker and the Polish women of Ascension parish.

Workplaces

In general, workplaces are shaped directly by larger forces of change—a factory is bought by a series of new owners and downsizes, affirmative action is formally instituted, city agencies come to be run by African Americans, and so forth. Yet each is structured by accumulated work-force history, and as a result very different alliances and cleavages develop. In Philadelphia, many workplaces are layered by seniority, with white ethnics working longest, followed by African Americans, and then by Puerto Ricans as the last hired.

The offices in which Ester and Inez worked reflected this. They were members of the last entering group into an oppositional dyadic structure of whites and African Americans. In the absence of other Spanish speakers, they were identified as white and developed long-term friendships.

In addition, the advent of African American political power in public-sector employment created the new experience of non–African Americans working in settings in which African Americans control supervision and policy. This last factor exacerbated the situation in Ester's office. One Latina talks about working for a publicly funded social-service agency in which she and one white worker were the only non–African Americans:

> I think he [the boss] tries. That's the reason I am there. But of course he is for the Blacks. Whatever he does, he does it for the Blacks. A lot of people in that office don't like whites. They accept Latinos, because of course Latinos are discriminated against just like they are. Some of them even think Latinos are of a lower scale, a lower ladder. People get hired because they are Black and they get fired because they are not Black. The [white] guy that left, he was harassed because he was white. . . . To me, it doesn't make sense, because a Black person knows what it is like to be treated unfairly because they are Black—so when they do it to a white person who has totally no fault. . . . You can't hold this guy accountable for what was done two-hundred years ago.

To the Latina, the harassment of the white worker was an unfair retaliation against someone innocent of historic oppression by whites. Yet to the organization, the worker was distrusted as a symbol of the still-dominant white power structure responsible for institutional racism.

Candy, a white ethnic woman, works in a public-sector workplace containing approximately equal numbers of African Americans and whites, with small groups of Puerto Rican and Asian workers. There is more camaraderie here between the established workers of both races than with any of the newcomer groups. For them, the main division is between men and women rather than Blacks and whites. Most of the employees have worked together a long time.

Candy sees her Asian and Latino coworkers as forming two self-segregated cliques of isolated language speakers. She is annoyed by the self-exclusion of the Latino workers because they are obviously bilingual and use English in their work. In her view, "They just do it to keep us from hearing what they are saying, and that is just plain rude." Yet these newer workers had entered a situation in which established whites and African Americans had already established tightly knit, gender-based ties that seemed to exclude them.

Yet recent events have created a rupture in the relations between Candy and her African American women colleagues. She once spent many off hours with her coworkers, either in African American bars and restaurants or at their homes or the homes of their relatives. Having grown up in mixed neighborhoods and dated African American men, she was not uncomfortable.

The following incident illustrates the different perceptions of friendship, group allegiance, and the use of civil-rights protections. When Candy was promoted, one of her African American friends filed a complaint with the Equal Employment Opportunity Commission (EEOC). When she heard this, Candy withdrew her application, expecting her African American friend to withdraw also. Instead, the friend was offered (and took) the promotion. Candy did not understand the strength of collective African American concerns about discrimination and the fear of racism based on lifetime experience. She felt that this was a betrayal of an intimate personal relationship of mutual trust.[6]

Many of the men we encountered worked in factories or in public-sector jobs like Jim Baker's, characterized by a parity or dominance of African Americans. With economic pressure coming from factory closings and public-deficit-related layoffs, their workplace relationships are influenced by economic competition. Close working relationships and solidarity on the job do not translate into the erasing of racial stereotypes. Jim praises and respects his African American and Puerto Rican coworkers, but he denigrates the groups they come from. This conflict is exacerbated by his experience with affirmative action in hard times.

Fay's husband, Tim, works for the public-transportation system. He too has been affected twice by affirmative action. He scored well on the police exam but was not hired, which he sees as a result of minorities being taken first. Second, in his present workplace there are forty African Americans and seven whites. Every year they take a test. He notes that

> if one of the seven whites fails we get suspended for five days, but if the Black ones fail it, they're allowed to take the test again the next week.

Yet his disapproval of affirmative action does not affect his personal relations. Like Candy, he and Fay are friendly with several African American coworkers and are horrified by the racial harassment they receive.

> We have a friend that works with Tim. She's a Black woman. Her name is Phyllis. She's much nicer than some of the white people we know. She moved into a white per se neighborhood, and so far they have busted up her car and burned a cross on her property. They busted her windows in her house. They have done everything to make it miserable for her. She doesn't deserve it.

Our white working-class informants see a pattern of favoritism for newcomers as well as for African Americans:

> Puerto Ricans come over here with the help of civil-rights organizations. They accept less money and knock whites out of their jobs. White people

are a minority now, and because of affirmative action, even a Puerto Rican who can hardly speak English becomes demanding and insists on jobs he is not qualified for.

At the same time, African American and Puerto Rican informants often mentioned that whites seemed to be put on a fast track in their workplace in comparison to people of color. At a factory fieldwork site with a white, African American, new Pole, and Puerto Rican labor force, two buyouts and movement to plants in Mexico had recently led to downscaling, which produced layoffs, rumors, and low morale. The fear of job loss at the factory was a major aspect of life that created solidarity among the workers, who blamed management and not each other. Both African American and Puerto Rican workers complained about the slowness of their promotions, listing the times they were passed over. However, although they were clearly hostile to management for what they saw as blatant discrimination, they were not angry at their coworkers.

Yet while colleagues got along extremely well during the workday, talking and joking through work and break times, these relationships did not diminish the strongly held group stereotypes of established white workers based on the African American/white dyad. Two field-workers, one with a group of white women and one with a group of white men, were regaled with stories about the weaknesses of African Americans and Latinos (as groups) while observing friendly, cooperative relationships as they worked side by side. Some were close friends away from work, especially those who had been hired at the same time and who shared experiences in the "bumping-down" procedures related to layoffs (Cohen 1994).

Many workplaces, then, are structured by the familiar three groups with the same order of seniority—Latinos adjust to a racially dyadic structure formed in part by the history of hiring. Yet, many other workplaces differ from this model. Localized workplaces in Kensington like the public school described by Goode, Schneider, and Blanc (1992) are not characterized by the citywide racial dyad because African Americans are only a small minority. Instead, the local white/Puerto Rican dyad emerging from the checkerboard segregation patterns creates a different dyadic structure that shapes work relations.

At the same time, many recent newcomers have little contact with established residents at work. They are employed in monolingual settings in construction, sewing factories, and enclave retail outlets and restaurants.

Impersonal Relations in Local Public Arenas

In addition to daily interaction with close friends, neighbors, schoolmates, and workmates, people come together in more impersonal public arenas in the neighborhood. While many of these settings for adult interaction bring people together in the same place and time, they have become the focus of issues of "ownership" and control, generating boundaries and questions of insiders and outsiders. Preexisting ties and conflicts over control make it hard for these arenas to engender close friendships. We have seen examples of this in the discussion of civic and home-and-school associations in Chapter 4.

Shopping Strips

These local settings have much more impersonal interaction, yet they are important settings for exchanges between established residents and newcomers. Here, interactions between owner–managers, workers, and customers shape ideas as people go through their daily local shopping rounds.

As we see in more detail in Chapter 6, the restructuring of retail shopping (suburban malls and downtown redevelopment) has transformed local shopping strips and prepared the way for newcomer investment. White ethnic owners have sold out to new immigrants, particularly Koreans.[7] Both new immigrant owners and the shift to chain-operated stores bring changes in the social nature of retail transactions. There has been a movement away from stores that rely on personal interaction and customer loyalty to self-service stores, which minimize direct interactions and increase distrust and the need for customer surveillance.

Exclusive Stores: Keeping People Apart

In Olney, there have always been some exclusive outlets that discouraged outsiders through locked doors or chilly social encounters. Examples are bars and taverns with "insider" clientele, hairdressers who require referrals from customers, or the cluster of shops catering to eastern Europeans who immigrated after World War II. Apart from these, most outlets were open to everyone.

Today, there are more exclusive shops, mostly oriented to specific newcomer populations, especially Indians, Chinese, Vietnamese, and Cambodians. They usually exhibit exotic merchandise as signals to specialized customers. The shops serve as places for newcomers to socialize and exchange information. Many established residents talk about occasionally walking into one of these stores by accident; after being ignored, they simply leave. Some of those who express enthusiasm for diverse cultures often want to buy merchandise and complain about the closed nature of the social environment and the need to be demanding to get service.

Of greatest concern to established residents are the limited-access Korean stores, which are either wholesalers catering to Korean retailers or retail outlets serving only Koreans. The rapid loss of much storefront space to these operations is seen as particularly threatening to the nature of the community and led to a major incident that is analyzed in Chapter 6.

Another confrontation involved an Olney resident who tried to eat at a local Korean Restaurant that saw itself as serving the Korean community.

If you go in there you feel like you're intruding, and it's supposed to be a business that anyone can go into. A friend of mine went in there and he was treated very nastily. They took their gripe somewhere [a community leader mediated] and then they [the restaurant] said they were sorry and gave him a free meal.

Open Access Stores

For the majority of owners, who depend on a mixed clientele for success, hiring workers from all major groups is a preferred but costly strategy. Established owners want to attract and facilitate trade with newcomers, while newcomer owners hope to deal more easily with the established customers. Employing "others" helps in adapting merchandise, in attracting customers, and in creating customer satisfaction. Such newcomer employees also act as buffers for the owners, shielding them from language problems and unpleasant encounters as they serve "their people."

Both white ethnic and Korean small-store owners use this strategy if they can afford it. However, increased competition forces many of them to limit themselves to relying on themselves and their families (Goode 1994). Koreans first began to hire African Americans as a result of community-group pressure and threats of boycotts in some African American neighborhoods, but it was found to be advantageous and is now widely practiced.

One Korean owner said he tells all recent Korean arrivals to use African American employees to handle "headache" customers until they are tough enough to maintain an upper hand. Two Korean owners talked about racist white customers avoiding their stores until they hired established workers to keep them happy.

While owner–operators of small stores were financially limited in their ability to hire immigrants, the supermarket we studied was also hindered by increased competition from hiring more bilingual staff or offering those whom they hired any career ladders. Recent downturns in the industry have led to store closings and the "bumping down" of recently hired workers by those with higher seniority. Only 7 out of 150 workers are Spanish speakers in the Olney supermarket, which has the largest shelf space in the city for Latino products (Gonzales 1987), and only 1 Polish-speaking cashier works at Aramingo.

Service Encounters

Service transactions are public performances. They communicate messages about economic and power relationships, engendering resentment and hostility that affect both the actors directly involved and the observers in the store.

Negative encounters between Korean owner–operators and established customers are the source of many anecdotes. Moreover, stories about refusal of service in Korean-only stores, the frequent discomfort of Korean merchants with using English, their fear of white racism, and their concern with security problems have generated a pattern of distancing techniques. Brusque encounters in which the merchant maintains a stiff and erect posture in order to keep the upper hand are frequently observed. One Korean woman in a discount store, when told that she was friendly, seemed upset: "Friendly no good," she said, "cold is better for business. I treat not too bad but not too kind." This runs counter to the established U.S. expectation of a personal, pleasant encounter, full of chitchat in small owner-operated stores. Such encounters are part of a traditional strategy of trying to cultivate a loyal customer base through word-of-mouth referrals.

In addition, Korean owners often try to set up their stores using self-service aisles to minimize the need for speaking in English. Fearing shoplifting, the merchants then monitor customers closely. This violates the expectation of established resident browsers who expect freedom. One established white customer complains, "I don't like the way he follows me around while I am looking." Another says, "they keep asking 'Can I help you, can I help you.' I don't like that. I want to look on my own."

Attempts to bargain also upset established customers familiar with fixed prices. This occurs with Koreans as buyers as well as sellers. In an established men's store where the merchant is trying to target Koreans, he complains about their bargaining. "Even when it's on sale, they want to bargain. I finally learned to bargain because I did not want to get a bad reputation among them." Another white shopper recounted a transaction in a store owned and operated by Koreans:

> I asked him to repeat the price since I did not understand it, and he thought I was bargaining so he lowered it. I felt uncomfortable, so I left.

Finally, the middle-class clientele is insulted by some of the security measures brought by Koreans from poorer neighborhoods where their former businesses were located. They resent the occasional use of bulletproof-glass windows. When a Korean merchant pulled a gun on some uniformed parochial-school girls, news of the incident spread rapidly throughout the established community. Little mention was made of the fact that they were cursing him with racial epithets. Nevertheless, this was an inappropriate response.

Contrast this to the experience with Korean owners on the strip near Spanish-dominant Norris Square. Here, the merchants brought a dead shopping strip to life, much to the delight of the residents. Since Korean owner–operators recognize their dependence on Spanish customers, they go out of their way to please them. This has led to very cordial relationships between Koreans as owners and Latinos as customers and workers.

Almost all Korean merchants near Norris Square have hired some Spanish help. They have learned numbers, colors, and greetings (and sometimes more) in Spanish. They often buy from wholesalers of Spanish products. The Goya Foods representative talks about his success in business here, and one Korean merchant claims to be the first in Philadelphia to have imported certain foods for Puerto Ricans (Gonzales 1987). Their Latino customers try to find similarities between themselves and Koreans, remarking, for example, that "they like fresh produce like we do." Both parties prefer perfunctory transactions that avoid much personal interaction and language difficulty, although bargaining is not deplored. Shoppers see Koreans as fellow outsiders, victims of racism. A recent study of Korean merchants in New York also found a preference for Latino neighborhoods and customers (Park 1990).

Yet, several blocks away on another major shopping strip in a white-dominated area of Kensington, white ethnic merchants fearful of crime often lock doors and restrict the access of Puerto Ricans and African Americans. This particular shopping strip has been identified as racist by one community organization and by a local city agency.

The experiences of new immigrants in small stores without mixed labor owned by established residents were often as dissatisfying as those in immigrant-owned stores were to white ethnics. These transactions emphasized personal service and mandated greetings, small talk, and farewells to cultivate regular customers and word-of-mouth referrals. The changing neighborhood broke down these patterns and forced merchants to find new customers. This is one more instance where African Americans have an advantage over newcomers, since white ethnic owners see them as being closer to their traditional clientele. Their language and shared interests in sports and politics help them to transact the typical pleasant store encounter and to become valued new regulars (Goode 1994).

Unless one can afford to hire immigrants as buffer labor, attempts at traditional interactions with new immigrants in small stores are uncomfortable for both parties. One day a small merchant struggled long and hard to chat with a Spanish-speaking customer whose young daughter was serving as translator. The transaction worked, but the small talk was a failure. As they left, he said, "This language business is really getting me down." Immigrants also report discomfort in these personal encounters. One Central American woman was insulted when an established merchant made a friendly comment about her child, which she took as a criticism of its behavior.

In contrast, newcomers find large self-service chains that sell groceries, drugs, and sundries to be safe places where one can preserve anonymity. The self-service nature of chains demands little reliance on language. The supermarket is used heavily by newcomers shopping in large family groups, which both insulates them from interaction with others and allows children to help with translation. Inez takes her Spanish-speaking mother to the market every Saturday morning: "It is the only time she gets out of the house and she looks forward to it."

For established residents, the chains also become important and comfortable arenas. They are community institutions where people meet regularly. A mini–police station is located in one Olney store. Those who shop frequently never fail to meet people they know from the schools and community organizations.

In such chain settings as the supermarket, diner, or fast-food outlet, established residents claim space and assert ownership by speaking loudly to each other across public space. Groups of oldtimers have taken over certain sections of the McDonald's in Olney and the Wendy's at Aramingo. African Americans, Asians, and Latinos sit quietly as whites yell at each other across tables. On the other hand, established residents feel uncomfortable when newcomers use the same technique. At the K-Mart at Aramingo, whites complain that Latinos speak Spanish in front of them, and they feel uncomfortable because they fear that the conversation is about them. They also ask, "Why are there Spanish signs and no Polish signs?"

White customers also claim ownership through chatting and using first names with cashiers and counterpeople whom they know. Ruth always chooses her two favorite cashiers. She chats with them, hugs them, and gives them Christmas presents. Customers in the line observe these warm personal interactions between white ethnic customers and white ethnic cashiers; these are followed by transactions in which immigrants and cashiers ignore each other while immigrants chat with their companions in their own languages. A lot of time pressure occurs at the checkout line. Misunderstandings about the Women, Infants and Children nutrition program, food stamps, coupons, the rules of the express line, and merchandise promotions occur, causing delays. Store workers share a view of Spanish speakers as argumentative about food-stamp regulations, and Koreans are seen as overzealously buying loss-leader sale items above the allowable limit. One day at a Port Richmond supermarket, a Polish speaker who spoke accented English tried in vain to challenge a cashier's register input; the cashier ignored her and dealt only with the customer's daughter, who spoke unaccented English.

The lengthiest transaction observed during the study involved an African American customer in the WIC program and a market basket filled with infant-nutrition products. A form had to be filled out for each item. A long line of customers watched the cashier struggle, albeit competently, to complete the complex paperwork. Although the interaction involved no small talk or smiling, it was not unpleasant. The cashier was not overtly hostile, and the customers in the line were patient and made no comment. Nonetheless, they probably registered annoyance internally. Sometimes impatient people in the line made critical comments about what persons with food stamps were buying. Such experiences reinforce resentment and stereotypes. For example, one woman said:

> I come across the Spanish in the Acme. I don't like to stand in line and watch people buy brand names with my money [tax-based food stamps] and then not packing the bags themselves. They have to be waited on, too.

Incidents of trouble are rare in the stores, but those that do occur also reinforce negative stereotypes. Shoplifting is common in self-service stores. Most shoplifters who get caught are adolescents, often African American or Latino, although people are careful to point out the incidents of white gang problems as well. While all teenagers shopping in groups are watched carefully, both African Americans and Latinos of all ages feel they are unfairly monitored. One incident occurred when African American customers loudly and angrily accused a white manager of racism for handcuffing two African American teens alleged to be shoplifters for two hours while they waited for the police to come.

All of these factors lead to constant contradictions on the strip. Few opportunities occur for sustained positive interaction either as worker or customer. Pleasant encounters are followed by negative ones. White ethnic stores inadvertently make newcomers uncomfortable with their tradition of personal interaction. Korean stores serve newcomers well, but some alienate established residents. Large chains please newcomers seeking anonymity and established whites who feel they control the public space, but performances at the checkout counter often subtly reinforce established ownership of this community space. Transactions in small stores owned by Koreans and white ethnics are performances of class difference, reinforcing intergroup resentment and language difficulties. The checkout counter of large chain stores provides an even more public arena for such performances.

Children and Adolescents

According to conventional wisdom (which we heard over and over), parents teach their children racist views and undermine the tolerance taught in the schools. One individual noted: "They spend five hours getting along fine because the authority structure won't tolerate racism. But then they go home. . . ."

Our findings indicate a much more complex process, with relationships patterned by the interplay of residential proximity, the structure of the school, and the family's adult kin and friendship networks. In general, the way in which school structure, parental control, and street life work together to shape children's friendships depends very much on such features as the nature of population turnover and the creation of oppositional structures. Boundaries formed in elementary schools influence the structures of the secondary schools to which they send students. As children get older, group identity and bounded structures become more salient. Yet in spite of general trends, differences between neighborhood structures and school policies create very varied social processes.

As we observed children, it was obvious that their social networks and interaction patterns were often developing spontaneously in the schools and on the streets. While they come to school and to the street with few preconceptions about difference, the ability to sustain a friendship depended on variables like neighborhood turnover and the structure of the school. If parents' networks consisted of a dense, tight-knit group of fellow immigrants or were characterized by long-term ties, this had an effect on channeling children's relationships. However, parents were not simply villains who taught prejudice or kept their children from playing with others.

In Olney and parts of Kensington, if the residential block was mixed, children were likely to have mixed friends at home as well as in school. However, in those parts of Kensington that are in the center of drug activity, parents are more guarded. One says:

> Most white children are not allowed to play with Puerto Rican children because it's not safe. The kids are nice but the streets themselves are not safe. Three kids next door were out playing, one got shot in the shoulder by drug dealers. . . . This [house] is the only place this [twelve-year-old neighbor] is allowed to go. Here and her home are her world. We are prisoners here.

While all parents monitor children's neighborhood relationships to some extent, on most of the mixed blocks we observed established children played freely across lines, and in almost all instances they had best friends from different groups.

Controlling Children's Networks

In these neighborhoods characterized by turnover and declining quality of life, all parents were preoccupied by issues of safety and danger, discipline, achievement, and drugs. While some individuals from all groups associated these problems with specific group stereotypes, most others saw danger as coming from strangers, people they did not know.

Peggy, a white ethnic woman, talked about the pressure she received from relatives and friends because of the "best friendship" between her son and a Puerto Rican boy. He almost lived at their home and was treated like a family member, being allowed to walk in and out without formal permission. Yet some of her relatives and neighbors expressed surprise that they encouraged the relationship.

At the same time, Ester Ramos was also upset when her son shifted his friends from a group of whites on the block (whose families she knew) to fellow Spanish speakers whom she did not know. "I was worried. I had to find out who their parents were," she said, indicating that "coming from a good family" rather than group identity was the key concern. In contrast, other Puerto Rican parents were more concerned about white racism as a result of experience and discussions with friends. They encouraged only Puerto Rican friendships.

The limiting of contact between children across groups by people of color who fear racism is common. Jenny Baker, whose ten-year-old daughter had close African American and Latino friends in school, was called by one of the African American friend's mothers to decline a birthday party invitation. When the white mother indicated that other African American girls would be there, the invitation was accepted, since her daughter would not be placed in an all-white setting. On the other hand, many aspiring middle-class established residents (such as Sally, the self-described "culture fanatic") talk proudly about the diversity of their children's close friends:

> Lee [Sally's son's best friend] is from Taiwan, and he is smart as a whip and so well-behaved. His father works so hard in the store.

Port Richmond girls often resist their parents' attempts to limit their contact with "others." On the steps of their parochial school, Polish American girls from Port Richmond talk about how they love to hang out at the Pizza Hut in Aramingo mall and flirt with the Latino boys. "Those Spanish boys are so sexy," says one. "Don't tell our parents. They would kill us if they knew."

Middle-class immigrants in Olney often try hard to keep their children within circumscribed kin and friendship networks, placing them in parochial schools with siblings and cousins, driving them to school in carpools, and involving them in after-school activities within the ethnic community. One day, two Portuguese girls complained that their parents' insistence on Portuguese language class and work in the Portuguese day-care center limited the time they could spend with their local school-based friends. A Portuguese girl tells how after her father found out that she went to the movies with a large, mixed gender, mixed racial group he threatened punishment if she did it again.

Both this example and the one from Port Richmond illustrate the concerns parents have as their children approach adolescence. Then, they will be freer to move around the neighborhood on their own, and there will be more concern about dating and cross-gender contact.

Adolescents

We have described elsewhere the structures of the four elementary schools we observed (Goode, Schneider, and Blanc 1992). A wide disparity in the nature of ethnic boundaries was traced to the stability of the school population, social class, and neighborhood structures. In the upper grades of all but one elementary school, African American, Asian, and Latino girls often talk about feeling closer to their own group and begin limiting their "best friends" to people they define in this way. At one Olney school, for example, the older Korean girls asked to form a Korean club after years of cross-group play and friendship. One teacher there observes, "As kids get older, they clutch [sic] together by group."

Two upper-grade children of mixed marriages—one with a Central American mother and an African American father, the other with a white mother and an African American father—talk about feeling more comfortable with African American friends. The mothers recall that in earlier years their daughters had many white friends. Both attribute the change to their daughters' "favoring their fathers" (identifying with and/or being inherently like them), rather than recognizing the template of U.S. racial categories that define anyone with any African American heritage as African American.

Yet even with the strong template, there is nothing natural or automatic about choosing an identity or a peer group to belong to. As children move on to high school (choosing among selective magnet programs, Catholic, and local schools), their social relationships, their feelings about their own identity, and general social difference become very complex. This movement of teenagers to a variety of high schools increases their spatial roaming range and potential social contacts. Each school contains different conflicts and alliances. Pupils now relate to old street friends, old school friends, their own new fellow students, and the new friends of their old friends. They often spread their ties from Kensington to Olney and take on different identities in different settings. Their accumulated relationships from the block, from school, and from outside activities have become complex and full of discontinuities.

For example, Jane, a white girl, has only a few friends in Borders High School (described below), known for its racial boundaries. She came from a stable public school where almost no group boundaries were formed and has kept her old ties, a group of mixed neighborhood friends from her elementary-school days. These old friends chose different magnet high schools but remain tightly knit. Jane prefers them to the homogeneous ethnic/racial groups, which exist in her high school. Moreover, she has extended her friendships through her old acquaintances. Her South American boyfriend, for example, is a new schoolmate of a friend from elementary school.

Maria, a newcomer Pole who moved out of Port Richmond after eighth grade, returned for the parish Christmas festival accompanied by Asian and established white friends. The parish school possessed strongly emphasized boundaries, but once they go on to high school many parish-school graduates develop friendships with other students in their classrooms.

Mrs. Randall's daughter, Beth, was the only white in her Latino parish school in Kensington, giving her a predominantly Puerto Rican social circle. As her mother recounted above, she is still protected (watched over) by her predominantly minority neighbors. She has a Puerto Rican boyfriend. Her whole family is involved with her in a local intergroup teen activity that includes Puerto Ricans, African Americans, and white ethnics. Yet she has limited her current best girlfriends to three white ethnic girls from outside the area whom she knows from her mixed Catholic high school.

Steve, who is white, lives in an area of Feltonville where his block and entire set of street friends gradually shifted from white ethnic to Puerto Rican. At a very mixed Kensington high school, he sits at an all-white lunch table. However, he also has two good African American friends with whom he signed up for the mixed teen leadership program in Kensington. There, he is treated as an honorary African American. He attributes his ability to relate to everyone to his growing up in a mixed neighborhood.

Boys, especially, at this age tend to form large groups and roam long distances. As students travel the city on public transportation, patterns of "rushing" on the subway occur. The teens report these as manifestations of interschool rivalries, while to adults they appear to be racial. The Latinos who attended a party in Port Richmond that led to the murder of Sean Daily (described in Chapter 6) were an example of the kind of widespread mixed networks and long-distance roaming created by the variety and complexity of high schools. In this instance, ties created at a Catholic high school and a public technical school brought the parties together.

Moreover, the very structures of secondary schools are shaped by ties formed in widely differing elementary schools. Thus, the cleavages and alliances created in secondary schools are shaped in part by the nature of the feeder schools. As children from single-race elementary schools mix with those from schools where mixed friendships have developed, the boundaries become more complex. This is illustrated by two junior highs in Kensington. One, in a white-dominated area, has an oppositional structure of white gangs and African American–Puerto Rican alliances formed to hold their own against the whites. While this is attributed by conventional wisdom to a natural white/minority dyad, it is more linked to the fact that the whites had formed their friendships in basically single-race feeder schools, while the African Americans and Latinos had developed ties in their mixed elementary schools.

Another nearby junior high in a more mixed area had much more fluid patterns of alliance, shaped by the street boundaries of the local drug trade. Here, Puerto Ricans involved with the street drug structure sometimes recruited whites to "go against" African Americans with whom they competed. Drug gangs that divide turf on the street also structure conflict over who controls particular halls and bathrooms.

Borders High School

This institution provides an example of a school with strong group boundaries. It also yields two examples of programs that link students from different groups. The school is often described as the most diverse in Philadelphia, with thirty-seven languages said to be represented. With thirty-two hundred students, it is also the largest in the city. The population in 1988 was 50 percent African American and 25 percent Latino, with the rest divided between whites and Asians, the fastest-growing group. Among the whites were a significant number of Portuguese and immigrants from the Middle East.

The school was desegregated in the 1970s, during a stormy time of community protest. As a legacy of the problems and school conflict related to this change, the school day was designed to provide little time for informal activity. No lunch periods are provided, and students leave at 1:30. Since desegregation and the advent of magnet choice, many local parents have avoided sending their children there, preferring Catholic and magnet schools.[8]

Everyone—students, teachers, and parents—described the school as internally segmented. One student says:

As far as the generalizations are concerned, this school is really different.
In a regular school you have groups like jocks and so on, but at this
school it's not divided like that. It's more divided along racial lines.

While everyone knows of cases of interracial dating, it is considered comparatively rare.

Most students and teachers describe a system of group control of space, largely generated by ESOL, which leads to block rostering for each language group and to the definition of spaces near language classrooms as "belonging" to particular groups. For example, one floor is generally perceived as dominated by Spanish-speaking Puerto Ricans, who play Spanish music and are "really into their culture." This area was referred to as Hicksville by some established Puerto Rican students, since "hick" is a translation for *jibaro*, or mountain peasant.[9]

Some of the segmentation can also be attributed to outside social-service programs run by ethnic interest groups, such as Aspira (which promotes Latino achievement) and an Indochinese community center, which have organizations in the school.

An incident that occurred just before our fieldwork began helped further structure the school into origin groups as human-relations groups intervened. A Latino student was stabbed by an Asian.[10] The new principal, who arrived at the school right after the incident, was immediately contacted by human-relations organizations offering to help resolve the intergroup conflict. The growth of clubs based on heritage, which had already begun, was extended. Demands were made that club announcements and information about everyone's holidays be made over the public-address system. The principal describes the effect of this growing segmentation:

> We have the Korean Club, we have Aspira, now an Indochinese club with a Vietnamese rep, a Cambodian rep, and a Chinese rep. There's the African American history group. . . . I want to take this thing one step further and convince them that we need to do things together once in a while. Because what I don't want is one giant competitive thing like which club can get the teacher's or the principal's or the counselor's favor. We've created a bigger monster than we started out with, and in the name of human relations we actually went backwards.

The segmentation creates problems for students who have to choose sides, such as Ester's daughter. Having gone to an elementary school where she had mixed friends, she feels comfortable with everyone. The white girls think she is white, and she does not want them to hear her speak Spanish. The Puerto Ricans complain that she "acts like she's white." Her mother tells her, "You must choose the group you want to go with."

In this school, two exceptions to the divisions are the honors program and the soccer team, which has been deliberately integrated. The honors program places high achievers from all groups together.[11] As one participant says:

> There are honors classes. They are kept apart, block rosters, so that we [honor students] can get to know the supposedly more intelligent students. And they're totally kept away from other students. I've been in regular classes, and let me tell you, it's like night and day.

Here again, young people are pressured to choose a loyalty. The larger school structure encourages loyalty to Latinos, while the honors program tries to shift allegiance to a mixed group with common goals. One Latino honors student responded to this by distancing himself from other Puerto Rican pupils:

> I live in a Puerto Rican neighborhood, but I don't associate with them much. I hang out a little, but I have different interests. They are proud of their F's, don't want to study, want to have a good time, be good athletes and dancers. They are obsessed with money. Most of my friends are Asians. They are humble and have a respect for learning, like I do.

Yet in spite of the solidarity of honors students, pressures to "go with" his own group are resolved differently by another Puerto Rican boy. He gradually moved from the honors group to become a leader among Puerto Rican students. In the first year of our fieldwork, he indicated that he tried to keep the *jibaros* on the third floor from knowing that he was Spanish. However, in the second year of the study, an incident resulting from a conflict between school ideology and Puerto Rican language assertion reinforced his Latino identity. One day he was talking to the Spanish-speaking counselor in Spanish. The counselor is known to "work hard for Spanish rights" and was involved in a campaign against some white colleagues who discouraged students from speaking Spanish in the school. During the conversation, the honors student was challenged by the white counselors for speaking Spanish to the Latino counselor. He responded to the challenge with a complaint to the administration. By the next year he was a leader of Aspira and had dropped out of mixed honors after-school activities.

Soccer is another program in which diverse groups participate. It is used to assert strongly the school's identity as diverse but working toward a common goal. The principal, describing the team, remarks:

> Black kids, white kids, Polish kids, all kinds, Portuguese, Korean. You went out to watch a soccer game, it looked like the UN all-star team. So we did a lot of talking about that around the league, a newspaper reporter shows up, we made the playoffs. Instead of writing about an improved [Borders] team, he did the whole thing on diversity. Great for the school, great for the kids. The kids had a map—the coach, smart coach—had a map of the world in the locker room. The kids each put a pin in it with a flag with their number on it.

The team is a successful example of highlighting both differences and common goals.

Other high schools we observed were not as segmented as Borders. In two other secondary schools, Latino teenagers form a swing group, sometimes allied with African Americans and sometimes with whites. Over time, the fights and alliances seem to be random and shifting. Dating follows the same patterns.

Conclusions

Exploring everyday life "on the ground" in the three neighborhoods reveals many aspects of complexity. Everyday life experiences play an important role in shaping people's ideas about social categories and group stereotypes among established whites, African Americans, and new immigrants. Both children and adults form close relationships across boundaries. Yet competition over work, space, and government services operates to challenge positive views of other groups in general. There is little connection between personal intimate relationships and interacting in impersonal institutions, which are often either contested or "owned" and controlled by one group or another. Each school, workplace, and shopping strip is structured differently, reflecting history and demography.

Children's ties are created by street and school structures mediated by parental control. They are more open to spontaneous friendships in their early lives, but their social worlds become as complex as those of adults as they move to adolescence and deal with their futures. The succession of schools, the transiency of neighborhoods, and the nature of boundaries within secondary schools all play a role in producing variability from school to school and neighborhood to neighborhood. The explanation that parents "teach racism" and undo the teaching of tolerance in schools that is part of the cultural-pluralism model, and assumptions about white racism, reduce this complexity to something that is both too simple and frequently inaccurate.

Adult social life is already filled with dense social-network ties based either on the exigencies of immigration or a lifetime in a localized network of kin and friends. Yet mutual concerns about children, the practice of interdating and intermarriage, and shared concerns about the block or church create intimate friendships between people of different backgrounds. Sometimes long-term work ties create intimacy as well. Neighborhood turnover and increasing exposure to diversity can sometimes lead to more trusting ties with others or to conflict, depending on the circumstances.

More superficial contacts between adults in such institutions as schools, stores, and workplaces create fewer opportunities for closeness, and they often lead to struggles for control and ownership. In responding to high turnover and economic pressures, these institutions often create boundaries that segment populations into opposing groups. Much of this is directly related to the citywide political economy, which generates such things as residential turnover in neighborhoods, seniority layers in workplaces, and overcrowding and transfers in schools, as well as the turnover of shopping-strip control. Encounters in these segmented or contested institutions, in turn, create a set of messages about class, culture, race/ethnicity, or immigrant status that contradict those experienced through personal relationships.

In everyday life, dissimilarities in neighborhood dynamics influence public life, as in the case of differences in the nature of contact and conflict among groups in community organizations and shopping strips in the three neighborhoods. Experiences convey contradictory messages, depending on which set of friends one is with or the nature of the setting. Everyday experience frequently contradicts the standard models of difference. Korean and Polish newcomers do not fit the "good immigrant" model. African Americans in control of the workplace do not fit the structural-racism model. Friendships and marriages across boundaries often teach people that the cultural-pluralism model oversimplifies reality, exaggerating some kinds of dissimilarities and ignoring real differences in life experience.

The focus events analyzed in Chapter 6 call models of difference directly into play. Sometimes they reinforce the experience of everyday life, but at other times what they say is contradicted by day-to-day realities. In Chapter 7, we explore how these contradictions are manipulated by individuals as they make lives for themselves in the complex social landscape of a changing city.

CHAPTER 6

Focus Events

The many different aspects of everyday life crystallize into equally complicated patterns during events that highlight diversity. These include formal events designed to bring people from different ethnic, racial, and national groups together to celebrate ethnicity or to create mutual respect. They also include crises such as a cross-group killing or an argument over community identity involving different groups. These instances evoke symbols beyond the actual occurrences, creating memories that reverberate throughout the community over time and patterns of behavior or organized efforts that alter the dynamics of local intergroup relations. These "focus events" necessarily draw the most sustained attention from citywide forces. This term refers to occasions that underscore group differences. The structuring, citywide contexts described in the first section of this book clearly affect the lives of individuals living in the neighborhoods. But citywide messages and actions are always mediated through the localities' own social processes. The concentration of the citywide organizations and the media on agendas that only partially involve local communities also leads to resistance. This chapter explores how different groups interact during these events.

We examine two different kinds of focus events: those deliberately created to celebrate difference, and community reactions to crises that involve race and nationality. The section on celebrations of difference examines a variety of events. Programs for children provide the purest example of the local use of the cultural-pluralism model. Events within a particular ethnic community show how understandings of immigrant status and ethnicity change through time and within different segments of a group. We focus on the Polish émigré and Polish American community, describing two performances (one geared toward each group), competing understandings of ethnicity and nationality as represented at the annual meeting of a Polish beneficial, and the way that the Polish émigré and Polish American community chooses to represent itself to the rest of Philadelphia. Finally, we explore multicultural events designed for entire communities, including a series of neighborhood ethnic festivals and a church's attempt to bring its very diverse population together through ethnic celebrations. The community events demonstrate the impact of class, immigration status, and internal divisions between insider and outsider. We also discuss two crisis events, one in Olney and one in Kensington/Richmond. They contrast the ways that crises are understood and handled by people from various classes and by ethnic groups with different kinds of resources, and how people respond to different sorts of intergroup tension.

Celebrations of Difference

Occasions specifically designed to bring people together across groups incorporate the messages of the citywide human-relations organizations. In some cases, events in local communities are fostered by citywide institutions. Like most aspects of intergroup relations in Philadelphia, the amount of attention that citywide agencies give to local activities depends on the link between them and local organizations. Thus empowerment-oriented community groups in Kensington and Olney that rely on foundation and city funds reflect larger societal agendas, while Port Richmond does not participate in these events because it has no network of CDCs, NACs, and settlement houses to write proposals for such programs.

Events in this neighborhood reflect concerns within the Catholic hierarchy and the ethnic community. That Port Richmond gets left out of programming on multiculturalism is particularly ironic, because Philadelphia's human-relations institutions consider it the neighborhood most in need of such activities. As explored in detail in Chapter 7, the human-relations community's perception of Port Richmond as racist reflects middle-class assumptions about a community characterized as white working class.

Programs for Children

Chapter 3 stated that much human-relations programming focuses on children. Examining these efforts illustrates the tenets of the cultural-pluralism and "good immigrant" models. Events for children also show institutional models of pluralism most clearly, since authority figures rather than the participants play a dominant role in designing the program. A play presented in Olney as part of the public schools' cultural-awareness week provides a familiar example. This assembly and all the other events were organized by the art teacher, a middle-class African American woman. She served as the announcer for the program and was dressed in a Mexican costume—a lacy shirt and a long skirt. The audience included the younger grades and a few participants' parents.

The announcer first introduced a group of Korean dancers. These students were older children, part of a formally trained group imported for the occasion, who performed at other events in the city. Six women, all in elaborate matching costumes of green and gold, performed a very slow dance to taped traditional music.

The next event was a skit, "So This Is America," created by the fourth-grade teacher and a student teacher from Temple University. It started with a narrator (an African American boy, an immigrant from the Caribbean) saying that the United States is full of many faces, people from different places. There were many people living together—different races and nationalities—and that is what the nation is all about.

A series of vignettes followed.

[A]   The scene started with the Statue of Liberty saying that she has been in America one hundred years, and had been an invitation to immigrants. The Statue of Liberty was a white girl. She was then joined by Benjamin Franklin [Vietnamese] and an "immigrant," also a white girl. The immigrant wore a long skirt, blouse, a shawl, a scarf on her head, and carried a shopping bag. Like the archetypal "good immigrant," she looked like a nineteenth-century eastern European peasant.

The immigrant kept asking the Statue of Liberty and Benjamin Franklin who they were. Finally Benjamin Franklin said that there are children from many lands in the school and asked the immigrant if she would like to meet them.

[B]   Next, a number of children came up in different costumes. Each introduced him- or herself as descending from a particular place. It appeared that each child was really "from" that place. The first one was an African American girl dressed in a costume out of *Uncle Tom's Cabin*. She said that her ancestors had no choice about coming here, but they were looking for opportunity. The whole group then sang a Freedom Trail song.

Next, a white boy: "My ancestors came from Italy. They thought that the streets of America were paved with gold. They didn't find gold, but they did find the opportunity to work."

The next child was also a white boy. He spoke about Jews and Europeans who came looking for peace and freedom of religion.

Another white boy said that his ancestors came from Ireland to escape the potato famine.

The next boy said that his ancestors were Germans who came to Pennsylvania in 1790 "on William Penn's invitation"[1] and settled in Germantown.

Another boy's ancestors came from Italy because the land was played out and they were looking for opportunity.

Next Ben Franklin said that now we were going to introduce Hispanic cultures. Two children came up, a boy and a girl. The boy said that he was Puerto Rican and the girl said that she was Mexican. They spoke about speaking different dialects, and then said that they were similar. Then the girl said that parts of the United States had been parts of Mexico. The boy said that Puerto Rico was a U.S. trust territory and that Puerto Ricans had been U.S. citizens since 1917.

Up until this point, all the children had been talking about places that their ancestors came from. Next, about six Asian children came forward and said in unison that some children don't have ancestors who were immigrants, but are immigrants themselves. They are the first generation, and "someday other children will call them ancestors."

[C]   At this point all the children marched to the back of the room. The children who had speaking parts, and about twenty others, including Benjamin Franklin and the immigrant, were then given paper flags. Each flag had a name on the back, an indication that these children were "from" these countries. Each child was also in costume. Among others, there was a little girl in a "Dutch girl" costume and a child from India. The "immigrant" was carrying an Italian flag. Benjamin Franklin had a Vietnamese flag. An African American boy was carrying the American flag. They then walked up the aisle by twos and arranged themselves on the stage. Benjamin Franklin and the immigrant were in the front. The whole group then recited the Emma Lazarus poem and sang "This Land Is Your Land." Finally, Benjamin Franklin asked the immigrant if she was ready to be an American and she said yes. Then the entire group sang "Shalom Chaverim."

These kinds of events highlight the model that all Americans share a common experience and common goals, while reinforcing a notion that each group has a unique ethnic culture that should be identified and celebrated—the hallmarks of cultural pluralism. The program was intended to teach children the value of each culture by illustrating characteristics of clothing and past experience from the country of origin. The program provided bits of data about the homelands, such as that Puerto Ricans are U.S. citizens. This information is meant to expand understanding of people from other groups.

Commonality of immigrant and ethnic experience is stressed through the statement that everyone came from somewhere else, seeking opportunity. The established white children were portrayed as immigrants like the newcomers, showing the similarity of all Americans as both immigrants and ethnics.

Even U.S.-born white children with multiple ethnic roots are identified as coming from one country through the use of ethnic flags and costumes. But the play's authors are not sure of how to fit the African American child into this model of equal ethnicity because they cannot identify a fixed country of origin. Instead, the African American child became the representative of "American" culture.

Such a choice is fairly common. It shows the ambivalence of whites toward the historical experience of African Americans by giving the child a U.S. flag rather than one from Africa. In this attempt to merge slavery into the "good immigrant" and cultural-pluralism models, the dominant society quietly ignores the very real differences between the way that immigrants adapted to the United States and the way that slaves were repeatedly torn from their families and countries. In this sense, cultural pluralists attempt to paint a happy face on the African American experience. Highlighting the American identity of peoples descended from slaves brought from Africa also has a positive side. Identifying an African American child as American reveals the reality of the transformation of many local African cultures into a uniquely American cultural pattern through the experiences of slavery, the economic exigencies experienced by most African Americans after the Civil War, migration to the North, and the crucible of the civil-rights and Black-power movements. In fact, each ethnic culture is created by the interaction of immigrant experience with the social and economic structures of the United States.

This skit shows many aspects of the "good immigrant" model. Newcomers emigrate to the United States in search of opportunity, as established residents once did. All faced some struggles, but will eventually fit into U.S. society. The emphasis on opportunity reveals the middle-class expectations behind this presentation. Each child is considered an equal who can succeed in the United States through individual effort. The cultural resources provided by ethnic heritage are portrayed as important in helping these children achieve their potential. By highlighting opportunity and ignoring such barriers as limited family resources, the presentation assumes that these children come from a class background that will provide economic support and connections. Having completed their education, they can take their place in the middle-class "mainstream" and achieve the "American dream" of steady income and a comfortable material lifestyle.

The same presentations seldom appear in working-class Kensington. Instead, the principal at the elementary school we observed admonished the parents at graduation ceremonies that they must help their children become flexible in an ever-changing economy. Opportunity was never mentioned.

The skit also reveals both expectations of newcomer subgroups that prevail throughout the society and patterns of interaction with newcomers in Olney.

The "Hispanic" and "Asian" youngsters were lumped together into racial categories used in the U.S. census. The Spanish-speaking children emphasized the similarities between very different cultures. The fact that the African American teacher who organized the events chose a "Hispanic" costume shows an attempt at bridging cultures, but her selection of Mexican dress as opposed to Puerto Rican clothing indicates limited understanding of the differences between people from Spanish-speaking countries.

Like the Olney organizations that deal with newcomers as a group, through brokers, newcomer children spoke in one voice about their difference from children born in the United States. Unlike the rest of the performers in the presentation, the Korean dance group was brought in from the outside through a broker. Newcomers are foreigners who become the ancestors of American ethnics.

The same patterns appear in numerous events. The International Club at another school in the area staged a version of *Alice in Wonderland* as their diversity event the next year. Like the immigrant, Alice was introduced to children from a variety of countries representing the backgrounds of young-sters in the school. Each child rattled off a speech about his or her country of origin. Again like the immigrant, Alice was looking for a home, which turned out to be a country that included a cultural mosaic from all these other places, the United States. The message for the children in the school is that, like Alice and the immigrant, they should learn that a positive cultural heritage is the basis for creating a strong nation. Acknowledging ethnic identity is expected to build self-esteem. Using music from different groups cements the idea of commonality of purpose within a plurality of forms.

Intracommunity Events

Exploring ethnic community events reveals yet another set of layered inten-tions, as groups use different sets of assumptions in creating occasions that attempt to define community both internally and to society at large. While events for a single ethnic community may exude a different ambience than specific multicultural programming, the same pattern of back-and-forth inter-action between goals and structures set by citywide forces and the local community prevails.

Issues of ownership appear in each of these events. Different participants view the celebrations as intended for different audiences. Who the organizers are, the language used, advertising, and many different aspects of presentation indicate which group(s) are insiders or outsiders at a particular event. Both audience members and performers maintain multiple understandings of the different symbols used; these contrasting patterns of control and interpretation are highlighted in Polish ethnic events. The various factions of the community each use the same general symbols—language, food, art, costume—to assert very different perceptions of community and to include or exclude different portions of the Polish émigré/Polish American population. The kinds of symbols used in these events reflect assumptions prevalent in the city and in the society about what constitutes ethnicity along the lines of the cultural-pluralism model. The various parts of the Polish émigré and Polish American community adopt the same kinds of safe ethnic markers used by Irish Americans, Italian Americans, and even Puerto Ricans and Koreans to show how they are different. But the meanings assigned to these familiar symbols of ethnicity differ for various parts of the community. Ethnic markers defined by the dominant society are transformed by the subcommunities that use them. Tracing the multiple use of cultural symbols throughout the events reveals the dynamics within the community.

Contrasting four events reveals the flow between structure and meaning as representatives of each faction use and portray events. Two are ethnic performances, each controlled by a different faction within the ethnic community. The other two events are meant as group gatherings. A beneficial-society business meeting reveals the internal dynamics of an occasion designed for the community alone, while a city-sponsored ethnic festival shows how community factions portray themselves in an event meant to present the community to all of Philadelphia.

Polish Emigré versus Polish American Performances

The children's dance recital sponsored by one of the beneficials contrasts with a performance by a folk-dance group imported from Poland. In this example, different factions control potentially similar occasions. Both events were held in the same place—the auditorium of the largest Polish nationality parish school—further underscoring the commonalities and contrasts between them.

The children's dance recital is an annual event for this beneficial, which considers programming for youth as a major focus (youth programming has become one way to build membership).[2] The beneficial sponsors Polish folk-dance and baton classes throughout the area. Each group becomes a club, and the recital brings them together for this annual event.

The teenage program combines cultural activities and lessons in Polish with a social-service program. Older children gather points for participating in folk-dance presentations at community events, such as ethnic parades or festivals, as well as through such social-service activities as volunteering at nursing homes. A certain number of points enables girls to be presented as debutantes; points also matter in the college-scholarship program.

The beneficial is an established-resident organization that includes a mix of Polish Americans and DPs in key positions. However, a fair number of newcomer families also participate in the youth programming, viewing it as a way to maintain Polish national culture and also being attracted to the scholarship program. These newcomer parents use a fundamentally American event to their own ends.

As a Polish American organization, the group's programming reinterprets Polish national culture as reified peasant style with significant U.S. elements. The dance costumes provide a key example. Like the dances themselves, the costumes are careful copies of folk styles collected in Poland. Like most invented traditions (Hobsbawm and Ranger 1983), these costumes take a version of clothing worn during one period in Polish history and present it as the way that all people in a given region dressed throughout time. The reification assumes an unchanging traditional culture that contrasts with the progress of the modern world. The costumes reflect the assumptions of newcomers represented by the "good immigrant" model. In fact, change is evident in even the most careful copies. Polish American parents, for example, substitute polyester blouses for the cotton and linen originals, adapting tradition to the current way of life. Even so, Polish American participants maintain that they are sustaining an unchanging ethnic culture by learning traditional dances and participating in an ethnic organization.

The same tension between a conscious effort to preserve ethnic identity through the framework of an ethnic event while Americanizing most elements of the presentation is evident in the dance recital. While children from all emigration waves in Philadelphia participated in the program, the ambience was decidedly Polish American. English was the lingua franca. Besides parents, the other audience members primarily came from the Polish American component of the community. Only half of the presentations on the program were choreographed Polish folk dances, depicting the culture as peasant style. Such presentations remain central to Polish American conceptions of ethnic identity. The youth group performed these particular dances for audiences throughout Philadelphia as representatives of ethnic culture, in accord with the cultural-pluralism model.

The rest of the program consisted of three polka presentations and eight baton-group performances. The polka is recognized within the community as the defining tradition for Polish Americans. It is characterized as a U.S. adaptation of a Czechoslovakian dance style. The polka culture has become a significant locus for socializing within the Polish American community. Its prominence in an ethnic-organization presentation shows the community's recognition of its own Americanization. The baton events highlight the patriotism and respect for U.S. values so characteristic of Polish American culture. None of the baton presentations had anything to do with Poland or Polish American traditions. Models focused on the United States ("The Stars and Stripes Forever" and "America") or on American life ("California Girls" and "Rock and Roll Is Here to Stay"). Even the incorporation of other ethnic traditions into U.S. values appeared here, with one group using the music of "La Bamba" to present a very American baton routine.

A performance by an imported Polish folk-dance group stands in stark contrast to the dance recital. This event was sponsored by a travel service that primarily serves the Polish-focused elements within the community. Much of the audience came from the DP and newcomer emigration waves. With the exception of the beneficial's youth group, whose members attended as one way to gather points, the Polish American community was decidedly absent. Polish was the primary language spoken during the performance and in the audience. Newcomers clearly owned this occasion.

Like all events within American Polonia, linkages between newcomer and established portions of the community appear here. The performance consisted of more-professional presentations of the same Polish folk dances performed by the beneficial dance clubs. A leader of the Polish American community introduced the event, attempting a speech in halting Polish before switching to English. The dance group and its sponsors viewed the event as presenting Polish culture to a U.S. audience. Both Polish and English appeared in the program, but English came first. The event was advertised both in English and through the Polish-language radio program. The group performed two traditional American songs, "Red River Valley" and "Goodnight, Irene." Yet these attempts to bring a version of Poland to Polish Americans highlighted the differences between the newcomer and established communities. Polish Americans chose to stay away from the performance, while newcomers saw it as a way to cement connections within their community, a safe place to speak Polish, and a reminder of Polish national traditions.

Multiple Interpretations of Ownership

The same kind of multiple use of similar symbols appears throughout community events. The beneficial's annual meeting is a case in point. Most of the delegates were established DPs or Polish Americans. The food consisted of standard U.S. luncheon catering: roast beef and chicken. The U.S. Catholic traditions of Polonia, such as selling chances and beginning and ending events with prayers, were also featured. Polish American priests were honored presenters at this meeting. English was the primary language spoken.

While English was preferred, and this meeting resembled any other U.S. organization's annual business session, Polish symbols and language were in evidence. For example, Polish ethnic dolls were raffled off, and all of the signs welcoming delegates were in Polish. Yet the delegates' discomfort with representations of modern Poland was evident when the Polish-language teacher, a '68 Wave newcomer, decided to give her report in Polish. Much of the audience fidgeted throughout the complex, rapid-fire presentation. As it turned out, many delegates could understand the report yet did not pay close attention. They understood the organization to belong to Americans of Polish descent, emphasizing familiar U.S. symbols within Polish ethnic packaging. In their minds, the teacher's use of Polish was inappropriate.

American ethnicity involves the use of familiar, Americanized symbols like language signs and dolls in peasant costumes to represent difference. The cultural-pluralism model stresses that each ethnic culture has its own unique elements, yet the elements are identical and equal. Since the expected symbols vary little from group to group, all groups become equal because each has its own identifiers representing the proud heritage of the members. But ethnic symbols are not so different that they remove the group from the U.S. mainstream. One nun, for example, reported being embarrassed to participate in Polish ethnic events as a child because they made her different. However, when she was sixteen she saw a Saint Patrick's Day parade and realized that "everybody does this, we were no different from anybody else." At that moment she decided that ethnicity was acceptable, something that made her similar to other Americans, not unacceptably "foreign" and different.

But speaking a language that some members of society may not understand is a clear way to indicate separation from average Americans. Even though most of the Polish American audience at the beneficial meeting could follow the language teacher's speech, they equated her use of Polish with the Puerto Ricans who speak Spanish in the supermarket instead of using English in public like "good" immigrants. When the language teacher spoke in Polish, she stepped outside the "good immigrant" model, which shows new arrivals as working toward becoming American. By using Polish to communicate instead of as a ritual symbol found only in prayers and welcome signs, she crossed the line between American "ethnic" and foreigner.

The language teacher, on the other hand, saw the gathering as a place to be Polish in the United States. She greeted people in Polish and chose to give her presentation in her native language (although she speaks English fluently) to cement her sense of connection between the homeland and the U.S. ethnic community. The same kinds of choices are true for many of the delegates, who learned Polish as children but almost always use English. Newcomers and established residents use the same symbols and events to mean very different things.

Internal Divisions, External Solidarity

Despite competing definitions within the community, Polonia attempts to present a united front to society at large. The Polish American festival is one example of the citywide ethnic events described in Chapter 3. It was organized by the Polish American Congress, and most of the booths were run by congress-related organizations. The event featured such typical Polish American symbols as polka bands, kielbasa, pierogies, and many booths selling chances. All signs were in Polish and English. The signage both identified the event as Polish and provided information to the few newcomers who attended. Newcomer organizations did participate: the sports club and a language class both had well-staffed booths.

The event was geared toward outsiders. Many organizations that are integral within the community, such as the established travel agencies, beneficials, and groups not associated closely with the citywide umbrella group, did not participate. Their absence confirmed that this gathering did not draw its primary audience from inside the community. Fissures within Polonia no doubt also helped determine which organizations participated. While people from all sectors of Polonia did attend, many in the crowd were tourists and Philadelphians who frequent waterfront events. It cost $500 to sponsor a booth at the festival. Knowing that it would draw little new business or membership, the established organizations chose not to pay such a high fee for representation. The arguments over ownership and the meanings of ethnic identity belong within the community, as each faction draws its own audience and organizes its own events. In events involving the whole city, people are content to let the citywide organization supply the image for the community.

Neighborhood Multicultural Events

The same multiple understandings of group identity and the importance of ethnicity underlay interactions among newcomers and established residents in multicultural events involving the whole community. Ideas about defining groups (as well as the nature of boundaries, differences, and relationships) are contested, negotiated, and socially reconstructed during the planning of these events. Such planning often entails competition over resources and divergent assumptions about audience and the meaning of symbols. The performance of the event itself produces intended and unintended messages as groups come together in stressful situations.

People who attend such gatherings have an additional understanding and use for the event. While many of these occasions are designed to introduce different ethnic groups to each other, newcomer Latinos and Asians, and even established African Americans, regard ethnic cultural events as a time to convey a subgroup or homeland identity, which they feel that they must push into the background in their day-to-day interactions. They come to enjoy their own food and company in a safe environment. While they are not hostile to the outsiders who attend, they focus on people they consider similar, creating a sense of camaraderie that can be viewed as cliquishness by longtime residents.

For established whites, intermarriage and the homogenization of ethnic culture created by the effort to use the same symbols as markers for different groups leads to a sense that ethnic identity is a shifting and peripheral part of self. Some established Puerto Ricans share this view. Established community residents join clubs or activities identified with ethnicity because they like the company and the activities, not necessarily because their cultural heritage is a particularly important part of self. The Polish beneficial youth group is the Port Richmond equivalent of the 4-H club. Members will participate in events that take place outside the community or that are geared toward other groups primarily because they have a role as part of an organization. They often see no need to use their scant leisure time to go outside the community for events labeled as ethnic. Nor are they drawn to gatherings within the community that feature another group. The opposite is true for the elderly, who welcome events as something to do.

The most direct interaction between citywide human-relations institutions and the local community took place in Neighborhood Human-Relations Projects, a program initiated by the citywide institutions. All the communities we dealt with had one or more such grants, except for Port Richmond.

The program sought proposals from community organizations for local projects.[3] While the grant administrator stressed that the program received a number of creative proposals, and that its design reflected community ideas, the funding criteria highlighted human-relations activities in accord with the cultural-pluralism model. These either involved bringing people together to celebrate positive aspects of culture from the "homeland" (mostly food, costume, and dance) through culture-at-a-distance performances or developing ways of dealing with crises. The funder–administrator strongly encouraged groups to offer ethnic festivals and presentations, along with workshops in multicultural sensitivity/awareness and mediation/conflict resolution, when negotiating proposals. While some groups resisted this format for a while, every funded proposal ultimately included these elements.

An analysis of the results of the neighborhood human-relations project grants in Kensington and Olney shows both positive and negative outcomes. In Kensington, the majority of community groups were concerned with issues of drug criminality, housing, and economic development. Reflecting the structural-racism model, most held that people did not get along because of fundamental economic problems and that relations between people could best be improved by equalizing opportunity through improving social conditions. In fact, this difference in focus—emphasizing economic and social-welfare concerns versus changing attitudes and providing information—lies at the bottom of the disjuncture between working-class and middle-class views of problems between groups. Kensington organizers are correct in saying that economic and social problems are the flashpoints for intergroup tensions in working-class communities. Resisting the guidelines of the project, they tried to propose activities more central to their missions. However, the funders remained strict in their interpretation, and the organizers finally accepted the funds on the terms offered.

These kinds of focus events show the limitations of a cultural-pluralism model that focuses on individual cultural traits while ignoring structural underpinnings of conflict or accommodation. Focus events also reveal that using a strict structural-racism paradigm is inadequate to understand events. In more middle-class communities such as Olney, where conflict is seen as resulting from different habits and "not knowing the rules," the cultural-pluralism model makes sense to many residents as a way of developing mutual respect and understanding. But in Kensington, where most people perceive their lives as a struggle for pieces of an ever-decreasing pie, programs that ignore the day-to-day realities of structural inequality have less currency. The ideas and values that people bring to a problem or celebration also affect how they participate in a focus event and the types of interventions that work in a given situation. In part, the variation in the ways that people from Port Richmond, Kensington, and Olney respond to focus events depends on the class-based resources and values that both newcomers and established residents bring to a situation.

Kensington

Here, three neighborhood groups received funding, and all created ethnic events along the lines of the cultural-pluralism model. We will concentrate on one group's activities. This organization mounted a massive, ambitious plan for a single two-day event intended to demonstrate through performances, films, arts and crafts, food, and games that every culture had similarities in experience and life. The message of the festival thus followed the cultural-pluralism model. Structural problems plagued this project, however. The local staff was not experienced in such events, and an African American woman who had run a festival elsewhere was eventually hired from outside the community to direct the event.

The board of the organization, which included both established community residents from working-class backgrounds and younger, better-educated, and more militant empowerment activists, was ambivalent about the festival. The working-class residents saw cultural programming as largely peripheral to their lives. Empowerment-oriented members also saw dealing with the economic deficits of the community as their major goal. On the other hand, these more middle-class residents saw cultural programming as a way to teach whites about the other cultures in their midst. All board members viewed the grant as a way to provide salaries for several of the organization's volunteers. Instead, the activity taxed the limited energy and resources of the group.

Deciding on which "cultural" communities to incorporate led to conflict. Several groups recognized as being in the neighborhood were impossible to recruit, since there were no brokers who could participate in the planning and deliver "cultural" commodities. This was true of both Palestinians and

Koreans, whose presence in the area is largely mercantile. Nonetheless, films from these groups were included. Ethnic subcommunities for the white population could not be "found" because there were no organized entities to represent them. Moreover, the whites who did participate were hard to define by ethnicity because they had multiple national ancestries. When it came time to amass cultural artifacts considered appropriate ethnic markers as per the cultural-pluralism model, the organizers were forced to turn to the official African American and Latino museums outside the neighborhood for their traveling exhibits and to Irish American priests who ran a local mission. The lifestyles of local newcomer Puerto Ricans rarely included "appropriate" ethnic markers that could be borrowed to represent their culture, and local white oldtimer residents did not identify themselves with single ethnic labels.

Conflict over the language of the advertising posters arose. The original poster used English to provide all information. Words for "Welcome" in seven other languages were used symbolically to convey the idea of cultural pluralism. This created a conflict when a leader argued that in this neighborhood it was common practice for information to be presented in both Spanish and English. For him, the attempt to portray a multicultural community using language as a mere symbol of difference conflicted with the exigencies of local life in a community in which Spanish and English language use were vital parts of everyday reality.

City agencies would not commit equipment, and more work time was spent borrowing and transporting other equipment than on anything else. In the end, the more mobile and convenient city equipment arrived anyway, only to be withdrawn without announcement just before an ecumenical service that had been carefully negotiated among local clergy. The service was ruined and feelings were hurt.

Turnout from the neighborhood was small. Many newcomers were on their porches watching the event from afar. The view of culture as the safe ethnicity of cultural pluralism did not reflect their experience as new arrivals on the U.S. mainland. The bulk of those actually on the site were university students and professionals from around the city. A mismatch between the types of booths present and newcomers' needs further limited the appeal of events. The vendors recruited for the fair came from groups that travel the circle of neighborhood fairs. They included many political activists, whose literature was mostly in English, and craft vendors, whose wares did not appeal to local newcomer Latinos. The exception was the roasting of a pig over an open pit, Puerto Rican style. Newcomers flocked to buy the roasted pork as soon as it was ready, and the supply soon ran out.

In Chapter 4 we discussed problems in the community with two groups of white newcomers, a church devoted to community service and a newcomer Polish priest's social-service organization. Members of the church became the most committed volunteers and participants. While grateful for their help in the festival, the one-on-one relationships did little to change Latino perceptions of the mission-oriented church. Despite the very positive interactions across these groups, the sponsoring organization continued to view the whites from the church as gentrifiers encroaching on their neighborhood.

Interactions between the local Polish émigré social-service organization and the community development corporation mounting the festival revealed how such labor-intensive events can cement existing negative perceptions across organizations. Despite past differences, the priest who ran this program and his representative became faithful participants in the festival. His associate attended most planning committee meetings and volunteered to create a play using neighborhood children. Working on the play showed the potential for positive interaction across different cultural groups, since Puerto Rican children were to be actors. The émigré group contributed cultural artifacts and food for a table at the event.

Circumstances, and the fact that the festival was peripheral to both organizations' main agendas, curtailed positive interaction in this case. The play was canceled because several key actors went back to Puerto Rico, which the sponsoring organization attributed to lack of interest. Although the émigré group had promised to bake Polish pastries for the festival, other priorities did not allow enough time to do this. Instead, the group brought only one type of pastry, which was placed with their art exhibit instead of with the other food. The newcomer priest's manner in appropriating supplies to set up his booth was interpreted as arrogance. In the end, his niece (a summer visitor from Poland who spoke no English) ended up in charge of the display for most of the time. The sponsoring organization interpreted the priest's absence as, again, lack of interest.

The two groups' interpretations of interactions between the Puerto Ricans and the Polish émigrés were very different. The Poles reported that people seemed interested in their booth and that one woman ate "half the tray of cookies." The Puerto Rican leaders, on the other hand, said that they were afraid to get near the booth and claimed that the Poles had refused to give two children some candy—an act that was interpreted as racism.

As in many encounters between newcomers and established residents, children crossed boundaries where adults could not. Community youngsters participated in programs run by the sponsoring organization, as well as in another long-standing, child-focused program. An elderly woman from the Polish organization ran some games for children at one program site during the festival. While the boys and girls happily participated in events presented by all factions, the adults maintained a studious lack of interest in and knowledge of activities run by other factions, even when they took place on their property.

The most successful, long-lasting result of the neighborhood human-relations projects in Kensington was a rumor hotline created by a second organization. While it began under the auspices of the local human-relations program, the hotline really took hold when violence drew attention to Kensington later in the summer. These events are described later.

Olney and the Saint Ignatius Festivals

The neighborhood human-relations project money in Olney was awarded to a network of organizations already collaborating on programming to increase understanding and resolve conflict. This program had the advantage of having more paid staff, and more volunteers committed to its goals, than was the case in Kensington. Moreover, its activities were already under way, and they were strongly tied to the central mission of the group.

The differences in the neighborhood led to very dissimilar long-term outcomes in this community. As the citywide agendas more readily fit community expectations, organizations expressed more interest in participation. The neighborhood human-relations projects did create a consortium of people in this area, and thus ongoing structures.

Funds were used for three initiatives. First, a series of ethnic nights was planned, celebrating one of the new immigrant communities or one of the older ethnic communities through music, food, and narrative events. While local representatives estimate that between thirty-seven and forty-five different groups live in Olney, the events focused on Colombians, Pakistanis, African Americans, and Germans. Choices appeared to hinge on the availability of contacts and cultural materials rather than on the demographic importance of the group in the neighborhood. After the ethnic nights, the program was discontinued because each gathering seemed primarily to attract its "own." As with the Polish ethnic events, cultural-pluralism events became a way for subcultures to celebrate their own identity rather than a forum for actively sharing culture. Most community residents from other groups had little interest in taking time to attend events that simply offered tangential information about outsiders. There were further difficulties in finding resources to represent the established ethnics. In comments about these events, the director said that "although interaction was limited, there was a good feeling in the room, . . . there was a sense of openness and sharing." On Colombian Neighbors' Night, one person commented that the event had raised the Colombians' self-esteem because they had been put in a position of authority.

In the second initiative, a conflict-resolution team was established. This effort responded to several block disputes, half of which involved no "cultural" differences, with some success.

The third, and most innovative, initiative involved a Welcome Express. Volunteers identified newcomer neighbors, presented them with packets introducing them to neighborhood institutions and services, and offered to serve as "buddies." The project got off to a slow start because volunteers found it difficult to identify the origin of newcomers and give them packets in the right language. A creative plan to get the information from real-estate agents failed because of a lack of staff. The packet translations, provided by local high-school students, were also found to be full of errors. Furthermore, the packets themselves were extremely expensive. After the project ended, the community group responsible worked for several years to resolve these problems.

A major arena for focus events in Olney was the Saint Ignatius parish. In need of new members for financial survival as oldtimers die or move away, the parish recruits them by providing separate masses, sodalities, and other activities for immigrants in their native languages. Recognizing the growing Spanish-speaking population, it is plugged into the citywide mission directed at Spanish speakers (part of the Hispanic mission of the Conference of Bishops). Since the parish also recruits Portuguese and Asians (particularly Indians), the priests and nuns try to make all newcomers feel at home. A parish calendar describes each cultural group, and separate ethnic festivals occur throughout the year. All whites (Irish, Poles, Germans, and Italians) come to each others' events and joke about how nobody is a pure ethnic anymore. The beneficial dance group described above was brought in from Port Richmond as the featured entertainment for Polish Day. The key parish kitchen volunteers have food service down to a system. They prepare it in the rectory, with the same women doing all ethnic groups and often even the same dishes—a version of sausage and sauerkraut, for example, serves both Germans and Poles. There is always coleslaw.

Newcomers do not come to established events. One day a Latina and her son walked in on Italian Day, (a Latino event was taking place at the same time downstairs, and they had come to the wrong location). They sized up the situation, looked flustered, and immediately walked out. Since parishioners assumed these events to be for an insider audience, no explanation of meaning was included for others. For example a Colombian family, personally invited by one of the priests, were the only outsiders at Irish Day. They did not understand the symbols of the event, and nobody talked to them (discomfort with language problems) except for one field-worker.

In an effort to break down boundaries, priests exhort established parishioners to come to newcomer events and sometimes bring them. Elderly established residents do frequently participate, enjoying the color and the chance for a different experience. Yet they most often sit together and are ignored by most newcomers. The latter also feel that they "own" their own events. At Puerto Rican Day, for example the typed program and menu was entirely in Spanish, and the emcee had to be reminded to translate what he said into English. To make up for this, he called on a white participant to draw the raffle winners, saying, with humor, "because nobody trusts Puerto Ricans."

The Spanish-mission activities, which include separate retreats and special rituals, as well as perceived preferential assignments of space and schedules, are resented by established parishioners, who see their own volunteer work as sustaining the church.

Worried by the increasing segregation of subcommunities and the expressed jealousies among groups, the parish established events to bring people together. A mass to commemorate the anniversary of the parish in the spring was designed to be celebrated in all languages; it was followed by a celebration of diversity in food and musical performances in the hall. We observed three successive anniversaries, as well as a fund-raising carnival one fall that shared the format of celebrating diversity in food and music.

The priest who organized the events clearly distinguished the newcomers ("the ethnics," as he called them) from the established residents as he assigned space for food. This stemmed from the different ways in which he dealt with oldtimers and new immigrants. While planning meetings were held, only established white volunteers came. Each newcomer group was dealt with through a broker. The priest would call the broker (invariably male) and tell him to arrange for the community's food. This was made at home, usually by one extended family, and brought to the church. The priest joked that he never knew what to expect or when to expect it. Similarly, performances were arranged by communicating with the leaders of the music groups.[4]

For the first anniversary festival, the priest assigned a table for "Hispanic" food and put up a sign. As the several Spanish-speaking nationalities arrived, they asserted their own identities by setting up handwritten signs designating their countries. The next year they came prepared, with lettered signs, flags, and maps. In the meantime, the Spanish choir had broken down into a Puerto Rican singing group. The Colombian dance group and the Colombians had asked for a special celebration of July 19 (their Independence Day) after conflict with the Puerto Ricans over who owned the Latino Day celebration. Since traditional Latino Day was scheduled during Puerto Rican Week, the Puerto Rican majority had appropriated it, leading the Colombians to walk out. At the same time, other immigrants from South and Central America whose numbers were too small for them to form their own groups joined the Colombians in their celebration. Like Polish émigrés, the Spanish-speaking newcomers asserted their national independence in the face of the native-born priest's attempt to fit them into large-group ethnic boundaries as defined by the dominant society. They participated in a cultural-pluralism event while redefining it as a way to celebrate their national identities.

The white groups moved in the opposite direction, toward an American identity. In the first year they went to their assigned tables as Irish, Germans, and Poles, but in the following years there was an increase in the display of food on the American food table, complete with U.S. flags. This change reflects the emphasis on patriotism among white working-class established residents.

It also shows resistance by people of mixed ethnic origin toward the cultural-pluralism model, which expects them all to have strong ethnic identities.

Each event created some competition for table space in displaying food and for time allotment and preferred position on the program. Groups pitted against each other for these resources complained during and after the event about perceived unfairness. Most striking was how each group tended to gather at their own food table and eat their own food, in spite of the intention that all groups pass by all tables in a line. In a similar fashion, there was a tendency to leave after their own group performed. The one highly successful event was a Puerto Rican dance performance in which each couple separated and went into the audience to pick a new partner. This produced tremendous fun and laughter and was the single best moment of community.

In this instance, since the event was repeated and critiqued, relationships among groups improved each year. There was more effort toward joint planning, with a deliberate attempt to deal with points of tension. Every group was represented at the planning meetings, and each was assigned a task that required collaboration and phone contact with others. The emcee was a member of one subcommunity, and he had to touch bases with all performing groups. Another subcommunity representative, an engineer, designed and controlled the table arrangements and the lines, which necessitated contact. Women were asked to set up food tables at the same time. Performances were arranged so that everyone had to stay. The mere number of occasions that people were together in planning the event increased facial and first-name recognition.

Even before the self-conscious attempts to correct separatism, several Latinas crossed the big divide and became part of the established women's kitchen crew. Employed in mainstream workplaces and having white friends, these women were at home both at Spanish-controlled events and among established residents. Arriving at set-up time for the fund-raising carnival, they were ignored by the close-knit group of established kitchen women. They quickly summed up what was happening and pitched in setting tables. Nobody spoke to them, or asked their name or relationship. However, after repeated participation, they were part of the kitchen team by the third anniversary celebration. That year, the celebration received a visit from the local archbishop and heavy media coverage.

The priest's adherence to a strict cultural-pluralism model created distance between groups, not solidarity. Attempting to lump Spanish-speaking groups into larger categories creates as much friction as attempting to parcel out mixed identities for established residents who see cultural background as incidental to everyday existence. Yet the ability of all parties to learn from past experiences has led to a series of events with the potential to create long-term relationships across groups.

All in all, festivals featuring "culture at a distance" did little to change things. While planning can provide an opportunity for more interaction between separate groups, it usually creates a pressured context for negotiation and competition for space and priority on the program. The event itself is often attended only by those already partial to the multicultural message or by people interested only in the food and performance of their group. Depending on whether messages were intended for audiences who were insiders or outsiders, symbols had different meanings or made no sense without explanation. Contrary to the assumptions of "culture at a distance" performances of pluralism, they did not lead to instant understanding. An even more severe problem was that, in all of these events, the "culture" performed was derived from a common place of origin, with little attention to the specific historical moment or class that reflected the real origins of the group. The Poland of the turn of the century and traditional agricultural South Korea before the "economic miracle" provided the images of immigrant backgrounds. These derived cultural presentations reflect the "good immigrant" model, but they hold little currency for established residents attempting to understand the ideas and behavior of newcomers of today or for newcomers attempting to convey the realities of their countries of origin and their past experience to established residents.

Crisis Events

These different understandings of ethnicity among newcomers and established residents, members of majority and minority groups, and people from different class and educational backgrounds become particularly acute when communities respond to crises. In these cases, both definitions of events and appropriate strategies to defuse tensions are contested. In general, the local community's relationship to wider societal contexts involves a combination of reaction and reinterpretation, as people in the neighborhoods respond to outside concerns and incorporate messages from the larger social world into their own systems of meaning and behavior. Some organization leaders and city human-relations workers focus on the racism of established residents. At the same time, both average residents and local organization leaders blame the media and outside political forces for creating or exacerbating neighborhood incidents. Nationality-based factions within the community fault both the white residents and citywide institutions. Ironically, each set of actors in these conflicts attributes much more control and intentionality to others than actually exists. Observers who focus on the overall picture accurately see patterns of structural racism, hostility toward outsiders of different colors, and media manipulation of local events. Yet the activities that create these patterns often reflect very different motives. The ways that these dissimilar views converge and diverge in each instance led to the necessity for different strategies to handle problems and to limited success for any standard means of reducing tensions.

The framework of negative focus events highlights class differences. White working-class residents of these neighborhoods are acutely aware that everyone expects them to be racists. Part of the interaction around focus events involves attempts by established residents to deny accusations of racism through such behaviors as absenting themselves from discussions of the topic, placing the blame for problems on "bad" outsiders, or mentioning cultural differences to soften references to intergroup problems.

This section focuses on two events, one in Olney and one that involved attempts by Kensington organizations to deal with tensions among people from their community, Port Richmond, and Feltonville, the increasingly Puerto Rican neighborhood between Olney and Kensington. Like Kensington, Feltonville has rising levels of housing abandonment and crime. It has some ties to Olney and is viewed by established residents there as an example of encroaching neighborhood decline. In both cases, these crystallizing incidents are only the most dramatic in an ongoing pattern of escalating tensions. The root causes of the two events are very different, as are the kinds of responses.

The Korean Sign Incident

In the 1970s Korean merchants began investing in businesses and real estate in Logan, just west of Olney, with an eye to making it a service and cultural center for Koreans, a "Koreatown." A model for such a concentration exists in Los Angeles, and the many Chinatowns in the United States (including Philadelphia's) are also used to legitimize the notion. Logan had long been a home to new ethnic groups. Once predominantly Jewish, it later housed Ukrainians and then South Asians, just before the arrival of Korean investment. As Logan witnessed more African American and Cambodian refugee in-migration in the 1970s, Korean investment moved eastward to Olney.

By 1980, when Koreans began to buy into the Olney strip, its nature had already changed. It had once been a middle-class area purveying food, hardware, drugs, and clothing in stores owned intergenerationally by small merchant families emphasizing personal service to regular customers. In the 1970s, as suburban malls and center-city development lured middle-class shoppers away, the strip shifted to self-service stores. These were owned largely by national, regional, and local chains, which often catered to lower-income populations such as those in Logan. The negative reaction to many of the changes on the strip generated by absentee ownership and downscaled merchandise were often mistakenly associated with the Korean influx.

Furthermore, the rapidity with which Koreans bought stores led to stories of a "takeover." Tales circulated about Koreans with briefcases full of money walking the strip and trying to buy all the buildings and enterprises. One merchant says, "I saw them coming and I bought the building my store was in."

If I didn't, a Korean would have bought it." Suspicions abounded about favoritism that these merchants allegedly received from banks and public agencies. When an established merchant was turned down for a bank loan, while a neighboring Korean received one, the story circulated quickly. In addition, it was generally believed that immigrants received both lump sums and tax abatements from the government.

Korean presence on the strip was of three kinds, one similar to Korean activity on strips elsewhere but the other two specifically directed at making Olney a center for the Korean community. In the first case, family owner–operators would take over established stores, often retain existing labor and types of merchandise, and cater to continuing clientele. On the other hand, stores with upscale merchandise for the suburban-oriented Korean community often excluded established residents by locking doors and otherwise limiting entry. One leader of the established community was once waved away from a clothing store when she approached to solicit an advertisement for a local publication. She reported being told that the store was for Koreans only, and "besides, these clothes are too expensive for you. You could not afford them." This story also circulated rapidly.[5]

In addition, the development of a dozen wholesale storefronts (also locked to walk-in customers) served the needs of Korean retailers from throughout the Middle Atlantic region. Customers came in vans after dark when the stores were closed, appearing surreptitious and secretive to established residents.

The resentment of Korean wealth and business practices documented in earlier chapters encouraged a local perception that these merchants were not committed to the neighborhood and were engaged in hit-and-run operations designed to make quick money and leave. Meanwhile, the Korean businesspeoples' initial experience in poor neighborhoods and advice from experienced merchants created often overzealous security strategies, such as bulletproof-glass barriers and visible guns, that insulted Olney residents. Other incidents arising from encounters between Korean merchants and regular customers exacerbated the problem.

On the other hand, most established residents had no idea that Korean merchants saw them as perpetrating racial incidents, such as the one in which a group of teenagers taunted a storekeeper, making fun of his speech and hurling racial epithets. The merchants also saw racism when adults ignored Korean owners, preferring to deal with employees already familiar to them. Moreover, while established businesspeople were happy to see Korean capital create a market for their stores, they were concerned about the invasion of wholesalers who would drive away the middle-class customer base.

Such was the context when, in 1986, a Korean running for president of a citywide Korean organization proposed as part of his platform to get the city to permit the erection of Korean-language street signs in Olney.[6] He used the relationship with the city government that Korean leaders had established through contributions and ceremonials to ask for and receive a permit for the signs. Not understanding the strength of local organizations, he assumed that, as in Korea, one goes to the top.

The most acceptable stated reason for wanting street signs in Korean was a desire to make it easy for newcomers and the elderly to find their way around. However, other leaders were open about wanting the signs to make it easy for Korean retailers from Pittsburgh, Baltimore, and other cities to find their way, helping the Philadelphia Korean community in its bid to become the major regional wholesale center. They assumed that locals would be pleased that Koreans were investing in the city. Shortly before the signs went up, a feature article in the Sunday *Philadelphia Inquirer* traced the move of Koreans from Logan to Olney and used the word "Koreatown" in describing their aspirations.

Established leaders in Olney were angry. Proper procedure, their frequent point of emphasis, had not been followed in getting a permit. Procedure would have required local hearings about such a change, and these would have allowed the community to protest. The incident typified neighborhood views that "downtown" interests were bent on changing Olney. The business association clearly saw the signs as related to the wholesaling threat and wanted to raise that issue. In an attempt at resolution, established leaders argued that Olney had always been a "Little United Nations" (albeit all-white) and was now even more international, "truly a melting pot." Thus it was not fair for one group to appropriate the center of the community.

A meeting was planned at which leaders of the Korean and established communities were to confer under the auspices of the city Human Relations Commission. However, a dissident established leader reportedly went door-to-door rounding up angry Olneyites. They turned up at the meeting—in a Veterans of Foreign Wars post where the bar had been mistakenly left open.

The session got out of control. Korean leaders were not allowed to speak. A white woman had written a letter to the *Philadelphia Inquirer* in which she said positive things about Koreans in Olney; she was cut off as she tried to read it. Angry residents shouted "Go back to Korea." One man said that his nephew had died in the Korean War helping the Koreans and now they were coming here and taking advantage of "us." Human Relations Commission representatives tried to make pleas for multiculturalism and understanding.

In the next few days the situation became polarized. Community leaders who defended Koreans received nasty phone calls. Yet these same establishment leaders, even today, play down the racist tone of their community. They emphasize that the opposition was not to the signs themselves but to the procedural violations made by the city in granting the permit (although, as we saw above, the signs themselves were seen as inappropriate). Koreans downplayed their real intentions of appropriating space and creating a "Koreatown" by talking only about racism.

Ultimately the leaders met again in secret and hammered out a pledge of cooperation. More meetings were held about how to get the signs down. Who would pay for removal, since the Koreans had paid for them to go up? How could this be done in a way that would allow the Korean leaders to save face in their community? However, before plans could be implemented, the signs were vandalized. The police never caught the perpetrators. Two more public meetings were held, resulting in a more conciliatory tone in the neighborhood.

We began fieldwork a few months after a major ceremonial dinner was held in a Korean restaurant involving representatives from both sides. Korean and established leaders ate together, had their pictures taken, and made testimonials. The dinner occurred a year after the crisis ended.

Newspaper and media coverage, both local and national, described the incident as an example of white racism. Established leaders called contacts in the news media to try to correct this image. They were particularly angered when a reporter (who happened to be African American) came to one of the last public meetings, held at an integrated recreational center. Every leader we interviewed (whether of traditional or empowerment orientation) said that the reporter remarked, "I can't believe this playground, I never saw kids get along like this. This is an unusual community. This cannot be a racial incident." However, none of this "good press" appeared in the ensuing report. In Korean newspaper coverage, which also reached other cities in the United States, the affair was called "one of the ten worst incidents of American racism."

On February 3, 1990, four years later, an article appeared in the *Daily Pennsylvanian*, the student paper at the University of Pennsylvania, about "Koreatown" in Olney. Its publication demonstrated that this was still a tender subject, largely unresolved. Word spread throughout the Olney leadership network, and it was discussed at every meeting. Mentioning "Koreatown" always sparked an immediate reaction from leaders. One said, "Don't say 'Koreatown.' Philadelphia is made up of small towns. This is Olney. There is Frankford, Bridesburg, and Fishtown. They all had lots of groups and were never named after one people." When asked why the notion of "Koreatown" was different from "Chinatown," the reply was that in the case of Chinatown the Chinese were there first and the area had been historically certified. There had been no tradition of a multicultural residential area.

Some people see the Korean sign incident as having had some positive outcomes—opening up Olney's awareness of its multicultural diversity, for example. After the event, storekeepers put up U.N. flags to celebrate the symbolism of this diversity until local residents, following the common white ethnic emphasis on patriotism, asked for U.S. flags to be added to them. However, most Koreans and established residents see the issue as never having been settled. Unresolved anger and resentment still underscore relationships between both groups.

One Olneyite summed up the views of many established residents:

You wake up one morning and the signs are up. What the heck's this stuff? They didn't even come to the [community organization] and say look, because there's so many of our people here that don't know how to read English, could we put up. . . . Something could have been worked out. The arbitrary way it was done. So because we made such a big stink about it, we're a bunch of racists. Where I contend that they are ignorant of not considering us. If we're supposed to consider them, it's a two-way street.

In many ways, this response resembles the resentment of Polish Americans toward new Poles described in Chapter 3. In that instance, there were neither racial nor nationality differences. In this case, ideas about racial and cultural differences and language barriers compound the situation.

Differences among Koreans

The Koreans' belief that the police failed to arrest the sign vandals because of racism and their memories of the public expression of bad will, exacerbate their fear of racist whites. They also resent not being appreciated for the economic investments they are making in Philadelphia.

There was also a clear recognition of a difference in interests and actions between those merchants more connected to the citywide Korean leadership, who were pressing for the signs, and local Korean storeowners, who served the general public. In fact, one white ethnic business leader who tried very hard to point this out got into trouble for "defending Koreans":

I defended [the local Koreans I work with] because I wouldn't allow anyone to say anything about them when I knew it was not the case. . . . They certainly weren't interested in anyone coming here to open wholesale businesses, because it would ruin the foot trade on the street.

This division was also reflected in the statements and actions of the locally oriented Korean merchants. One such businessman reflected on the mistake of the citywide group in erecting signs without having talked to the community:

Korean way is top–down. That is what [the citywide leader who initiated the idea of the signs] did. In America that is not enough. Here you have to build good relations with neighbors. That is the grassroots. You have to lobby to be accepted.

In contrast to the citywide leaders, the incident brought these local Korean merchants closer to the established community in their own business interest. They have abandoned the mechanism of a separate Korean group, which had formerly been linked to the strip association through a single spokesperson. Now they have become active in the strip association themselves, making up nearly half of the board when the research ended.

Differences among Established Residents

The incident also revealed the divergence between traditional community leaders and the new empowerment leadership described in Chapter 4. While they worked in concert and with great energy during the crisis, they defined its significance differently, and this continues to create a rift. To established leaders, the city was to blame for the incident, having circumvented proper procedure in issuing the permit. This was the old argument, "The law is the law," obvious and incontrovertible. In blaming the government, the leaders could avoid blaming Koreans: "They did not know any better. They have to learn the rules here, and the city did not do it by the rules."

The empowerment group saw the incident as a community-condoned public expression of racism. One leader said that the fundamental import of the crisis and its aftermath was "the fact that it was done in a group; the peer group gave support for the public expression of racism." Another said, "The central issue was certainly the racist response because of the inhumanity of that and the prejudice and destructiveness towards other people." However, they also blamed the city for granting the permit. One empowerment leader said the problem was that the city, by not holding hearings, had deprived the community of consultation among all segments and the creation of a dialogue.

The issue of wholesaling was never fully resolved. In 1989, a traditional business leader reported that the problem was under control. When new wholesalers were brought to the business group's attention, one leader said, "We're not making too much of an issue—the residents will misinterpret the whole thing and we do not want to do it" [start another racial issue]. However, in 1990, as more and more wholesale operations appeared and it seemed that action was necessary, the business leader was forced to make the issue public.

When the worsening wholesale situation was raised as a real emergency at an empowerment organization meeting, it was permitted on the agenda only because leaders were concerned that it would "lift the lid off racism" again. One empowerment leader said later of the traditional leaders who had reluctantly raised the issue:

> [They] represent the interests of racism in the neighborhood. While [they were] very good in handling the Korean sign incident, it is when you see [them] in a setting like this that you begin to see the racist aspect.

In an empowerment setting, where minorities were always seen as victims, the interpretations of traditional leaders, who saw some newcomers as having significant economic power and changing the neighborhood, was always suspect. One empowerment leader privately admitted that the wholesaling issue was a serious threat to the nature of the community. He recognized the role of citywide Korean leaders in setting up the conflict, but to him this issue had to take second place to eliminating "local racism," which was seen as ingrained in the whole community.

Crespo and Daily

Cross-group incidents are becoming increasingly frequent in the working-class areas of North Philadelphia. In the summer of 1989, more than forty events were reported within a five-mile radius of the Kensington area. Many of these episodes occurred in border or high-traffic areas. Toward the end of the summer, four white men attacked two innocent African Americans waiting for public transportation at the corner of Kensington and Allegheny in retaliation for the mugging of the girlfriend of one of the men by a male African American earlier in the day. Other events took place in mixed neighborhoods. A playground located in a Puerto Rican, white, and African American district several blocks away from Kensington and Allegheny has become the locus for a number of incidents. White male members of the playground sports team developed a vigilante attitude toward the drug activity and deterioration in the neighborhood. White children see these boys as "good kids who fight with their hands, not knives and guns" and who protect the playground from bad elements. Since these whites see most problems as caused by Puerto Ricans, "protection" frequently translates into hostility toward people of color. They have attacked Puerto Ricans playing video games in nearby locations, hurled racial epithets, and thrown bottles at people they dislike, especially Puerto Ricans; lifeguards at the playground have also refused to let "Spanish" children into the pool. Working-class residents attributed the rising tensions to frustration over the increasing competition for jobs and grant money for college. Human-relations workers more frequently blame the problem on the fact that "racism is on the rise in America."

The Events

The incident that drew the most media attention involved Puerto Ricans going into Port Richmond. The killing of Sean Daily on May 20, 1989, was the end result of a series of events. Two weeks before this incident Rafael Droz, a Puerto Rican youth, had attended a party in this predominantly white neighborhood at the request of a girl who lives there. It is unclear whether the newcomer was simply a guest at the party or part of a drug-supply ring working in the area. There is also local debate about the relationship of the youth involved and an area Puerto Rican gang. Some say that the young people who participated in the incident were gang members, while others claim that they were "good kids, supporting their families and going to school." In fact, the group may have included both kinds of children, or young people who were both associated with a gang and continuing in school.

The young Puerto Rican got into a fight with an African American resident of the neighborhood at the party. He left the neighborhood angry and proceeded to tell his friends that he was looking for revenge. Two weeks later, he returned to the area with three carloads of friends armed with baseball bats. By this point, the goal had become "getting those whites" as opposed to finding the African American with whom he had fought. Seeing a group of youngsters hanging out at a local playground, they got out of their cars and started smashing windshields. Most of the white youths ran, but the victim was caught off guard and became the focus of the attack. He was beaten severely with baseball bats and then shot in the back, dying shortly thereafter.

The response of the police was quick and all too typical of their behavior in this neighborhood. There were massive interrogations of Puerto Ricans, with thirteen suspects rounded up over a two-week period. All were held without bail, and the district attorney called for the death penalty. The incident, apprehensions, and pretrial hearings were all reported in gory detail in both local newspapers. The Puerto Rican and white communities were hurt and angry.

The situation was further complicated by another incident over the July Fourth weekend (a month later) in Feltonville, the neighborhood above Kensington where many of the Puerto Ricans implicated in the Daily murder lived. Coming upon a number of Puerto Ricans preparing to strip a stolen car, a group of whites gave chase. During the pursuit a Puerto Rican youth threw a lug wrench at them. Francis Skullin threw it back, hitting Stephen Crespo in the head, which ultimately killed him. To his credit, Skullin stayed with the wounded Puerto Rican youth after the incident. On the other hand, the Puerto Ricans would probably not have been pursued so vigorously had they been white. Stephen Crespo's brothers were trying to find out what happened when the police arrived. Seeing the Puerto Ricans standing over their brother and kneeling Skullin, the police drew their nightsticks and approached them instead of the white youth. Police were slow to respond to the Crespo family, and the case was not declared a homicide until three days later. Nor did the police record the racial overtones of the incident until citywide antigang workers, responding to rumors in the community, brought the case to their attention. Skullin turned himself in and was set free on bail. He was returned to custody several weeks after the killing, having gotten involved in a barroom brawl with racial overtones.

In Port Richmond, a catering hall owned by a Puerto Rican that brought nonwhite outsiders into the neighborhood for events became the lightning rod for local anti–Puerto Rican sentiment following the two incidents. Some white Port Richmond residents tried to shut it down, and the police received bomb threats on the property. They responded by assigning a police car to guard the catering hall. This made matters worse for both sides. Young Puerto Ricans used its presence as a safety net, pointing to the squad car and taunting white residents along the lines of "Ha, ha, you can't get me, I'm Puerto Rican!" Whites, however, saw the police protection for the caterer as an example of favoritism for the Puerto Rican community at a time when services to their neighborhood were being cut back by a city government that they defined as African American and working for people of color.

Media Involvement

Unlike the many other incidents surrounding these murders, the Crespo and Daily killings drew sustained media attention. They became front-page stories both because of the violence of the events and because additional information continued to come to light. The media reporting exacerbated already rising tensions in the communities, and rumors flew about continued retaliations surrounding the two events.

Media images became a key issue in the Puerto Rican and white communities. Sean Daily was portrayed as a "good kid" who liked baseball and who happened to be at the wrong place at the wrong time. Stephen Crespo was referred to as a young man with a long police record who liked to tell jokes and did not like school very much. His killer was characterized as a good student who wanted to join the FBI (*Philadelphia Inquirer*, August 6, 1989). When the *Inquirer* published a positive story about Francis Skullin, elements in the Puerto Rican community accused the paper of racist, biased reporting. They also said that Sean Daily had participated in acts of vandalism in his neighborhood and that his father was known as a racist cop. When Skullin was arrested for fighting a bouncer in a New Jersey bar and shouting racial epithets, the Puerto Rican community saw justification of its original claim that the Crespo death was racially motivated.

As discussed in Chapter 7, the "truth" of each set of statements is not the key issue. In all likelihood, the positive and negative reports of people involved in these incidents have some basis in fact. Here, we focus on the ways that multiple images are used and understood in community reaction to publicized events. As is true in many cases, the sequence of events and perceptions of them create compounded problems. For example, *Philadelphia Inquirer* reporters tried to do a nuanced portrait of the youth involved in the Daily killing, similar to the positive article about Skullin. Out of long-established fear of white media and white police, Puerto Rican families refused to talk to the reporters, and the story was never written. The absence of positive reporting on the Puerto Rican defendants was, in turn, used as further evidence of the racism of the media.

Both human-relations experts and local residents quickly blamed news organizations for stirring up events. The media frequently become the target for community frustrations over conflicts between groups, and negative responses to media coverage were in the foreground during all crisis incidents. Blaming someone else for inciting violence is a favorite strategy to avoid accusations of racism. One Port Richmond resident said:

I think a lot of people really aren't prejudiced. I think because the news said it was a Hispanic kid who killed a white kid . . . if it was a white kid from Northeast Philadelphia it would have come down as "Youth Killed—Gang-Related, Accident." And that would have been it. But a lot of people hear this [and it] triggers off "It's a racial thing." But it isn't. It's a misunderstanding between kids. My heart goes out to the parents of the boy who pulled the trigger. Whoever they are, I would love to sit down to talk to them. In my wildest imagination I can't even come close to what they must be feeling. I have no idea of what it must be like to say my son killed someone. It's got to be a hard thing to deal with.

The press is also blamed for creating negative stereotypes about people of color. In the words of a community leader in Olney:

I keep going back to the press, media. When you say drugs usually, now it's getting to be Jamaican and so forth, but there for the longest time it was Hispanics. So they equate drugs and pushers and so forth with the Hispanics. The ones that are moving into Feltonville, the Spanish-speaking people, we tell them [white established residents] at the meeting all the time that they [Hispanics] want a better life for themselves and they [Hispanics are] moving from the 8th and Butler area because they don't want their children living down there and exposed to that. Just as many of us [whites] have moved from one area to another because we wanted to move out of a bad environment.

Human-Relations Responses

Workers from many citywide agencies were involved in the cases from the start. Since the Daily incident inflamed an already tense community, human-relations workers from throughout Philadelphia attempted to develop ways to reduce the tensions. Since they had long-established contacts with Kensington organizations sharing the same vision of intergroup relations, city human-relations workers asked them to help form a coalition to address the problem. This new group made a sustained effort to draw in grassroots support from all communities involved. Initial meetings included people from the playground-advisory committee in Port Richmond (where the Daily murder occurred), one of the neighborhood sports clubs, and a variety of community residents, in addition to the human-relations-agency personnel and clergy who routinely take part in these efforts.

Meetings were held in Kensington because Puerto Ricans would not travel to Port Richmond, fearing racist attacks like the one on the catering service. This location caused problems for Port Richmond residents, because they were asked to go into another district for meetings, which violated their clear sense of territory based on neighborhood.

Despite genuine concerted efforts by citywide antigang workers and a Kensington community development corporation to reach people in Port Richmond, attempts to create a truly representative coalition were limited by the different kinds of social structures that exist in Port Richmond, community resistance, and the organizers' time and staff limitations. Coalition organizers sought representatives from defined groups similar to the kinds of organizations they traditionally work with in other neighborhoods—CDCs, town-watch or block-captain structures, or other groups with ties to citywide programs. At this point, however, Port Richmond was just forming a town watch and had no CDCs. The former was organized by a person who had just moved into Port Richmond from Frankford, a mixed white and immigrant community to the north that contained more settlement house and antipoverty institutions than Port Richmond. The organizers approached the highly active playground-advisory group at the city recreational facility near the place where Sean Daily was killed and found several representatives. The two major Port Richmond sports clubs were also contacted. Members of one group that was already integrated joined in some meetings, while the other (run by Sean Daily's father) declined to participate, saying that feelings were too raw in that sports club. Organizers initially failed to contact either the churches or ethnic clubs, which form the basis for social activity in Port Richmond.

During the first meeting, members settled on three standard strategies to address local problems: holding a church service to stress unity, creating a crisis-intervention network, and developing a program to bring youth together to improve relations. These approaches drew mostly on the cultural-pluralism model of sharing knowledge about cultures. Over the next few weeks the group and various subgroups held numerous meetings to develop plans. The church service was put on hold because it was complicated to organize. Most of the planning for the youth program was completed before committee members realized that there was not enough time to gather participants before summer recess. The crisis-intervention network was eventually activated by the CDC, which took responsibility for this initiative.

Attendance at coalition meetings shifted over time. Initially, few people came other than agency workers from the Latino community. While organizers found support in Port Richmond from the integrated sports club and from women concerned over playground violence, the agency's message of combating racism through direct discussion of attitudes got little response from the churches, one of the main organizing institutions in the community. For example, the priest running the Catholic youth organization in the neighborhood retreated behind a busy schedule to avoid participating in something that he considered separate from his main agenda. The agency workers had neither the time nor the vocabulary to convince church officials to join the coalition. The same constraints on time led other community residents to miss meetings. The staff people organizing sessions failed to make the two or three calls required to reach participants. Part of the problem here involves the differences in time schedules between established and empowerment organizations. Staff people who worked at the latter were trying to reach volunteers at home during times when they might be working or dealing with household needs. The volunteers often did not have answering machines or someone to take messages. Agency people also quickly found themselves saturated with meetings and began to drop out of the coalition.

The tone of meetings shifted after the Crespo incident. A very vocal young Puerto Rican woman attended the next session, proclaiming that "it was time that the Puerto Rican community became angry" and that she was "tired of her race being treated like trash." She drew on African American nationalist strategies. The same model was picked up by Puerto Rican nationalist elements, which organized a sustained and highly vocal attempt to focus attention on conditions in their community as examples of racism. This group sponsored rallies at city hall and well-attended town meetings. Coalition organizers found themselves faced with the nearly impossible task of negotiating the different messages of structural racism versus cultural pluralism throughout the various efforts to bring people together to develop community responses to rising tensions.

Most of the Port Richmond participants had dropped out of the coalition by the time of the Crespo incident. While claiming time constraints and illness, they privately complained that they felt intimidated by the educated agency workers, especially Latinos who spoke about racism. Like most white working class residents, they interpreted discussions of racism as directed at them. Afraid that they would be called racist for attempting to bring up problems caused by Puerto Ricans coming into the neighborhood, they eventually came to feel that the group was not addressing their needs. In addition, some people within the neighborhood saw participation in the meetings as consorting with hostile outsiders, and they threatened some group members. The fact that concerned Port Richmond residents could be dissuaded from participating in efforts to ease tension in part by fanatic, racist elements in the neighborhood shows the power of a violent minority in these communities.

The working-class residents of these neighborhoods are experts at the techniques of passive resistance. "I'm sick" or "I'm too busy" are just two of many standard ways of getting out of an uncomfortable situation; another is claiming not to have known about a meeting. The real problem for community organizers becomes sorting out the mixture of reality and resistance in such responses. Mail often gets lost in these neighborhoods. The community organization's staff members are often too busy to do much more than leave messages regarding meetings; quite frequently, they do not have the time to follow up on nonparticipants or to send minutes to people who could not attend. On some occasions, concerned individuals find that they must call the organization to request information. Community residents sometimes misinterpret this lack of information as indicating that the organization really does not value their participation. When neighborhood representatives claim that they did not receive information, it could mean that (1) they really did not get it, (2) they did get it but either lost the flier or forgot about it and now assume that it did not arrive, or (3) they are lying. That these residents dropped out of the activities means that they were not willing to make the extra effort required to stay involved.

As events became more heated and the first coalitions ran up against obstacles, a second CDC stepped in to organize a church service as an effort to calm the community. It was fundamentally a top-down effort by local clergy to create a community event. A highly professional and well-attended service, it stressed unity while highlighting the two local cultures by the use of Spanish and English. While this event created much-needed momentum, participants mostly included those already predisposed to the diversity message. For example, while all local churches were contacted regarding the event, no extra effort was taken to include those in Port Richmond. Fliers never made it to the community, probably because the church secretaries, who open the mail, saw no need to tell residents about an outside event. The church service also brought in African American representatives, even though the event was primarily about a conflict between whites and Puerto Ricans. African Americans were included because they constitute an important part of the racial dyad and the discourse on race relations in Philadelphia.

After the church service, the same CDC created another coalition to explore long-term solutions to racial problems. Participants included a more professionalized group of community organizations and leaders, in addition to local CDCs, but grassroots representatives were not involved. This group created a number of task forces to address different populations. It succeeded in interesting a local foundation in funding proposals; before the nationalist elements in the Puerto Rican community, however, were able to draw support away from these efforts by talking about separatism and suspicion of white racism. The two CDCs began similar efforts on a larger scale again the next year and are still attempting to create long-term efforts.

The final event of the year was organized by the first CDC. When incidents continued, its members developed End the Racial Violence Day. Drawing on an expanded network of leaders and grass roots representatives involved in the first coalition, they carefully organized a march and rally that went through both the Puerto Rican neighborhood and Port Richmond, convening at the shopping strip at Kensington and Allegheny. Organizing the event was a slow, careful process. The same problems plaguing the first effort recurred as the Port Richmond representatives failed to appear at some key meetings, later claiming that they did not have the authority to represent the community and that they could not support an event labeled as "combating racism" that started from the playground where one of their own was killed. Puerto Rican nationalists insisted that the event highlight racism directed against their community. City officials wanted to stop the event, fearing violence.

In the end, the parade went off as planned. The organizers compromised between white and Puerto Rican constituencies by having it start from two locations, one in each affected community. The Port Richmond end began with only white organizers from Kensington and citywide human-relations people; residents either ignored the parade or watched in silence as the marchers moved through their community. The Puerto Rican organizers were able to draw a larger grassroots contingent. By the time they reached the corner of Kensington and Allegheny, the group included a noticeable number of participants and drew some audience from the Saturday shopping population. No violence occurred.

As the parade approached the intersection of Kensington and Allegheny, members of the playground group that had caused much of the trouble that summer joined it. The young people were genuinely there to support the efforts of the human-relations worker who worked with them, but they saw the event as a way to stop the *violence*—meaning drugs and crime in the neighborhood—rather than the racial violence that they had helped escalate. The same multiple interpretations appeared in other aspects of the event. For example, middle-class organizers had wanted music, meaning hymns and peace songs; instead, the group was treated to a rock song about Kensington. The organizers got their music, but the community got its own sense of appropriate entertainment.

Community organizers and citywide human-relations representatives responded to the event with solutions based on assumptions that groups needed to understand each other better. The focus on cultural-awareness training and celebratory events is itself a contradiction, given that most of these organizers understand the complex dynamics of race and class in these neighborhoods. Most of their work focuses on dealing with the realities of inequality and frustrated youth. They turn to these standard strategies to bring people together because they realize that the citywide organizations and concerned community residents will quickly lose patience with long-term processes and that all parties need some marking event to show concern regarding violence. Church services and workshops are usually easy to put together. In addition, since these meetings draw representatives from numerous human-relations groups from throughout Philadelphia, the standardized human-relations discourse dominates the conversation. When citywide and community activists turn to developing long-term strategies, they find that energy has dwindled, funding for such projects is limited, and that other agendas intervene.

Puerto Rican Community Views

While police, media and white established residents in the neighborhood point out the differences between the two cases—the killing of Sean Daily clearly involved intentionally hunting people down because of their race, whereas the killing of Stephen Crespo was an accident involving people from two different backgrounds—the Puerto Rican community was quick to equate the two events and tie them to a series of cases related to injustices in Philadelphia. The widely understood account of the Crespo murder among Puerto Ricans is very different from the reports in the media and the white community. The Puerto Rican recounting highlights the whites chasing the Puerto Rican youth and reports that Francis Skullin and his friends were shouting racial slurs and actively attacked Crespo.

The Crespo murder occurred in the middle of the pretrial hearings for the Daily murder. It came soon after the mayor's Puerto Rican Task Force publicly and angrily disbanded amid claims that the African American and white power structures of the city did not care about the Puerto Rican population (*Philadelphia Inquirer*, March 29, 1989). The police further exacerbated the tensions surrounding the Crespo incident by stating that Francis Skullin would have been a hero for turning in a car thief had the boy not been killed. The organized parts of the Puerto Rican community leapt on this case as the quintessential example of the very real differences in the ways that police handle this minority group. This led to several angry town meetings and rallies at the district attorney's office (e.g., *Philadelphia Inquirer*, July 13, 1989, and August 4, 1989).

People of color throughout Philadelphia view the Crespo and Daily killings very differently from the white working-class residents of Kensington and Port Richmond. Part of this different view involves misinformation or selecting among contradictory facts. First, few people of color knew that an African American resident of Port Richmond had started the original fight. African Americans and Puerto Ricans widely believe that Sean Daily was involved in the original fight and that Stephen Crespo was deliberately struck down because he was Puerto Rican. Some people equate the two stories and see the Crespo killing as revenge for the murder of Daily. Following the structural-racism model, whites are usually seen as the aggressors and people of color as the victims of white racism.

People of color see the other side of the historical confluence of race and class. Many have experienced hostility from whites at first hand. Firebombings and cross burnings are continuing reminders of the way that people of color are intimidated by whites. Police behavior in the Crespo and Daily incidents is yet another example of the very different ways that people of color are treated by the authorities. In the Daily case, police rounded up any Puerto Rican who vaguely fit the description of the youths who participated in the killing, and there were accusations of police brutality in questioning suspects.

Based on historical experience, these people assume that all working-class whites are racists. Every action that excludes people of color or any unkind comment about a newcomer neighbor becomes another example of white racism. For this reason, some Puerto Rican participants in the coalition to end tensions in Kensington and Port Richmond demanded that the primary focus of the event be resolving racism toward their community.

Yet the Puerto Rican and African American understandings of the Crespo and Daily incidents acknowledge or ignore as many contradictions as they attempt to resolve. None of the people of color questioned the fact that a Puerto Rican boy would come into Port Richmond for a party. The same people who see all whites as racists admit that they have friends from other groups and that much mixing occurs.

White Working-Class Views

The notion of insider and outsider pervaded the understanding of these incidents in Port Richmond. Community residents blamed the troubles on bad elements—both white and Puerto Rican—that were coming into the neighborhood. The fact that meetings to reduce tensions were held outside the community underlined these perceived divisions. When driving into Port Richmond became the macho thing for Puerto Rican youth to do that summer, feelings that cross-group problems were imported into this insular neighborhood by outsiders, who then blamed the white residents for problems beyond their control, were further enforced. Their vocabulary of difference avoided the direct discussion of race as a motivating force behind actions. Such efforts, which highlighted a volatile subject while ignoring insider/outsider conflict and real economic and infrastructural problems, became anathema in the neighborhood.

Part of the anger at the media on the part of Port Richmond residents reflects the white working-class viewpoint that the power structure, as represented by the press, holds them accountable for racism. When whites are the targets of violence, they feel that stories which report white hostility toward people of color are cases of blaming the victim. The reporters see their documentation of cross-group tension as balanced reporting. They are telling the whole story. And in reporting that white racism is one of the causes of violence between groups they attempt to avoid being accused of racism themselves. Recall that the Puerto Rican community regarded the continued reporting on the Daily case as yet another example of racism.

The end result of this mutual blame shifting is that everyone feels that someone else causes cross-group tensions. At the same time, communities are left without a way to address problems openly that arise either because the perpetrators happen to come from a different group or because newcomers or established residents behave in ways that hurt people who are different. Sensitivity toward racism is a necessary element in any mixed community. Yet both newcomers and established residents have difficulty negotiating a balance between sensitivity and simply avoiding overly "hot" issues.

Conclusion

While all of the crises are seen as cases of antagonism between racial or national groups, there are other bases for these conflicts. Community insiders compete with outsiders regardless of race. Korean merchants who behave like insiders are accepted and given roles. The young African American who started the fight that precipitated the Daily murder is considered an insider by Port Richmond residents. The Puerto Rican youth missed this racial difference when planning revenge because he equated being white with community membership. Media reports (and some Koreans, human-relations representatives, and empowerment leaders) miss the cordial interaction among people from different backgrounds when calling all established residents racists.

The most frequent citywide human-relations prescription in the aftermath of a crisis is to present the discourse of cultural pluralism largely through the medium of "culture at a distance" performances or by encouraging whites to search their inner selves and eliminate racism. This prescription for breaking down barriers is fraught with problems. As illustrated by the multicultural events in each neighborhood, various community members understand and use events in ways completely unintended by their organizers. Thus an event meant to bridge boundaries by teaching others about a group becomes a celebration of subgroup unity or a contest over meaning, resources, and priorities.

A large part of the problem with using a strict cultural pluralism model to decrease tensions or to build community lies in some of the basic assumptions about cross-group interaction inherent in it. Most people involved in human-relations efforts assume that individuals from different groups have little contact with each other and develop negative stereotypical opinions because of this lack of contact. While Philadelphia is still a very segregated city, the amount of interaction across groups varies dramatically by class. Unlike the "diversity seekers" who live in Olney, many middle- or upper-class whites may have limited contact with people from other groups. Residential segregation and structural inequality limit minority participation in the workplace and, to a lesser extent, in some of the elite private schools. "Culture at a distance" is an entirely appropriate way to introduce these individuals to people from different groups.

Incidents like the Crespo and Daily murders become the focus for media attention and community concern because they are examples of intergroup hostility, both expected and feared by people concerned with the state of relations among groups in Philadelphia. Yet, as described in Chapters 4 and 5, these neighborhoods differ from expectations because of the high levels of contact. Even these blatant testaments to cross-group violence contain numerous contradictions.

Consider the following oppositions in the killing of Sean Daily:

While the Puerto Ricans who killed him deliberately sought to attack a white youth—making the incident a blatant act of aggression against another because of difference—the events that led to Daily's death began with a young Puerto Rican *voluntarily* coming into Port Richmond to join a mixed-race party.

Even though, subsequently, the Puerto Ricans intended to retaliate against whites, the insider Port Richmond resident who started the original fight by punching Rafael Droz at the party was an African American.

Apart from the massive reporting that the Puerto Ricans intended to "get those whites," white Port Richmond residents repeatedly downplayed the racist aspects of the incident. Instead, they blamed the media for turning Daily's death into an issue of cross-group tension.

White Port Richmond residents begin any discussion of diversity with such statements as: "Everybody is equal. There really is no difference between people. I don't care who moves in next to me, he could be purple, as long as he takes care of his house." At the same time, some residents threatened to firebomb the Puerto Rican caterer's building in their neighborhood, and Port Richmond is considered one of Philadelphia's most hostile neighborhoods toward nonwhites.

During the incident, the Puerto Rican caterer was seen as a hostile outsider who brought African American and Puerto Rican troublemakers into the neighborhood. Yet he had worked for an established white catering service in Port Richmond for twenty-five years before starting his own business, and he had provided service for events held by established white residents of Port Richmond, as well as for African Americans and Puerto Ricans. Many Port Richmond residents considered him an insider in the community. The caterer's worldview is similar to that of other established residents. In fact, his "Spanish" menu consists of tacos and enchiladas, not traditional Puerto Rican foods.

The Puerto Rican community saw the handling of the Sean Daily affair by the police and the district attorney's office as a quintessential example of structural racism directed against them. At the same time, white Port Richmond residents saw the police protection of the Puerto Rican caterer as an example of favoritism toward that community, as yet another example of how the African American city establishment prefers non-whites over whites.

Chapter 7 concentrates on these kinds of oppositions. We explore the contradictions within the models of cultural pluralism, structural racism, and the "good immigrant." Then we look at how people use and understand contradictions in their everyday lives.

PART III

Restructuring Diversity

Simultaneous Contradictions

We have documented contradictory beliefs and actions throughout this book. Residents of Kensington, Olney, and Port Richmond hold both positive and negative views of newcomers and established residents, of members of minority and majority groups. As in the case of the Korean sign incident, people can work together amicably on a daily basis, yet devolve into angry subcommunities when an issue strikes them in a particular way. People who have friends from different backgrounds can distrust and malign the same group as a whole or the city officials or organization representatives who come from outside their neighborhood. Like the friendly mixed-race gathering that precipitated the murder of Sean Daily, positive actions toward others who are different are sometimes followed by negative behavior. As in this case of violence against whites by Puerto Ricans, cross-group tensions do not always involve majority group members attacking minorities.

Even in a mixed marriage, perhaps the ultimate crossing of boundaries, partners hold diverse views of the treatment of people in this country. Consider the very different ways that Patrick, a white factory worker from Kensington, and Gladys, his newcomer Puerto Rican wife, answered the question "Are there any groups who seem to be getting favored treatment from the government?"

> GLADYS.   Americans. For example, if you go to the hospital and you don't speak any English, they would delay you, until they look for someone who speaks Spanish. They would take care first of English speakers.
>
> PATRICK.   Puerto Ricans are getting more attention from the government now.

Contradictions run through every level of U.S. society—the social, economic, and political structure; dominant belief systems; power arrangements in neighborhoods, organizations, institutions, companies, and homes; and individual beliefs and actions. People react to the contradictory nature of social life in two ways:

1. *Developing categories to understand reality and becoming frustrated when these do not work.* Individuals often attempt to create a unitary response to a problem. Trying to find one solution to racism, and believing that all Puerto Ricans are lazy or all whites are rich, are both examples of Philadelphia residents' attempts to push a complicated reality into simplified categories. When these single ideas run counter to events and beliefs, people become frustrated and angry, either lashing out against those who defy expectations, harboring hidden resentment, or simply avoiding situations that do not fit expectations.

2. *Accommodations to simultaneous contradictions.* Often people move through the contradictions in their world comfortably. Such oppositions are not simply anomalies in individual lives, but a primary part of existence in a confusing and fragmented society. Understanding the dynamics of cross-group relations in these communities involves tracking the interaction among the many contradictory elements that appear as people move through society.[1]

We realize that these two reactions to contradictions are themselves opposites. Analyzing the many-faceted aspects of cross-group relations involves comprehending the tension among contradictory elements as part of a dialectical whole. (The theoretical understanding of dialectics used in this book is described in Schneider [1989].) The concept of dialectics resembles the structure of an atom—like protons and electrons, contradictory elements exist in a constant, moving tension within a complicated system.

People can develop intimate relationships across groups, yet adhere to negative stereotypes of the same groups as a whole. Others assume that only whites perpetrate racism and that people of color naturally bond together against white oppression. Yet power dynamics vary from situation to situation and there is a wide economic, social, and political range within all groups. The competition between two minorities—African Americans and Latinos—for political power and resources, and the many intermarriages between whites and African Americans, indicate that racial boundaries regarding power relations and intimate bonding do not always adhere to a single pattern. The visibility of the Korean community throughout Philadelphia, as compared to the equally economically successful but less visible Indian community, shows that people do not react uniformly to high-achieving newcomers. The relations between these two nonwhite immigrant groups and native-born people of color highlight the contradictions inherent in expectations that the world is simply divided into whites and nonwhites and the confusion linked with forgetting the many kinds of power available in the United States.

Contradictions are not problems to explain away. They are integral parts of daily life that cause frustration, anger, and sometimes hatred among people from different backgrounds. But contradictions also contain the seeds of change. People move forward by readjusting their understandings and actions in their social world as they negotiate the inconsistencies in their lives. Take, for example, the comments of one man regarding Koreans:

> They come over here and they want to take your business but they don't want to be friends with you. . . . It's their culture. They are narrow minded. They're living in the United States. They should adopt our culture, just as we should adopt some of theirs. I was in the service and you go all over the place. And you have to respect individual cultures. I find it interesting. How does the other half live? It's a history of the world. But you have to share.

This man's experience in the military expanded his expectations of the world—he has learned to value difference. When confronted with newcomers who attempt to shut him out, he reacts not by wanting them to become more American or to leave but by wanting to share with other people. Another man expresses similar anger at the Korean community related to the Korean sign incident, but he has warm feelings toward the Latinos who helped his family when he was sick. His antipathy toward successful, middle-class Koreans as compared to the poorer Latinos is the opposite of that expected of native-born whites. Experiencing this contradiction showed him the range of behaviors and people in the "minority" community. He changed because of the contradictions.

This chapter examines some of the key contradictions we encountered in this study. As with people developing stereotypes and single solutions to problems, analysis must necessarily examine pieces of the puzzle of intergroup relations, developing categories along the way. Analysis starts by outlining the confusing aspects of social structure and belief systems. We also explore individuals' frustrations with these disparities. Next, we show the unintended effects of certain actions. Finally, we describe simultaneous contradictions. As described in Chapter 6, developing solutions in a complicated social world involves going beyond political economy or the individual's belief system. Attempts to change hostile and unequal intergroup relations must address both the social structure and individuals' understandings of it. Such change also means acknowledging positive and negative parts of the social world. Our analysis looks at both the effects of the macrostructure and of microlevel interactions. As described in Chapter 8, we propose seeking to better intergroup relations through an equally complex process.

Contradictions and Confusion

Social Structure and Common Ideological Models

The structure of U.S. society contains contradictions on many levels. Many immigrants comment on the openness of the society. For example, a Polish émigré said that she had left the relative economic safety of the former West Germany for the United States because she knew that she would always be considered a second-class citizen there. Indian immigrants have made the same statement regarding Britain. It is relatively easy to obtain material goods and create an abundant lifestyle here as compared to many parts of the world. The educational system is far less rigid than in many other countries. People who have the skills and resources can succeed in both the educational and economic systems.

Yet exaggerated expectations of unlimited mobility in the United States highlight the fact that the socioeconomic structure is more rigid and difficult than in many other societies. New immigrants, native-born people of color, and even the white working class encounter subtle class structures and developed networks that limit access to the power centers of society. It is much harder for women and people of color to succeed in the United States than in other places. Since the United States does not provide basic income and health care as much of the developed world does, it is much easier to fail here. The contrasts between wealth and poverty are much greater than in many other countries. The expected roads to success are relatively limited.

Both newcomers and established residents react to these contradictions with confusion. This section outlines some major incongruities highlighted by our research. As appropriate, we contrast the viewpoints of people from different backgrounds: immigrants and native born, various groups of people of color and whites, and middle class versus working class.

Open Society Versus Taking One's Turn or Knowing One's Place

Much confusion rests on the contradiction between the supposed openness of U.S. society and the reality of limited access to both social hierarchy and specific places. Every person in the United States is supposed to have equal opportunity. Yet we have any number of expectations about fairness and taking one's turn.

Examples of Openness.   Established residents' understanding of immigrant progress in the United States shows inconsistency in beliefs about openness. Such institutions as the media and schools, as well as many established residents, applaud the new immigrants who succeed as proof of the openness of U.S. society. The many articles on Asian success in the United States are one example of this view. In fact, immigrants are seen as restoring the ethos of hard work and ingenuity expected in the United States:

Koreans are very hard workers, and I can see that each generation that's here in this country works a little less. And I've seen it—especially among my Jewish friends. . . . The parents had a store and they worked six or seven days a week and then the kids took the business over, and it was really running and flourishing and they say "I don't have much business. I'm going to open at ten and close half a day on Saturday," and some are closed all day on Saturday. It just seems to me that each generation that's here in this country gets more lazy.

Koreans also adopt these Horatio Alger aspects of U.S. opportunity, seeing themselves as using the possibilities for success in the United States. This is the positive half of the contradictory standard U.S. immigration story. One young Korean commented:

What [poor native-born people] don't realize is that when they come in with their food coupons, my parents worked so hard. They came here with $400 in their pockets. And now they've got a condo, three cars, and a store. I believe the U.S. is the land of opportunity, but you get out of it what you put into it.

Taking One's Turn.   Contrary to these expectations of openness, the mythologized road to success in America remains a very narrow path. New immigrants are expected to be like the poor, uneducated "peasants" of the "good immigrant" model. Like their prototypical ancestors, these immigrants should also struggle before succeeding in the United States.[2] As the economy declines, the feeling that immigrants should start at the bottom is magnified. Economic pressure is exacerbated by the difference between the reality of more educated and skilled newcomers with middle-class expectations and the expectations of peasant immigrants based on turn-of-the-century images. According to the established residents, the newcomer Poles and Koreans who succeed quickly are breaking the rules. The fact of higher education and resources is contrary to the expectation of "wretched refuse" that the United States as a haven for immigrants must take in. We expect gratitude and hard work from newcomers; we do not expect them to gain economic and political power too rapidly.

Koreans who have stores in working-class communities become particularly aware of the contradiction between expected immigrant behavior and their own economic success. Poorer established Americans constantly question where Koreans get the money to start businesses. Many complain that the newcomers must be cheating in some way. Confusing Korean immigrants, who are entitled to no government funds, with Southeast Asian refugees, who do get some government assistance, established residents claim that the government must be giving them money. Over and over we heard about tax-abatement programs for immigrant businesses that accounted for their frequent turnover. "They do not pay taxes for five years, then they give the business to someone else and he doesn't have to pay taxes for another five." We heard from numerous sources in several neighborhoods that all Asians automatically received ten or twenty thousand dollars. Special welfare benefits and housing giveaways were also mentioned. Such specific and consistent anecdotal information was often disseminated through radio talk shows and then spread by word of mouth. The following example reveals both the disparity between foreign and domestic policy and established residents' view of successful newcomers:

> A lot of the veterans that fought in Korea and Vietnam were peeved because we [the United States] turn around and pour money into a country and try to defend it. We get our butts shot up and stuff like that. We defeat them. And they turn around and ask us for millions. . . . So they bring refugees from Southeast Asia and they don't pay taxes for a number of years, they're given all kinds of stuff. They go on social security, which they never put into. I've been busting my butt for years. I fought for the country, yet I don't get half the benefits they do. These foreigners come over and we give them a welcome basket of open doors. . . . If these people want to work for what they are getting, great. That is what I had to do.

Few established residents realize that, although some Koreans may come to the United States with little money, they do bring middle-class understandings of business and access to community capital through the loan clubs—the latter a resource that is beyond many established residents. In addition, access to different levels of capital and knowledge of working the system has given some Korean businesses access to loans from the U.S. Small Business Administration (SBA), partially confirming the view that Koreans get some help from the government not easily available to others (Young, personal communication [1989]). Yet Korean businessmen do not get SBA loans because the government is giving them special treatment, but because they have the skills and resources to apply successfully for a generally available asset. The people who assume that Koreans get special privileges see only part of the picture.

In addition, Koreans increasingly bring large sums of money with them when they emigrate to the United States. During the 1970s, when the amount of money allowed out of South Korea was limited, immigrants brought capital over in small batches, sending funds with different relatives or bringing additional money out on different trips between the United States and the homeland. The facts about these relatively wealthy and educated newcomers contradict the standard U.S. immigration myth that all newcomers are poor and uneducated.

The different class values of urban, educated newcomer Poles led to similar problems:

Pre–World War II immigrants didn't look like this, for a long time, till they could really afford it. But the new immigrants, they might not have anything but they will dress well, and so the Polish Americans who are here are jealous. Look what they have, they have only been here one year.

Not Taking More than Your Fair Share.   But it is equally unacceptable for newcomers to fail in the United States. For established residents, the "good immigrant" model also means working hard to succeed. Puerto Ricans who remain poor in the United States or Polish refugees who take welfare are perceived as bad immigrants who do not want to become Americanized. Newcomer Poles adopt the same stand toward Puerto Ricans as established Americans do. Since they are working, they complain that the "Spanish" are lazy, living off welfare and not learning the language like the newcomer Poles. All immigrants should be able to succeed by their own initiative. Those who ask for help are asking for unfair special advantage.

Both people of color and working-class whites perceive special programs and funds for refugees as unfair in comparison to their perception of their own parents' and grandparents' immigration experience.[3] The many statements documented here about favoritism toward newcomers and immigrants receiving special help from the government reflect this view. In addition, the fact that established residents note that government programs seldom serve the general population while some newcomers receive special government support adds to the feeling that immigration policy is unfair. However, it is important to note that community residents seldom stated that immigration should be restricted, only commenting on perceived special treatment of newcomers. They question the fact that some newcomers receive the benefits of the United States while the working and middle class pay taxes but are excluded from such benefits as college-loan programs and free clinics because of income. One person commented that the clinics are "always full of foreigners." While the neighborhood health clinics are technically open to all, they are perceived as resources for the poor. As native-born residents are increasingly pressed by rising costs and diminished government services, they are even more likely to resent newcomer use of government resources. For example, one woman who is active in helping elderly community residents said, "We can't even take care of our own anymore," implying a priority commitment to long-established tax-paying citizens.

The same attitudes hold when institutions give special attention to a newcomer group:

The priests started shoving down your throat—accept the Spanish. You were going to church and every Sunday it was the same thing. Pete's [husband] mother died then, and the first Mother's Day after she died I really wanted to walk out of church because the sermon was not about mothers as it usually is, but about accepting the Spanish people. I had never had a problem accepting them. My kids went to school with them. I worked at the school with them but it got to the point where you're saying, why are they so special? There's a whole lot of nationalities in that parish. And I'm thinking, What's the big deal?

Then I was talking to the priest once and I said, Why? This is really infuriating. When we had a fair once, they worked their own wheels. They didn't want anyone working with them and they didn't work with anyone. And I thought, that's not fair. And then I heard that they had their own CYO [Catholic Youth Organization]. And I thought why are these people telling us to accept and yet giving these people special privileges. My husband got infuriated that [the mass they went to] was one where they sat us in the basement when the Spanish have the upper church. And then the tuition changed over completely from what it was when we started here—and then all of a sudden it was this humungous tuition. And I said to the priest once, "Can I ask you why the changeover?" And he said to me, which took me by surprise, he said the Spanish weren't contributing voluntarily. They paid tuition but they would not necessarily contribute to the church so they had to raise tuition. That was the only way they could get the money. So what I'm doing is paying the high tuition *and* contributing. It just didn't seem fair.

The same perceptions of fairness play into the way that some white established residents view affirmative action. Many of the whites encountered in this study understood that African Americans should receive special training and consideration in order to give them equal access to society. However, many of them felt threatened by the way that affirmative action played out in their own lives. Some felt that a generation of change under civil-rights legislation had gone a long way toward leveling the playing field between working-class whites and African Americans. These individuals felt that working- and middle-class African Americans should no longer receive preference in allocating college scholarships or promotions. They believed that giving people of color preference when they had educational backgrounds equal to those of whites betrayed the expectation of openness and equal opportunity.

Recall the incident described in Chapter 5, where a close friendship between white and African American women broke up after the African American woman gained a promotion through affirmative action. The white woman followed the line of equal opportunity and cooperation between friends, which holds that cross-group friendships take precedence over affirmative action, and withdrew her name from consideration for the job, assuming that her friend would do likewise. When her African American friend drew on the logic of affirmative action—believing herself entitled to the job because of past discrimination—the white friend felt betrayed. Like many working-class whites, she appealed to the ethos of equal opportunity and individual effort. In her mind, her African American friend betrayed this rule by putting group privilege ahead of concepts of individual merit. But her African American friend relied on another definition of racial justice, based on the weight of her overall lifetime experience with racism in Philadelphia.

Building on the argument that whites control the power structure of society, those in the working class are considered to blame for the impoverished conditions of portions of the African American and Puerto Rican populations because they benefited from the racist policies of whites in power. Yet white working-class residents see themselves to the same extent as victims of an unfair power structure. Equally accurate contradictory messages led to dissolution of the women's friendship.

New immigrants who do not succeed also violate societal expectations of openness. If those who are successful are continued proof of the belief that everyone can prosper in the United States, immigrants who fail show that the U.S. social structure is not completely open or fair. Some established residents react to this evidence of inequality by blaming the immigrants for their lack of success. White resentment of poor people of color is also based on the same set of assumptions. This is particularly true of the working class, because its members see themselves as only one step above poverty. According to this logic, if they must work hard with no support from the government in the form of social programs, immigrants and people of color must do so too. This kind of resentment increases in hard economic times.

Openness and Exclusion.   The same confusion between ideas of openness and knowing one's place also shows up in discussions of physical space. Olney residents' anger over Korean stores that are only open to Koreans or over the presence of wholesale shops on a commercial shopping strip also reflects views that space should be open to everyone. To quote one Olney established resident who again evokes the importance of mutual sharing:

> The good part of the change is the coming of so many different groups [cultural pluralism]. The bad part is that some of them are not letting everyone in their stores. If we are willing to share our country with them, they should be willing to share their stores with us.

When asked if there was any setting where he felt out of place, one white Port Richmond resident described an experience in which African American workers at a pizza parlor outside his neighborhood ignored his family until they went away. He felt that he did not belong in this restaurant because of his race.

But whites use the same subtle behaviors over and over to show ownership of physical space in contested territory. Recall white established residents claiming space on the Aramingo shopping strip by talking loudly over tables.

This behavior tells people of color that they are out of place. Given the prevalence of this kind of action in Port Richmond, it is no surprise that Rafael Droz forgot that the neighborhood resident who attacked him was African American. The individual's actual race did not matter. Given the cultural dynamics of this community, Port Richmond means white, and "those whites" have a documented history of racist behavior toward people of color. In the language of youth interaction in these communities, retaliation against "those whites" was completely appropriate.

Recall also how the floors at Borders High School are segregated by group. Likewise, the cafeteria at the Kensington school is strictly portioned out to members of particular groups, and to sit at one table is to be part of that group—the rest of an individual's identity becomes irrelevant. In these cases, space defines identity. The contradiction of actual color, or the ways that people may switch allegiances in different settings, is ignored, given the importance of the context.

Strength through Unity versus the Sanctity of the Individual

Notions of openness and inequality are often linked with contradictions involving individuality versus strength through unity. Members of majority and minority groups, as well as newcomers and established residents, are confused by disparate societal messages about "strength through unity" as opposed to the dominant U.S. view of "the sanctity of the individual."

The Positive Side of Strength through Unity. The models of structural racism and cultural pluralism recognize that people often have a common bond with others who have had the same historical experience. Like new immigrants' realization that they are very different from their native-born hosts, different histories of particular groups in the United States yield a sense of peoplehood and, sometimes, of similar cultural styles. As one African American community worker put it:

> You can go back in time to slavery. We had to stick together. That was the only way to be let out of bondage for freedom. You sort of had that family closeness.

Bonding of networks and historical experience through group solidarity has been a common strategy throughout U.S. history. The Polish beneficial organizations were formed at the turn of the century to provide insurance and loans to new arrivals who were excluded from the power structure of mainstream society. Today, they serve to provide services for their members and to create and cement ethnic identity. The many Korean churches perform the same dual role.

"Strength through unity" implies that there is power in recognizing and celebrating subgroup status. In the cultural-pluralism model, people build self-esteem by recognizing the value of their individual cultures. The structural-racism model documents oppression of people of color by whites. Creating a just society involves redistributing power and resources to minorities. People of color can achieve power by forming groups and demanding resources. Many of the strategies for redistribution involve defining people as groups competing for resources. African American and Puerto Rican nationalist efforts are an extension of this argument. Korean strategies to present a united front to city government and local communities is another example of this trend.

Members of minority and majority groups recognize that there are many positive reasons to build group solidarity. In the cultural-pluralism model, recognition of culture is the key to building positive relations across groups. During attempts to generate youth programs to combat intergroup tensions surrounding the killings of Stephen Crespo and Sean Daily, one Puerto Rican participant kept asking if the whites understood the culture and history of Puerto Rico. He felt that problems would go away if groups understood each other's culture. The various festivals described in Chapter 5 rely on the same model.

Pride in racial or ethnic identity is often combined with the collective action of the structural-racism model. Recall that Puerto Ricans, stating that "I'm tired of my race being treated like trash," proclaimed that police behavior in the Daily and Crespo incidents was a clear example of the discrimination that their community suffers at the hands of the white-dominated establishment. The incidents became a rallying point for the nationalist faction among Puerto Ricans. Community outcry led to much-needed public hearings on the plight of the Puerto Rican community in Philadelphia.

Much of the organizing effort within the nationalist faction involves creating work, housing, and other resources, along the lines of the model that promotes solidarity in the African American community. The strategy recognizes historical inequality and promotes in-group solidarity as a means to combat poverty. One community development corporation dominated by Puerto Ricans has combined creative programming with a solidarity agenda to create a program that allows community members to learn building skills on the job while renovating housing for the community. Through this program, the CDC teaches skills, creates jobs, and improves the living conditions of the neighborhood. At the same time, the program builds community and ethnic solidarity.

Negative Aspects of Strength through Unity.   Ideas of unity built into the structural-racism model assume that the white establishment intends to exploit people of color. Even comparatively wealthy Koreans and Palestinians are subsumed under the general label of people of color oppressed by the white power structure. Models of exploitation build on the long history of structural racism in the United States. Present-day inequalities also show the many ways that a white-dominated power structure hurts people of color on a daily basis. Taken to extremes, this view justifies hostility toward whites.

The anger associated with feelings and experiences of exploitation causes problems in multicultural settings. Recall the African American mother who refused to let her child go to a birthday party until she heard that other African American children would be there. She feared white racism even in a context of friendly mixing and needed the assurance of others from her race to allow her child to participate in this event. There are two integrated football teams in Philadelphia's Northeastern Suburban Athletic Conference, one in Olney and one in Port Richmond. That a Port Richmond team has been comfortably and consciously integrated since its founding in 1961 is yet another contradiction, given the real and assumed white separatism of this neighborhood. A team representative reports that his multicultural squad has problems only when playing against teams composed wholly of African Americans:

> Once we get in and we're along the sidelines they'll [African American teams] make sure that we're surrounded. They literally surround us. If there's a pile up or something they'll make sure that they get in a couple [of] digs. They just intimidate. When we're there, naturally the kids are a little afraid. They [our white kids] only see us and they picture a race riot. They're intimidated. But I'm sure when they [African American players] come down here they may feel the same way.

Cross-group animosity quickly turns into anger toward people who attempt to cross racial or ethnic boundaries. This is the negative side of sticking together with people from one's own race as a way of staving off discrimination. The football team's representative reported that his biggest problem was how the children on African American teams treated his African American players:

> The all-Black team is out to hurt our Black kids. I see it happen because they're [African Americans] playing with white kids. I see them spit in their face when they went down. Right in front of us. And our kids, we come back to the club, and after you tell them to line up they don't want to shake hands. I don't blame them. I seen it happen. You can hear them—"You want to play with them whities?" They are out to hurt them. That's a fact.

An African American woman described this tension between groups as follows:

> Like when you see a couple walking down the street and one's Black and one's white and you automatically turn. Most people feel like you're betraying your race. When I was their age we used to have names for people like that—coconuts and oreos. That's what I grew up with. That's the way I was taught. This isn't coming from home, it's coming from peers. You learn that you don't betray your own. With anything.

The same problems sometimes occur between Latinos and African Americans. Recall the woman who was made to feel like an outsider in her all–African American workplace. African American board members calling Puerto Rican workers at a CDC prejudiced, and Puerto Rican parents accusing the African American security guard at the Kensington school of displaying racist attitudes against their children, are two additional permutations on intra-group solidarity or hostility. Yet in other contexts African Americans and Latinos present a united front against the alien and hostile white "other."

Sanctity of the Individual.   The idea of "strength through unity" clashes with common views regarding the sanctity of the individual. Dominant society teaches that all people are equal and that the ultimate objective, in which personal merit thrives, is a color-blind society. This message appears in both the cultural-pluralism and structural-racism models. In cultural pluralism, people recognize commonalities by valuing difference; in the structural-racism model, structural inequality is caused by the historical confluence of race and class in the United States.

The contradiction occurs when in-group solidarity conflicts with the notion that everyone should have equal access to resources. For example, the CDC that developed strong programs for Puerto Ricans claims to serve all people in the area. Although programs are open to everyone, the fact that Spanish is the dominant language in this setting contradicts this expectation. One African American board member commented, "If you are working for nonprejudice, don't do prejudiced things."

Unexpected Power Relations

Contradictions between an open society versus ideas of taking one's turn and having a fair share, strength through unity versus equality of individuals, flare into anger when expected power relationship are turned on end. The fact that the city government throughout the 1980s was thought to be run by African Americans exacerbated already existing tensions between center city and the neighborhoods. White Port Richmond residents' complaints that the African American mayor was protecting the Puerto Rican caterer (when Puerto Ricans had "caused" the Daily murder) is one example of the perception of unfair allocation of resources for people of color. The notion of special treatment became more acute after Stephen Crespo was murdered:

> We were told that there was a moratorium, that the police were not
> allowed to arrest Puerto Ricans right now. And they know. That is why
> we have thirty-six cars of them [Puerto Rican teens] with bats and clubs
> because now all the cops just come around and slap their hands and say,
> You shouldn't do that. Because of the tension over this child's [Stephen
> Crespo] killing right now they are receiving preferential treatment right
> around here.

When the Human Relations Commission was slow to release the report from the Puerto Rican community hearings, Puerto Ricans saw the delay as lack of government interest in their community.

The Korean street-sign incident is another example of power relationships turned on end. Much of the anger surrounding this affair focused on the fact that Koreans had relatively strong economic power on the shopping strip. That they could negotiate with the city government to get Korean-language signs put up without discussion with the rest of the community highlighted this power. The same anger appears in African American communities when they see Koreans buy stores in the neighborhood. The latter are "supposed" to be poor immigrants, not store owners in an established-resident community.

But anger at Koreans focuses as much on their visible control over businesses in the city as on the fact that they have have moved up the ladder of economic success "too quickly." That Koreans present a united front and are currently attempting to build political power is another unexpected strategy drawing established residents' attention. Indian immigrants are even more likely to be middle-class professionals than are Korean newcomers. But the fact that Indians are not as visibly in control of local economic power as Koreans means that they do not receive so much attention, praise, and anger from the media and from established residents.

Creating an Ethnic Identity

In Philadelphia, the primary dynamic between newcomers and established residents is race and ethnicity, not newness to the United States. Following the "everyone has an ethnic identity" aspect of the cultural-pluralism model, new immigrants quickly learn to highlight separate identities and cultures. This phenomenon simply reinforces the difference they experience as newcomers anyway. For example, Korean businesspersons used the idea of understanding each other's culture as a primary way to increase understanding when critiquing *I'm Not Prejudiced, But . . .* , the videotape on Korean–African American relations in Philadelphia:

> I think we should emphasize our cultural background. Korea has five thousand years of history as a nation. Throughout that history, Koreans have successfully avoided being culturally absorbed by China. That was possible because we have maintained our unique cultural heritage.

> I would add the importance of our family system. Many aspects of Korean culture are deeply rooted in Confucianism. Among other things, it emphasizes the importance of family. It is a family-centered way of thinking.

The ethos of cultural pluralism declares that everyone has an equally valid culture that should be celebrated. In this view, we should be working toward a color-blind society where everyone has equal opportunity. Prejudice comes from people knowing too little about the people around them. If they discover the good things about each culture, and learn that inequalities of resources are not indications of inferior culture, the United States will become the true land of opportunity.

Yet the assumption of ethnic identity implies that every individual is different from the next. While encouraging contact across groups and building self-esteem, emphasis on ethnicity can create and reinforce boundaries between people. Those who welcome communication across groups can also inflame divisions. The Saint Ignatius festival shows how events designed to bring people together instead accentuate boundaries by defining each national or racial group as separate. As described above, the priests' efforts to get white residents to welcome the Latino church members caused more, not fewer, divisions:

> The priests did a big error there. They alienated a lot of people. You shouldn't say that one nationality is better than the other when you are in a mixed parish.

The Borders High School's principal's comment that the creation of many ethnic clubs served to heighten divisions is another example of this unintended consequence of highlighting diversity.

In *Streetwise* (1990, 40–41), Eli Anderson describes two types of middle-class African Americans: those who think that maintaining racial identity is primary and always suspect that whites are racist, and those who consider class more important and, while maintaining mostly African American close friends, move comfortably in mixed-race, middle-class circles. Our research showed similar phenomena. African Americans and Puerto Ricans learn to expect racism, while whites are careful to avoid accusations of racism and uncomfortable with the cliquishness exhibited by some people of color. New immigrants often adopted similar assumptions about white racism and African American bonding.

Another contradiction in the cultural-pluralism model appears when the descendants of turn-of the-the-century immigrants who have intermarried find themselves having to choose an ethnic identity or re-create traditions to fit an ethnic label. One boy in the Polish nationalities parish school described himself as being of Hungarian, German, Polish, Irish, and Italian descent, yet was highlighting his Polishness in the context of the school, saying that "it's in our blood but we don't speak it." Another family, which claimed no Polish ancestry, adopted Polish holiday traditions and became active in the Polish beneficial when they moved to Port Richmond from Kensington; they enrolled their children in the nationalities parish school because they felt that it had the best reputation in the area. This family knows that they have no Polish "blood," yet they became Polish because it fits their needs. Contradictions regarding ethnic identity are ignored when they conflict with selecting an environment that will create the best future for this family.

The same group of women prepare all of the "ethnic" dishes for the various Olney parish European ethnic festivals regardless of their own heritage. Here the assumption of primordial ethnicity contrasts with the ways that established residents with mixed ancestry negotiate identity (Yancey, Ericksen, and Leon 1985). The fact that third- or fourth-generation white Catholics can move among ethnic cultures highlights how difference becomes a way to create a unified American identity. These established residents are all one-tenth X and one-fifth Y, emphasizing the bit of heritage that makes sense in a given context. Seen as a whole, their lives are greater than the sum of the various ethnic parts. Their ability to use real or imagined background characteristics to their advantage shows how the interaction between contradictory elements creates more options for established residents. Fragmentation becomes a creative tool in negotiating U.S. society.

Competing Definitions of Racism

Further confusion surrounds the many different ways that people in these three neighborhoods define racism. Both societywide models and patterns of practice in everyday life reveal contradictory definitions. Problems arise when individuals react to different definitions of racism. Very few people in these neighborhoods consider themselves to be racist. On the other hand, everyone is afraid of being accused of racism. The ongoing dynamic centers on multiple interpretations of statements and actions as either racist or not. Frequently, people avoid being accused of racism by either defining their own behavior as nonracist or simply avoiding the topic altogether.

People of Color and Middle-Class White Definitions of Racism

Characterizations of race vary by class and color. We found two definitions of racism used in these three neighborhoods. Middle-class diversity seekers from all backgrounds and many people of color from all classes use elements of the structural-racism model to define racism. Recall that all whites are held responsible for structural inequality in such an analysis. Based on this framework, all whites are automatically suspected to be racists until proven otherwise, and the burden of proof against accusations of racism falls on them. Such proof comes from working for change and from challenging both the private perjorative statements made about other groups by one's friends, neighbors, and fellow citizens and the public expression of these views. Those who do not work for change are part of the problem. Inequality based on race exists as much because the whites in power do little to change the power balance as because of direct behavior or attitudes that discriminate against people of color.

A corollary of this view is that acts of hostility by people of color are necessary as self-protection. Following this logic, one middle-class Puerto Rican stated that "people of color can not be racist because they have been victims of a racist society in the past." Racism is defined as discrimination against other people based on color. For this reason, some Puerto Rican participants in the coalition to end tensions in Kensington and Port Richmond demanded that its primary focus be on resolving racism directed toward their community. Acts of racism range from thoughts, to statements in private settings, to public expressions, to more threatening actions that involve verbal harassment and attacks on property and person.

In this view, when whites make people of color unwelcome in any way they are actively practicing racism. White youth terrorizing people of color who move into their neighborhoods is one example of racism. Taken to extremes, retaliation against whites by people of color is justifiable protection of the subgroup population from bigots. Rafael Droz was able to recruit three carloads of Puerto Ricans to "get those whites" in part because the community contains so much anger against that population. That anger is understandable given the actual experience of Puerto Ricans with whites in their communities. But the violence is also fueled by the repeated assertion that "[white] racism is on the rise in America."

Since saying that people of color are responsible for problems in a community can intimidate subgroup members, complaints about everyday quality-of-life problems with newcomer neighbors who are not white can also be interpreted as racism. Witness the comments by empowerment leaders that established residents in Olney must be racist for talking about problems with newcomers in the community. This second example includes elements of the cultural-pluralism model in defining racism. In this view, complaints must flow from negative stereotypes about people of color, which come from lack of appreciation for the cultures of people who are different. By extension, any negative statement about someone from a different group is an example of racist stereotyping.

Many people of color take avoidance of mentioning racial differences as yet another example of racism. They assume that whites think that racism will go away if they do not discuss it. Not talking about race is seen as one way to do nothing about it. This view highlights aspects of power and racism. As with all contradictions, avoiding discussion of race has both positive and negative results.

White Working-Class Definitions

Other residents counter this definition of racism with an alternative definition and way of behaving on the subject of race. Most white working-class established residents reject the structural-racism analysis because they observe that they do not hold power in this country. Statements like "My grandparents weren't even here when slavery happened, how can I be responsible?" are commonly repeated in these communities. Such statements reveal the common view that structural inequality was created in the United States by Southern slaveowners more than a century before the arrival of the ancestors of these white working class Philadelphians. Their personal experience and understanding of history from their grandparents' struggles as immigrants in this country tell them that life is an uphill battle for success. They do not see how they are accountable for current inequality in the United States.

Part of this view involves failure to see the very real prejudices and differences in resources that people of color experience every day in the United States. But this sentiment also reflects the reality that only a small percentage of whites control the power structure of this country. The white working class also feels that set-aside programs go against the ideology of equal opportunity for all. When white residents of Port Richmond begin a discussion of diversity with such statements as "everyone is equal" and "everyone should be treated as individuals," they are appealing to hopes that they should have an equal chance to succeed in the United States as well. They see themselves as bearing the brunt of efforts to create equality in this country through programs like affirmative action.

Working-class whites define racism as hostility toward people from different groups. To them, racism includes explicit negative statements or actions against others. They have learned to censor their own negative comments or to preface them with disclaimers. A Puerto Rican woman uses aspects of the same definition when she begins a statement critical of African Americans with assurances that "I don't feel that I'm prejudiced, per se." In this definition, the failure of the African American pizza parlor employees to serve whites is an example of racism. Rudeness on the part of nonwhite employees in stores can also be defined as racist behavior.

This alternative definition embraces an understanding that most middle-class people point to the white working class as the primary purveyors of racist thoughts and actions in the United States. The best way to avoid being accused of racism is not to talk about it. White Port Richmond representatives dropped out of the coalition addressing race relations in their neighborhood in part because they were afraid that they would be accused of racism if they brought up the ongoing problem of Puerto Rican teenagers driving into their community in an attempt to goad white youth. The tendency of many Port Richmond residents to refer to the Daily killing as a problem between "good" and "bad" kids, explicitly denying that it had anything to do with race, is one example of this strategy.

Another common way to avoid the sensitive topic of race is to highlight other kinds of difference. For example, during a preparatory class for the

general-education-degree program at a community organization in Kensington, women of all colors began a discussion of difference by focusing on
disabilities and then on differences in sexual orientation before finally getting
to the topic of race an hour later. The taboo against saying bad things about
individuals from other groups has become so strong that people are afraid to
make negative statements even in single-race settings. For example, during an
interview between two white women in a closed room, one woman whispered
that African American youth caused most of the problems in her neighborhood.

The white working-class definition of racism as not saying or thinking bad
things about other individuals leads its members to avoid talking about racial
categories. This, in turn, creates a fissure between them and human-relations
experts attempting to quell tensions in these neighborhoods. Event organizers
ask white established residents to highlight the very thing that they define as
racism: talking about racial or national differences. When organizers stress
positive aspects of difference while defining discussion of problem-causing
behavior by other groups as racist, white established residents become confused, defensive, and alienated from potentially useful programming. Ironically, by not talking about race these established residents are adhering to
human-relations experts' advice that they should "Say UH-OH to the uh-oh"
and censor damaging thoughts and speech. In addition, the positive aspects of
culture used in most of these programs have little to do with the lives of either
newcomers or established residents.

New Immigrant Adaptations to Existing Definitions of Racism

New immigrants quickly incorporate both definitions of racism into their
understanding of racial dynamics in the United States. Korean references to the
sign incident in Olney and attempts to create political alliances with African
Americans follow the definition of racism as structural inequality perpetrated
by whites, the one used by most people of color and by some middle-class
whites. Consider the following statement by a Korean leader:

> If Blacks consider themselves disadvantaged, so do Koreans. We are
> victims of bigotry and prejudice too. Sometimes it's white people against
> us. Remember the Korean street sign incident on 5th Street.

On the other hand, the same leader went on to say:

> Remember the Georgie Woods incident on the talk show? If Blacks
> would talk about bigotry, they should consider their own bigotry toward
> Koreans.

The Georgie Woods incident and the statement that African Americans
should consider their own bigotry follows the white working-class definition

of racism as acting hostilely toward people from different groups. The arguments of the African American radio personality Georgie Woods about boycotting Korean stores echoed much of the dialogue about white economic power reinforcing poverty in the African American community typical of the structural-racism analysis of U.S. race and class relations. The Koreans interpreted the statements against their community as racism, here defined as hostility to people from other groups—identical to prejudice against African Americans. Georgie Woods was equating race and economic power, including Koreans as part of the white power structure. These multiple understandings of cross-group obligations and inequalities, as well as different interpretations of the word "racism," highlight the confusion regarding "appropriate" ways to think about and behave toward people who are different in multicultural settings.

Class-Based Differences in Experience

Much of the confusion around racial divisions, and the contradictory beliefs by different newcomers and established residents about who is racist in what contexts, crystallize around the ways that race, class, power, and poverty come together in these neighborhoods. The crux of this contradiction involves the ways that people interpret and act on real and perceived differences in income, lifestyle, and access to resources. Take the statement that more crime and housing abandonment occurs in racially mixed Kensington than in adjacent Port Richmond, which is largely white. Depending on how, when, where, and by whom this statement is made, it either becomes a plea for empowering an oppressed minority or a racial slur. The dynamic of cross-group interaction in these neighborhoods involves multiple contradictory interpretations of phrases like this every day. Since different actors adhere to different rules about the appropriate contexts for such statements, community residents are always caught in the double bind of negotiating the right words to avoid accusations of intolerance. Issues are further complicated when actions and beliefs fail to match, as well.

Middle-Class Experience with Difference

Recall the statistics on income and poverty in the three neighborhoods included in this study. Both Olney and Port Richmond consist primarily of middle-income households. Most people work and homes are kept up. In reality, income levels among the neighborhoods are very similar. Yet the populations differ in several important ways. Olney includes a group of immigrants and newcomer whites from relatively educated, merchant-class or professional backgrounds. While these individuals may struggle financially, they share the historical understanding that they will succeed in this country, which is the traditional hallmark of middle-class ideology.[4] The many statements about opportunity presented in the Olney school play described in Chapter 6 are one example of this optimism. The success of immigrants and diversity are other aspects of this positive outlook, and residents value them as proof that the individual can prosper in this country.

All whites in the United States tend to be sensitive to accusations of racism. The middle-class white diversity seekers in Olney reassure themselves that they are not prejudiced by embracing elements of newcomer cultures. They also repeatedly highlight positive statements about people from different groups. Their perspective reflects experience with people of color which is different from that of many working-class whites. They know middle-class African Americans, Puerto Ricans, and immigrants from a number of countries who are successful people just like themselves. They also have the educational background to understand the historical and present-day structural inequalities that keep a disproportionate percentage of the minority population of the United States in poverty. Unlike the working class, they can more easily disconnect the relationship between race and poverty that permeates this country. Their political viewpoints bolster this attitude. Furthermore, a smaller proportion of middle-class established residents are likely to have daily personal contact with impoverished people of color. It is thus much easier for them to have a positive attitude toward poor African Americans and Puerto Ricans, since they experience less frequently the levels of anger toward people with resources evident in these communities. Yet the same ambivalence about race and class is exhibited when middle-class whites face situations where race and poverty come together. For example, Anderson (1990, 147–149) describes how a middle-class white mother tried to decide how to react to a poor African American school friend of her son's. She expressed concern over the child's well-being while, at the same time, fearing that showing too much of the house might later endanger her property and fearing that her concerns about whether the child had eaten breakfast were themselves racist.

Working-Class Experience with Class and Difference

Port Richmond, Kensington, and Olney contain a group of white descendants of turn-of-the-century working-class immigrants. In Port Richmond, white ethnics form the majority. These individuals may have incomes similar to those of middle-class professionals (indeed, they often refer to themselves as "middle class"), but their outlook is very different. Consider this description of his childhood lifestyle in Port Richmond by one established resident:

> We never wanted for anything. But we never had anything extra. There was always enough food and we were always treated well. We went to the

movies and things like that, but we never had any extra money for extravagances.

These white ethnics perceive the world as far less forgiving than do the middle-class residents of Olney. Since many either work in industry or are one generation away from work in a factory, they have experienced deindustrialization personally. They may not want for anything, but they perceive their economic conditions as unstable—it only takes one layoff to become impoverished. They fear any element that could imperil their hard-won lifestyle, particularly their homes, which are their primary asset. In the mind of many white ethnics, decline is symbolized by Kensington and North Philadelphia. The statistics on poverty in these communities show the partial truth of this perception. The white residents of Port Richmond and Olney correctly perceive that more people of color live in these economically depressed neighborhoods. But instead of focusing the blame for decline on factories leaving the city, redlining, and the movement of more-affluent whites to other neighborhoods, these residents often link conditions in the communities to the color of their inhabitants:

> I don't want to live in a racially mixed neighborhood. Because I lived in a racially mixed neighborhood and it became a slum. Those houses weren't slums when I moved in, they are now. I don't want my neighborhood to become a slum.

This clearly racist statement is based on lived experience, not simply on stereotypes taught by racist parents. These individuals connect race and class. In fact, negative images of people of color sometimes develop late:

> I was never prejudiced until I moved into this neighborhood. Before I got married, one of my best friends was a colored man. I never saw color or age. I saw people. If I liked a person I made friends. But when the turnover came here with the Spanish, then it became a slight problem for me, more so for my husband.

The same person who does not want to live in a mixed neighborhood bolsters this viewpoint by reporting on the "Spanish" who use food stamps in the Acme. But even in this case, racist views are contradictory. In this person's experience, all "Spanish" are bad, but African Americans can be either good or bad:

> I don't like North Philadelphia. But look at Germantown and Mt. Airy. Those [African American] people take care of their neighborhoods. I don't see a lot of Spanish neighborhoods that are kept up like that.

This person knows that the working- and middle-class African Americans who live in Germantown and Mt. Airy also have pride in property. But he has no positive experience with Puerto Ricans. Would this person condone violence to remove a nonwhite resident from the neighborhood who was perceived as a threat to property values? Probably not. But he would also do little to speak against violence should it occur. Few individuals in Port Richmond stated that they would not want people of color to move into their neighborhood, however. On some level, most recognize that there are "lazy" people and "good" (i.e., hardworking) people from all races. The following dialogue is more typical:

> If they take care of the houses and live like me I could care less. As long as they take care of their properties and don't cause any trouble it makes no difference to me.

> Do they?

> Yes and no. It's just like whites. I call them white trash if they don't take care of their houses. If a couple [of] families move in I think they're fine. I tend to think they blend in and take care. But I've seen places, public housing, and up in the far Northeast, those places are just ripped apart by whoever. It was public housing so it's probably whites, too. Whites, Blacks, Hispanics. That's what I don't like.

Working-class residents of all colors are more likely to see the negative side of intergroup relations. As with Ruth in Olney, people who live in neighborhoods where classes and races mix are proud of their middle-class, professional neighbors who come from different races and countries. White factory workers in Kensington and Olney also expressed camaraderie with their hard-working coworkers. But they recognize that all African Americans and Puerto Ricans do not behave in the same way. One Puerto Rican established resident stated:

> With the Blacks it's hard to have much in common. I don't feel that I'm prejudiced per se, but I've had so many experiences being around them. I have really good friends at work, but the less educated they are, the less friendly or more aggravated they seem to be.

The negative confluence of race and class remains in the minds of many working-class residents. They honestly believe that some people of color make good neighbors. At the same time, they perceive Latinos, and the majority of African Americans, as members of the underclass, who do not maintain their property. Their fear that the "good" families from other races moving into the neighborhood would draw the "bad" elements leads to hostility toward people of color that can easily erupt into violence. It only takes one or two openly hostile members of a community acting from this pervasive ambivalence to terrorize a newcomer. When people throughout the city then label the neighborhood as "racist," the residents respond that they are not racist, stating that they really do not care who moves in next door. In reality, the disjuncture of knowing that class variation exists within racial groups, while seeing impoverished people of color every day, leads to contradictory attitudes toward persons who are different. In one situation, white established residents genuinely are not racists; they can exhibit extremely racist thoughts and actions in another situation. The combination of positive and negative understandings of race governs their lives.

In integrated Kensington, similar feelings that people of color are responsible for decline center on rules for fighting and drug use. The playground clique of white teenagers responsible for numerous racial incidents has been described as "good kids who don't use drugs and fight with their hands." Fighting only with hands is considered a key rule for white working-class boys. Whites see themselves as protecting the neighborhood from drugs and violent crime, perpetrated primarily by Puerto Ricans. When Puerto Ricans fight with knives or guns they break established community rules, reinforcing assumptions that newcomers bring crime and violence into the neighborhood.

The people who live in Kensington, Port Richmond, and Olney balance these various contradictory aspects of intergroup dynamics as they play out their lives. When class, color, and experientially based notions of social structure or definitions of racism clash with each other, community residents often react with frustration and anger. Yet in other cases people move with little comment through different contexts where understandings and behaviors regarding difference vary radically.

Newcomer Responses to Established Structures and Expectations

Being a newcomer to the United States means constantly feeling out of balance. Always unsure of language ability—we have seen numerous times when newcomers stayed away from events or settings, afraid that their English would not be understood—they also fear that they do not quite understand the rules of this country. Every day brings a constant comparison between life in the homeland and the way of life here, a feeling held by middle-class Poles and Koreans, in particular. For example, one young Korean woman reports how her uncle became bitter because he had to work long hours in his small store here to earn a living, compared to a more professional life in Korea. Poles enjoy the abundance of goods, yet decry the level of education their children receive, dirt on the streets, and the lack of high culture.

Newcomer Networks

Newcomers often respond to the uncertainty and the contradictions between the promise of their new lives in the United States and fond recollections of home by seeking out the culture and people of their homelands. One '68 wave Polish émigré reported:

You're in K-Mart, you know, an American store, and you hear someone speaking Polish, you chime in and the next thing you know you start saying "Where are you from?" and so on. . . . So these people who are from Poland, they kind of feel like they're not alone.

The most popular event at a Kensington festival was the traditional Puerto Rican roast pig. Both the Olney and Saint Ignatius ethnic nights drew mostly people from the country whose culture was being celebrated that evening. At the joint Saint Ignatius event, people from different countries mostly ate food from their homeland.

Newcomers respond to the contradictory messages that they should work hard and achieve in the United States yet not eclipse their American hosts by pulling farther into their own networks. Established residents, in turn, see this turning inward as cliquishness or failure to assimilate. To them, the new immigrants are violating the "good immigrant" model by failing to become American. They also view insularity among newcomers as violating rules of fairness and, in some cases, as a kind of racism. On the other hand, established residents have their own cliques based on long-standing networks and fear of decline. The new immigrants are also likely to view established residents' unease with foreignness as further reason to maintain and strengthen ties with the homeland.

Children were sent to language school to keep up the connections between generations and with the homeland. Adults kept friendships within the group and encouraged the same behavior in their children. As one Polish man reported, "People from Poland have the same values." A Korean remarked:

I have American friends [meaning white] and I like my American friends. But I am not as close to them as I am to my Korean friends—you sleep over at their house, you tell them everything, you are really, really close.

Even for these children of newcomers, who fit into U.S. society, life involves moving through contradictory situations. Older immigrants find that they want to embrace their new country, yet the actions of established residents and their own yearnings for home propel them into situations and feelings that keep them apart from native-born residents. Like this young Korean, many newcomer children and youth have ongoing friendships with established residents, yet feel more comfortable with people from their own background. These multiple interpretations of the behavior of both immigrants and the native born leads to contradictions that serve to accentuate ethnicity and to push the younger generation toward acting more like established "Americans."

As they negotiate the back-and-forth relationship between immigrant culture and U.S. society, the children's lives become an example of creating a unified existence that embraces many different contradictions. Their attitudes and behaviors reflect this double existence. Both perceptions of homeland culture and ways of being American are transformed as newcomers meld old and new.

Foreign-Language Use

Language ability is a particular problem for newcomers. Most note that established residents are generally intolerant of people who speak broken English, or even of those whose grammar and vocabulary is good but who speak with an accent. Newcomers quickly realize that established residents equate an accent with the stereotypical uneducated, impoverished immigrant (Schneider 1990b; Schneider 1988a and 1988b). Like Gladys, they find that established residents will make newcomers wait for the few overworked multilingual employees, rather than try to communicate directly with them. Gladys's view that established Americans' lack of ability to deal with other languages smacks of favoritism is fairly common, and this assumption further pushes newcomers toward people from their homelands. Newcomers often react to established residents' assumptions that inability to speak English perfectly means no fluency at all by staying away from English-dominant settings. Others will come, but not participate in the conversation out of fear that their opinions will be discounted. A woman of Polish descent who had grown up in South America complained that she had to try twice as hard to become involved in an established organization because "they think that you are stupid if you speak with an accent."

Other immigrants intentionally use their native language as a way to identify familiar people from home or to cement ethnic solidarity. The Pole listening for Polish in the K-Mart is one example of this trend. During a conversation between two staff members at a Puerto Rican organization and a Puerto Rican field-worker, the three women changed from Spanish to English constantly, often within the same sentence. Since all three were completely bilingual, the change of language served to cement solidarity among Latinas as well as to ease communication.

Much of the perception of foreignness by established residents focuses on language. Those who speak only English worry that newcomers are intentionally excluding them when they speak their native language. Candy described her coworkers as rude and suspicious when they spoke Spanish at work. An established resident boy in the Polish nationalities parish school reported that two Polish boys must be talking about him when they spoke to each other in Polish. In schools and workplaces, on the street, and in their homes, established residents in all three neighborhoods voice the same concern about newcomers speaking their own language. Most feel that newcomers should speak their own language in their own homes, but use English in mixed settings if they are capable of speaking the language. While Philadelphia does not have the same kind of formal "English only" efforts as other places in the United States, similar sentiments are expressed by working-class established residents of all colors.

Established residents' fears that the Koreans were "taking over" by erecting the Korean street signs is another example of this view. They also stated that the "government" did not provide foreign-language signs for their ancestors when they came to the United States.

Like Patrick, many feel that the Puerto Ricans or "Spanish" are favored. White established residents in particular see multilanguage efforts as demonstrating preference for nonwhites. Poles complain that the signs in the stores are in Spanish and English, but not in Polish. Sometimes complaints about Polish versus Spanish are combined with perceptions of the differences between past treatment of immigrants and the present situation:

> When my mother and father came here they had it very hard. But these Spanish people, they have everything written for them in Spanish and English.

Established émigrés from Poland, especially people who came to the United States during the 1950s, are particularly angered by special efforts to provide services to newcomers in their own language. People who adapted to the United States during the crucible of the McCarthy era, when any "foreign" behavior or connections revealed the taint of "anti-Americanism," especially resent special efforts to accommodate people who speak another language. They expect newcomers to have to become American quickly, as they did.

Defining Insider and Outsider

While established organizations crave newcomer participation, they make it hard for them to feel welcome at meetings. People like the Polish woman who had grown up in South America described above find themselves moving between cultures—working to be American in the context of the school, yet making sure that their children learn about their Polish heritage at home.

Like this woman, some émigrés will try twice as hard to become part of an established organization. Participation is key to the contradiction. While newcomers feel that their foreignness is highlighted in established settings, longtime residents sometimes do not even recognize those who participate regularly in established organizations as newcomers. For example, in one conversation the school principal called the Polish woman an established resident and had no idea of when she had come to the United States. She also characterized one '68 wave family in which the parents did not participate in the school as newcomer. Another family, where the wife regularly volunteers in the library and teaches English as a Second Language, were considered established residents. In reality, both families came to the United States around the same time, both speak Polish at home, and the bilingual children in both families are used as "language buddies" for newcomer pupils in the school.

Since she teaches ESL, this '68 Wave émigré is thought of both as newcomer and established resident by the school. While valued for her newcomer characteristics (among them her ability to speak Polish), her participation in school activities with native-born parents makes her an established resident in the eyes of the school. Contradictions come together to make a unified whole: school staff recognize the newcomer status of this woman when necessary, yet ignore it when attempting to define newcomers as people who do not participate in the school. Staff easily move between labels without worrying about contradictions.

The Tyranny of Context

Time and again we found that an immigrant was defined as either "foreigner" or "insider" based on the amount of time for which she or he participated in an event. The Latinas who worked at the Saint Ignatius festival are one example of this trend. Since the immigrant participants in these events strongly note that they feel like outsiders even as established residents increasingly trust them, this is another example of contradictory interpretations of the same behavior. These examples also show unintended consequences as established residents' genuine desire for newcomer participation is contradicted by their expectation that recent arrivals must play by the established residents' unspoken rules.

Our description of everyday events highlights ways that individuals develop very different relationships and act in very different ways, depending on the context. In Port Richmond, people have African American, Puerto Rican, Korean, Polish, or white friends at work, home, or school, yet stick with those from their own race or nationality in their neighborhoods. On the other hand, residents of mixed neighborhoods in Kensington and Olney get along well, yet fear African Americans and Puerto Ricans who live in other neighborhoods. In each case, contradictions appear when the realities of the context differ from expectations established in different settings.

What longtime residents expect of new immigrants clashes with the realities in multicultural schools. Poles complain that everyone thinks that they are stupid, yet the Polish émigré children are recognized by Polish American teachers as the best students in the school. One newcomer Polish eighth grader responded to her frustrated ESL teacher's question about why she did not speak English in school (although she had mostly monolingual, English-speaking, established resident friends outside school) by exclaiming, "Everybody knows that I don't speak English here." Her contradictory use of language became logical when viewed in the context of school expectations of newcomers. Out of school, she is rapidly becoming American. She takes public transportation to the malls, speaks English, dresses like an American teenager, and has native-born friends. But in the context of the school, these behaviors and perspectives blend with her behavior and view of herself as a foreigner. The school's practice of assuming that newcomers do not speak English bolsters this contradiction. Instead of encouraging children to learn English and blend into the established population, school messages instead divide newcomers from established residents and encourage new children to use Polish instead of English. Like Mary Hanson and others described in Chapter 5, context also determines behavior for established residents.

Our research highlights the complexity of intergroup relations. On a day-to-day basis, individuals respond to contradictions with confusion and occasional anger. Well-meaning people in schools, workplaces, or institutions bravely attempt to develop solutions to complex problems. As in the various examples of unintended consequences discussed here, deliberate efforts to cross boundaries can backfire. Like the mixed responses to foreign-language use, individuals' attempts to negotiate their world can also have unintended effects. Yet our research shows that people do traverse the complicated landscape of intergroup relations in Philadelphia successfully on many occasions. This ability to maneuver in a contradictory world shows the human power to adapt, as well as highlighting the importance of simultaneous contradictions in everyday life.

Simultaneous Contradictions

Most established residents view newcomers to their neighborhoods with a combination of positive curiosity and fear of the unknown and different "other" (Goode 1990). For example, at the annual Olney doll show an older established resident switched back and forth from positive to negative judgments. After commenting that Koreans made lovely dolls, she said that the new "Chinese" (Korean) neighbor's house "looked like a storefront," and then added that the Korean children in her neighborhood were better behaved than the "little white hoods" of a generation before. Newcomer whites in Olney welcome the diversity of new immigrant families while complaining about strange cooking smells and people who put out the garbage on the wrong day. Recall the Polish American children's fascination with posters in Polish, even as they expressed fear about newcomer language use. Individuals play out different aspects of these contradictory feelings and actions depending on the context of the moment.

Each attempt to blame someone else for problems among groups relies on one set of elements in a complex and contradictory situation. In all cases, each statement about people who are different is partially correct. The white working-class residents in Olney, Kensington, and Port Richmond can behave in ways that hurt people of color. The Korean street sign incident was an example of whites defacing property because it represented a foreign "other." White youths at one Kensington playground have repeatedly attacked Puerto Ricans in their neighborhood. But people of color from all groups can behave in ways that hurt whites as well. The killing of Sean Daily is but one example. Koreans creating closed shops intended exclusively for other Koreans and telling established residents that they could not possibly afford to make purchases there is also a form of discrimination. All races and nationality groups practice hostile behavior toward others.

Power relations differ among groups in different settings. White established residents dominate many organizations, yet newcomers or people of color can control settings as well. The contradiction between Polish American control of one dance program (described in Chapter 6), while another troupe performed in the same room, with the same general goal, and before some of the same audience members shows how control can vary from context to context. People move through these different settings, changing their own actions to fit the environment.

More important, the same people who talk and behave in prejudiced and exclusionary ways can also often appear completely open to persons from other groups. Like one Kensington girl who plays jump rope with African Americans and Puerto Ricans on her block but makes prejudiced comments in the Polish parish school, it is possible to be friendly toward newcomers in one context and prejudiced in another. Mary Hanson's ideas and behavior change as she moves from her block to the antiracist group where she volunteers. Peer pressure and variations in rules in different settings shape behavior at a particular time, although they do not explain the whole range of behavior.

Recognizing difference can have both positive and negative connotations. At one factory, workers from different races joked about differences in physical appearance based on race in an ongoing, friendly banter. Remarks (laced with sexual innuendo) about stereotypical racial traits became a bonding device for men working together. Equivalent joking about difference occurs in the mixed teenage clubs. But the same statements become ethnic slurs and bigotry when used by teenagers from one group against people in their neighborhood from different ones. Both newcomers and established residents find that they walk a fine line between perceptions of prejudice and accommodation. Any remark can be interpreted as either racist or a sign of rapprochement between people from different backgrounds.

The Puerto Rican youth who incited the killing of Sean Daily came to Port Richmond to attend a multiracial gathering—a clear example of friendly mixing across groups. Both the Puerto Rican youths and the members of the playground gang in Kensington responsible for violence against Puerto Ricans in their community are "good" kids: they go to school and work, and few are active in the organized drug gangs. These youngsters are at once "good" and

"bad," depending on the situation of the moment. To quote a union representative in a very mixed factory:

> I've never been prejudiced a day in my life. With some of the work force
> that we have, most of them are real good friends inside. While outside
> they might kill each other, using that terminology. Maybe that was the
> wrong thing to say, that was not a good statement. In here they can be
> best of friends, but when they leave the plant, the whites go their way,
> the Blacks go their way. That's the way they live.

Everyone in these communities is prejudiced some of the time. Attempts to
avoid accusations of racism cause as much confusion and contrary statements
as not. The contradictory nature of class and race relations in the United States
adds to the disjuncture. Like this union representative, most working- and
middle-class whites in these three neighborhoods know African Americans and
Puerto Ricans who are friendly and hardworking—the working-class definition of a "good" person. They successfully work and study together in
multicultural settings. Yet the majority of people from all groups live in
largely segregated neighborhoods. They differentiate the "good" people from
other groups (whom they know from workplaces, schools, and shopping strips)
from the "bad" people from the same groups who live in the run-down
neighborhoods nearby. In the parlance of African American and Puerto Rican
Philadelphia, "bad" means the racist white working class. In mostly white Port
Richmond, "bad" refers to the crime, drug, and housing-abandonment problems evident in Kensington and North Philadelphia. As demonstrated in the
quotes about concern over neighborhood decline, it is possible for a man who
is active in multiethnic settings to fear that the movement of too many African
Americans and Puerto Ricans into his neighborhood will bring down property
values. Even in multicultural Olney, established residents fear that the "bad"
African Americans and Puerto Ricans will move in from other neighborhoods.
Looking at their views on people from different groups as a whole yields
numerous contradictions. African Americans also fear "street niggers," and
some established Puerto Ricans complain that "they don't like the Spanish."
No group represents a unified perspective.

Part of the contradiction in these communities is that no appropriate
language exists to bridge gaps between groups given the multiple messages
associated with race and class in the United States. On some level, both
working-class and middle-class people recognize differences within groups.
African Americans talk about "street niggers" giving African Americans a bad
name; whites talk about "white trash" who cause problems in their neighborhood. While African Americans were the feared "other" of the last generation
in Port Richmond, the "Spanish" are seen to cause most of the problems today.
As with any label, connotations that a particular neighborhood is bad are as

unfair as stereotypes about race. Yet they are used again and again in certain contexts.

Contrary to assumptions that racism is an attitude learned from prejudiced parents, people from all groups garner positive and negative understandings of race and nationality from their own experience:

> I can't understand my mother. I was raised not to be prejudiced. We had a very tolerant home. But now all my mother does is to complain about the way the Spanish are treated at the church. She says they do nothing for the church but get the best of everything. I can't believe I am hearing such prejudice from her.

Whites have actually seen neighborhoods decline as they become integrated. African Americans and Puerto Ricans experience hostile behavior from whites. Koreans who fear their African American patrons have experienced problems with them. One Korean who owns a store in a poor neighborhood commented that "even [some of] my good patrons shoplift. When I catch them, they just smile and put it back on the shelves." In each instance these views are reinforced by negative statements about people who are different from families, peers, teachers, and those depicted by the media.

Yet each set of these negative stereotypes confronts a different and equally positive set of beliefs and actions on all fronts. The residents of Port Richmond really do believe that situations and people should not be judged by class or color—witness the repeated statements that everyone is an individual and the denial of racial antipathy—even as they fear their neighbors from other groups. The levels of intermarriage and interracial dating attest to friendly mixing across all groups. Even the girls at the nationalities parish school state that "Spanish boys are sexier" and talk about going out with them. Symbols associated with the "Spanish," like the music of "La Bamba," are used over and over in events in Polish American Port Richmond. Polish émigrés are both the pushy foreigners of today who should Americanize quickly and the source of pride regarding ethnic identity. Koreans are both succeeding too quickly and failing to play by the rules, even as they are seen as acting out the American dream.

As they move through their daily lives, both newcomer and established residents in these neighborhoods alter their opinions and actions about others like chameleons. The most important point about simultaneous contradictions (Schneider 1989) is that people in the United States today are comfortable living contradictory lives. Everyone negotiates his or her way through disjointed settings without concern. People are aware of the contradictions in their lives, yet make no overt efforts to reconcile contradictory views or actions. We use contrasting models to make a particular point. No one seems overly concerned that elements of even the most binary oppositions contain internal features that contradict each other. We understand our world as made up of disparate parts that work together as a whole. For Port Richmond residents, the Puerto Rican caterer is a representative of violent outsiders when they need a lightning rod for anger about an act of aggression against one of their own; in another context, he is a nice local businessman. For Olney residents, Asian neighbors both make beautiful dolls and keep houses that look like storefronts.

Adults as well as children switch easily back and forth between descriptions of society based on structural inequality and those based on assumptions of equal opportunity for all. Most know at some level that there are very real variations in class within all racial and national groups. Most also believe that opportunity exists in the United States. Most community residents have encountered situations that exemplify both inequality and opportunity. These contradictions become an integral part of their lives. It is the interaction between the various contradictions that creates both positive and negative interactions among people from different groups in these communities. In Chapter 8, we examine aspects that influence the mix between positive and negative interactions among newcomers and established residents. We also suggest ways that organizers and policymakers can use these contradictions to create better communities.

CHAPTER 8

Strategies for Action

Interaction patterns in Philadelphia between new immigrants and established residents, whites and people of color, are complex and contradictory. The economic and social history of the city shapes the ways in which people from different backgrounds come together. New immigrants come to a city with historically defined white ethnic neighborhoods and a segregated African American population. The prevalence of affordable housing in Philadelphia allows upwardly mobile people of color and new immigrants to move into neighborhoods once dominated by whites from a variety of backgrounds. At the same time, a white population whose image of African Americans and Latinos rests on a perception of historical poverty in those communities reacts by either facing newcomers with fear and hostility, moving away to newer and whiter neighborhoods in the Northeast or the suburbs, or accommodating newcomers. As the city's infrastructure deteriorates—because of economic shifts, changes in federal urban-funding policies, increasing pressures on city services related to the drug epidemic and increased poverty, and management problems—all residents react to a city bureaucracy increasingly seen as allocating city resources along racial lines.

Understanding the factors that promote harmony or create tensions among people from different countries, races, neighborhoods, and classes in Philadelphia is itself a complicated procedure. As documented throughout this book, the life choices, strategies, and perceptions of individuals are profoundly affected by both historical and present-day economic structures and power dynamics. Citywide models involving immigration and race relations further shape both activities and ideas about people from different backgrounds. Yet macrolevel factors alone do not determine events in a local neighborhood, school, factory, or household. City- or worldwide economic structures or ideologies are experienced through the prism of the local neighborhood and the primary institutions that people experience in everyday life: the block, workplace, school, shopping strip, church, and so on. Each of these institutions offers individuals a divergent view of power, along with many examples of the lifestyles and beliefs of people from different groups. For example, Inez Gutierrez and Ester Ramos align with the whites in their workplace against African Americans. In Ester's office, African Americans are dominant in the power structure. On the other hand, the Puerto Rican nationalist organizations align with other people of color against a white district attorney and the white working-class residents of Port Richmond, who are seen as "the other side" in conflicts between Latino and white youth. Established residents of Olney and Kensington see middle-class Koreans and Indians in control of shopping strips, yet compare them to struggling refugees. New Poles provide much of the low paid labor in Port Richmond, but they are also the successful, "pushy" newcomers who demand higher standards from the parish school while not contributing to the church.

Individuals form and re-form their understandings of people from different groups based on power structures and economic realities present in the larger society, combined with the many different power relations existing in the settings in which they live out their lives. They also bring personal views of the world and the people in it derived from growing up in a particular class, neighborhood, and ethnic milieu. The result is interaction among many-faceted individuals living in a contradictory world. These complicated dynamics reveal the need for analysis that incorporates both macro- and micro-level dynamics.

Our data also show the flexibility of individuals. The people described in this study have experienced much change and been exposed to many different dynamics. They are capable of learning and changing regardless of age. But their potential for growth is rooted in their pasts. It is impossible to deny earlier negative or positive experiences with economic structures or people from different groups. These past interactions profoundly influence strategies for change. It is also imperative to understand the many economic and social pressures that people living in the United States encounter everyday. These are busy people, balancing the needs of work and home in an increasingly precarious economy. Their response to persons from different groups—and especially to organized efforts to increase harmony—reflect these pressures.

Factors Influencing Intergroup Dynamics

This chapter focuses on strategies for change. First, we review the factors influencing these strategies.

The Economy

The changing economy limits financial opportunity and lifestyle for some residents of Philadelphia. As factories move away and are only partially replaced by service industries, which offer fewer benefits and lower salaries for workers with limited skills and education, people from all groups feel increasing stress. The changing economy disproportionately affects people of color, who have historically been denied entry into education and employment, and new migrants from Puerto Rico and countries throughout the world, whose resources are limited by lack of education and skills attained in their native countries, lack of contacts here, or structures that pressure them into low-level jobs (Sassen-Koob 1980; Portes and Bach 1985; Schneider 1988a).

At the same time, other new immigrants enter the United States with competitive skills and capital from home under changed immigration laws. People of color move into professional and managerial jobs through limits on discrimination and affirmative action. Korean merchants thrive in retail trade throughout the city. People from India and some Latinos and new Poles quickly move into professional jobs. These new developments alter the economic and social landscape of Philadelphia, running counter to established residents' expectations of newcomers and people of color.

Race, Ethnicity, and Immigration

The various dynamics of racial and ethnic-identity formation and cross-group interaction in Philadelphia are equally confusing. Both newcomers and established residents live in a country where resources and power relations have historically favored whites and limited possibilities for newcomers and people of color. The legacy of racial divisions continues in ongoing class disparities and discrimination. Yet changes in the past twenty years have complicated the picture of apartheid described in the model of structural racism. The civil-rights movement has broadened the spectrum of intragroup class divisions, which have always existed in the United States. At the same time, the Black-power movement and the resurgence of ethnicity among people from European backgrounds continually reinforce the idea that all Americans have a subgroup identity and that resources are allocated according to race and ethnicity.

The multiple experiences with race of the last thirty years have created several definitions of racial groups and numerous strategies for creating balance among U.S. citizens. Individuals and groups characterize race and racism, equality and privilege, and rights and responsibilities in different ways. In addition to understanding varying economic and social situations, people must negotiate multiple definitions and deal with the fact that different actors in a conversation about intergroup relations may not share basic definitions, much less conceptions of appropriate solutions to inequality.

Newcomers and established residents respond to these pressures in a variety of ways. As with the African American Creole population in Louisiana during the 1970s (Dominguez 1986, 172), some people consolidate identity into the racial dyad of white and people of color, claiming rights to resources based on group identity. Puerto Ricans, stressing nationalism and poverty, build structures to aid their community. Koreans attempt to face the world with a united front, complaining about racism directed against them and responding to other people of color with scholarship programs and award dinners designed to ameliorate tensions based on economic inequity. Newcomers respond to the supposition of a racial dyad by absorbing existing prejudices or insisting on their differences from available categories. Like Haitians asserting their national identity when portrayed as African Americans (Stafford 1987; Foner 1987; Glick-Schiller and Fouran 1990), new Poles remind people that they are Polish, not Polish American, and people from Central and South America show through actions and words that they are different from Puerto Ricans. Both children and adults come to understand that they should have an ethnic identity. They also learn quickly that appropriate expressions of ethnicity include special cultural presentations, holiday traditions, and food, but that speaking another language in public generates expressions of hostility, fear, or superiority from many established residents.

Like the priests at Saint Ignatius, the human-relations experts from throughout the city, and the whites who see the variety in their midst as either exotic or a threat from alien "others," established people and structures can reinforce divisions across groups. When established residents repeatedly refer to persons from different backgrounds as members of separate groups, newcomers develop comparable structures in response to these categories. Like the situation in Borders High School described earlier, a proliferation of separate groups sometimes creates more distance between people from different backgrounds. Individuals in diverse settings find themselves walking a fine line between celebrating diversity and fostering intergroup antagonisms.

Both newcomers and established residents develop their own patterns of resistance to people or institutions stressing boundaries they consider inappropriate. Established residents emphasize a national identity through requesting U.S. flags on streetcorners and at ethnic food tables, displaying heightened patriotism, resisting discussions of race, and labeling themselves as "American." Newcomers stress that they come from a specific country, resisting attempts to lump all groups together. Latinos speak Spanish in mixed settings to show solidarity in an English-speaking world.

Variety and intragroup divisions continually crop up to complicate the vision of an economic hierarchy divided simply along subgroup lines. People from all groups recognize class divisions within populations historically defined as monolithic. Although whites talk about good and bad African Americans and consider new immigrants outsiders in one context and insiders in another, they work, study, and live amicably with people from many groups. As documented throughout the literature on white ethnics (di Leonardo 1984; Waters 1990), established whites pick and choose identities from mixed backgrounds to fit a contextual need or expectation of identity. Contradictions abound among macrolevel structures and ideologies, microlevel contexts, and individual beliefs and actions.

Neither race nor class alone accounts for the social and economic patchwork of present-day Philadelphia. Race, nationality, and class come together in a constantly changing dynamic to affect life chances and interaction patterns for newcomers and established residents. Olney, Kensington, and Port Richmond each contain "white ethnic" established residents with similar educational backgrounds and work experiences. Yet the whites in each neighborhood understand people from various groups very differently. The Koreans and Latinos in Olney are very unlike the Puerto Ricans whom Kensington and Port Richmond residents encounter every day. The structural dynamics of each neighborhood, school, and workplace influences who develops friendships with whom, where, and why.

Creating equal justice would be simple if, like in the parable by Derrick Bell (1987, 215–20), the discovery of "slave scrolls," which gave African American people resources for pride and ingenuity, could transform people of color who have lived in poverty for generations. If all whites hated people of color and did everything in their power to maintain superiority, it might not be easy to create equality and harmony, but the solution would be simple and clear: give power to the disenfranchised people of color. But class and race relations are not uniform or simple in the United States—vast ranges of both power and attitudes exist within all racial, national, and immigrant groups. History and present-day conditions at once contradict and compound expectations and day-to-day realities. New elements are added as new groups enter the United States; the responses of political and economic structures to movements for equality further complicate the picture. Residents of these three neighborhoods move through contradictory contexts and ideologies, picking and choosing responses depending on structural needs and their own understandings of events. Creating positive movements for change must take this complexity into account.

Intergroup Understandings and Responses to Cross-Group Tensions

The patterns of day-to-day interaction and the contradictory attitudes and actions concerning race and nationality described in the last three chapters reveal complicated and shifting understandings of diversity within the three communities that we studied. The groups and contexts that individuals experience in their daily lives are structured by kinship and friendship networks, work or school contexts, neighborhood, and worldview. Positive and negative behaviors and attitudes shift with age and the setting. None of the individuals or communities encountered in this study displayed a monolithic or unitary understanding of race and nationality.

Definitions of "friend from a different background" and "hostile alien other" change over time and depend on context. Even the most prejudiced people (from all backgrounds) often live in mixed neighborhoods or work and study in mixed settings. The neighbor, classmate, or coworker is classified as "good," while people from the same group who live two blocks away remain hostile outsiders who may breed crime, neighborhood deterioration, or racism. Incidents of tension across groups, such as the killings of Stephen Crespo and Sean Daily, often involve youths from adjacent neighborhoods attacking others from a different group whom they may never have met or know only from brief encounters. On the other hand, the talk about racial or ethnic attributes, which is either carefully hidden in many mixed settings or becomes the source of humor among friendly associates, often rebounds as angry slurs when neighbors or close associates fight over an issue that may have little to do with race. The prevalence of such talk fuels the use of racial epithets among people who rarely think about each other in terms of background characteristics. Police and human-relations workers constantly report disentangling disputes over cars or other simple matters that take on racial overtones that may be regretted the next day. Contradictory ways to talk and feel about difference are a constant source of confusion. Yet most encounters in mixed settings are genuinely positive.

These contradictions highlight the importance of understanding specific dynamics when addressing issues of race, class, and nationality. Contact alone is not the solution to intergroup tensions. Negative views of Korean store owners in Olney and of Puerto Ricans in Kensington come from day-to-day negative experiences with people from these groups. Whites in Port Richmond have no opinion of Asians because they have little contact with them. At the same time, however, the same whites have positive perceptions of African Americans from their experience of them as coworkers. The same confusing dynamic is true of Puerto Ricans who have both positive and negative views of whites and African Americans. It also applies to Koreans, who protect their stores against expected hostility from African Americans with bulletproof glass or who pull guns on rowdy white schoolgirls in Olney, while developing positive relationships with Puerto Rican customers and employees in Kensington.

Each of these examples highlights the changes in the three neighborhoods. A generation ago, whites in Port Richmond and Kensington "would draw down their shades and not answer the door" if an African American came into the neighborhood. Now people in these communities hold both positive and negative views of African Americans. Latinos are the new "hostile other," but even this dynamic continues to change. Attitudes in Olney are even more complex.

The dominant models for encouraging positive interaction across groups rely on assumptions that prejudice is an overweening mind-set, one learned at an early age that lurks just below the surface for adults negotiating their way through increasingly diverse life situations. The objective in workshops on "unlearning racism" or "exploring cultural diversity" is to replace negative stereotypes with positive information about people from other groups.

Programs for cultural diversity are often targeted at young children, because experts think that stereotypes are developed at an early age from messages taught at home. Yet, as described in Chapter 5, children get along amicably with people from all groups. They are often the brokers between adults from different populations.

Children learn early to save face by moving between positive interaction with people from other groups and professing group solidarity. For example, one white Kensington resident attending the nationalities parish school in Port Richmond regularly plays with African American and Puerto Rican children on a multicultural playground. The African American jump-rope rhymes that she has learned from these children make her particularly popular in her all-white school. Yet when discussing her neighborhood at school, she insists that her block is all-white and that all of her neighbors are prejudiced. In the educational context as she perceives it, being prejudiced is a good thing.

But as these children reach the age of eleven or twelve many start to break up into more racially and ethnically divided cliques (Goode, Schneider, and Blanc 1992). They express prejudices against people from the same groups that they played with as children, and they fear for their own futures. Teenage cliquishness contradicts the friendly mixing of children, and it is often in itself contradictory, since these same teenagers maintain some friends across groups.

Like the African American youngsters who belong to the integrated football team, subgroup teenagers learn to move between contradictory contexts when negotiating everyday life. The team representative reports that the African American players are "fine" the day after experiencing insults from African American children on other teams. In the mixed context of the football club, they have learned to get along well with their peers from other groups. The Puerto Rican youths responsible for killing Sean Daily probably moved comfortably through mixed settings as well. The Daily case is a particularly stark example of people living lives full of contradictions. These "good" kids became violent perpetrators of racially motivated aggression. The same thing occurred in the Crespo killing. Francis Skullin and his friends initially helped the Puerto Rican youngsters push the stolen car off the street. The shift shows how individuals both practice prejudiced behaviors and thoughts and try to reach accommodation with people from other groups.

As Barbara Fields (1990, 101) reminds us, "since race is not genetically programmed, racial prejudice can not be genetically programmed either but, like race itself, must arise historically." In other words, racial prejudice comes from the experience of individuals raised in a society divided unequally along color lines. Attitudes tend to reflect historical conditions, but they also change as society changes. The social and economic structures that individuals in Olney, Kensington, and Port Richmond encounter as they live out their lives reveal a collage of mixed messages. Fields goes on to say:

> It will not do to suppose that a powerful group captures the hearts and minds of the less powerful, inducing them to "internalize" the ruling ideology. To suppose that is to imagine ideology handed down like an old garment, passed on like a germ, spread like a rumor, or imposed like a dress code. Any of these would presuppose that an experience of social relations can be transmitted by the same means, which is impossible. (1990, 113)

Neither ideology nor social structure is a fixed and immutable element. The residents of these three neighborhoods explain how their communities have changed over time. Their descriptions of change and the ways that they re-form their lives based on these alterations show mixed positive and negative understandings of the relationship between diversity and change. Nor can focusing either on ideology or social structure alone resolve the tensions evident in cross-group relations in the United States. The answer does not lie simply in self-help (Brooks 1990) or in teaching about diversity through "culture at a distance."

Standard models designed to teach youth about diversity assume that if people improve their self-images through personal empowerment or learning about their own roots, their terror of others who are different will slip away. We also caution against the emphasis on self-esteem in many of the programs on diversity. For example, as noted in Chapter 6, an event organizer commented that Colombian Neighbors Night raised the self-esteem of participants, even though few outsiders came to share the festivities. For new immigrants, the issue is rarely self-esteem, but attempts to gain respect from established residents who view them, according to the "good immigrant" model, as uneducated peasants looking to succeed in the United States. Strategies should target sharing information with established residents on the actual backgrounds of new immigrants in order to generate understanding of actual experience rather than on celebrating heritage.

Issues are more complicated with African American and Puerto Rican young people, who experience hostility based on class and race every day. The whole African American cultural dynamic of "Are you dissing [disrespecting] me?" centers on a lack of respect, not simply low self-esteem. Untangling the issue involves facing the rage experienced by these youths. It also means understanding where the concept of "respecting yourself" intersects with acting in a way that is respected by the "dominant white culture." Creating programming to celebrate heritage is an important and powerful way to establish a base for people. But living in the United States increasingly means crossing cultures and classes every day. Individual self-esteem must connect with mutual respect and responsibility—promoting efforts to create communities, not simply demanding rights or encouraging people to respect themselves while they live and work in situations where they receive no respect from others.

Suggestions for Action

This book has described a number of persons from varying class, race, national, and ethnic backgrounds. Since our neighborhoods were very mixed, individuals had frequent and very diverse experiences with people from other groups. The people of Kensington, Olney, and Port Richmond included:

Working- and middle-class whites with limited experience in growing up with people of color who nonetheless sought contact with persons from other groups. This category also includes some whites who grew up in integrated settings. These individuals generally approached newcomers and people of color with eager curiosity and sometimes a certain naïveté about the range of feelings toward whites held by some newcomers and people of color and about class structures among different groups.

Poor and working- and middle-class whites who encountered people of color and new immigrants in mixed settings but who lived in primarily white neighborhoods. These are the white ethnics most often accused of racism. As discussed throughout this study, these individuals may retain hostile attitudes toward people of color based on a combination of negative experiences and prejudice taught by family, peers, and others. But they also usually have friends and contacts across groups, some mixed attitudes toward others, and a general perception that "everyone should be judged as an individual."

Working- and middle-class African Americans and Latinos who live and work in mixed settings. While networks of kinship and close friends are usually segregated by race, these persons are generally open to interaction across groups and sometimes hostile toward the poorer portions of their own communities. On the other hand, some of the most articulate supporters of race- or nationality-based organizations are middle-class people of color.

Poor established African Americans and Latinos. The economically disadvantaged people of color encountered in this research had experience with whites because they either lived, worked, or went to school with them. We found a high level of frustration with and suspicion toward whites and middle-class people of color among this population.

But, like their white counterparts, their attitudes and actions also contained many contradictions.

Middle-class immigrants. Newcomer Poles, Koreans, and Indians who can translate their skills or educational resources into success in the United States either bring negative expectations of African Americans with them or quickly absorb them upon arrival. This is particularly true of the Koreans and Poles who work or travel through poor African American communities frequently. Some nonwhite immigrants also learn to fear whites, particularly working-class whites. While less suspicious of them, these newcomers feel the general U.S. intolerance of different languages and cultures. They constantly perform a mental balancing act between two cultures, languages, and countries. Their children also experience two worlds, with varying difficulty translating between them.

Poor and working-class immigrants. Newcomer Latinos, Poles, Southeast Asians, and Koreans with fewer skills and less education than their middle-class compatriots who worked in the informal economy or the secondary sector for men and women from their homelands were perhaps the most isolated persons encountered in this study. These newcomers generally fear people from other groups and are cautious because of their inability to speak English. They are also the most economically vulnerable population that we studied. However, their children generally cross group boundaries and frequently become culture brokers for their parents. As teenagers, the poor newcomers from Asia, Puerto Rico, or Central and South American countries often adopt the racial attitudes of established African Americans and Puerto Ricans. In some cases, this includes an assumption that all whites are racist and strong support for the structural-racism model.

The Changing Relations Project did not include people with little contact with persons from other groups:

Working-, middle-, or upper-class whites with little experience with new immigrants or people of color. In the urban United States, the number of persons who grow up in almost completely white settings has decreased steadily over the last decade. Yet Philadelphia and its suburbs maintain a high level of segregation. Many whites live, learn, and work in all white settings. But a large number of the students and workers find themselves in increasingly mixed settings over time. As expressed in studies at Berkeley (Duster 1991), these individuals, like the "diversity seekers" in Olney, are often curious about people from different backgrounds; they are also sometimes cautious of people of color because of media images of the underclass or negative experiences.

Whites who moved away from integrating neighborhoods. We encountered some people from this group in the stories of friends and relatives of those who had moved away from Kensington and Olney as people of color moved in. These individuals are most likely to fit the stereotype of the racist white. But as stressed throughout this book, these attitudes reflect actual negative experiences coupled with a prejudiced worldview absorbed from a variety of sources.

Economically disadvantaged people of color who live in segregated neighborhoods. If current economic trends continue, these individuals are likely to remain the most isolated and vulnerable population in the United States. Work related to this research has included teaching workshops on racism for youths in the juvenile-justice system. Children in these classes uniformly expressed anger toward whites and middle-class people of color who "acted white." Since whites had "got it over" on people of color "back in the day" of slavery, people of color now had a right to "get one over" on white people—a variation on the structural-racism model. They assumed that all whites were racists. Since the only whites they were likely to encounter on a one-to-one basis were public employees or workers in the criminal-justice system, their hostility toward whites and the middle class in general was not surprising.

The various groups described here require the use of very different techniques to develop intercultural understanding and awareness. Whites and people of color who have limited experience with persons from other groups but who are generally positive about interaction need to be exposed to different information and experiences from whites, newcomers, and people of color who have generally negative experience or understandings of those from other groups. As described in Chapter 7, middle-class people are generally more supportive of the idea of diversity than working-class or poor populations, who see themselves as struggling with other groups for crumbs from a very meager economic pie. Attempts to build community among people who live, work, or study in mixed settings require very different programs from attempts to bring people from segregated communities and different classes together.

Creating Appropriate Diversity Workshops

In our critique of "culture at a distance" programs in Chapters 3 and 5, we observed that these events sometimes foster competition and conflict rather than understanding. We showed how these presentations generally rely on safe aspects of reified culture like food, costume, and holiday traditions. In addition, "culture" from the country of origin generally portrays static, preindustrial traditions. These are very different from the cultures of societies transformed by modern technology and familiar with U.S. cultural artifacts, which generally supply new immigrants to this country. A host of academic studies supports our observations that the day-to-day lifestyles among both newcomers and established residents are shaped as much by conditions in the United States as by culture from a home country. As succeeding generations grow up here, their subgroup habits are increasingly transformed by residence in the United States.

Discussions of a group's experience in this country should take into account the class and cultural background of a particular immigration wave, as well as its experience in the United States. As with the various Polish immigration waves, common bonds grow from shared historical experience and familiarity with a particular lifestyle rather than from a few cultural habits or ideas taught at home. Presentations on diversity should incorporate these understandings of group formation and change, rather than recite different cultural styles.

Nevertheless, there are particular differences in habit, style, and belief among both newcomer and established residents from different backgrounds. The best way to introduce people to diversity is through personal life stories and a range of experiences rather than a fixed set of cultural attributes. Economic and social history is just as important as present-day culture. Understanding the processes that shaped a country or subgroup and the class range of people who emigrated to the United States or migrated from one area of the country to another partially explains current socioeconomic dynamics.

Having individuals tell their life stories is a way to break through the "us versus them" dialogues that often develop in communities where a negative focus event, such as an interracial gang fight, has occurred. Bringing people together in small groups to share stories and expectations about the alien "other" creates empathy and begins to work through the frustrations that lead to violence. Talking through different aspects of racial dynamics by using stories and personal experience also gets past the fear and ambivalence Americans experience when asked to discuss difference. Discussions that rely on personal stories and shared talk also get past the idea that there are carefully chosen "right" and "wrong" answers about race and nationality.

In encouraging discussion, it is important to understand the positive and negative experiences that all people in the United States have regarding group boundaries. Our examination of newcomers seeking faces and cultural attributes from "back home" and the examples that we have presented of development through group solidarity show the positive aspects of people from similar backgrounds working together for the betterment of all. But turning in toward one's own people can lead to feelings of moral superiority for both newcomers and established residents. Newcomers sometimes see the lifeways of their homeland as better than the unfamiliar U.S. culture. Established residents facing loss of their familiar world as the economy changes and new people move in cling to known rules as the "right" way to think and behave. Newcomers and established residents and members of majority and minority groups have all experienced these negative aspects of group solidarity as exclusionary and often discriminatory. It is important to validate these feelings while touching on the positive aspects of group solidarity.

Affirmative action and antidiscrimination legislation came along at the same time as deindustrialization. Since these changes in public policy were quickly followed by recessions and the Reagan-era attack on funding programs for education (which had encouraged economic mobility for the white working class), many whites see minority gains as directly related to a downturn in their own economic prospects. People of color view the same historical events as reinforcing expectations that whites never really meant to open up society to people from different races. These feelings cannot be ignored or discounted as racism. Persons discussing the issue of equal opportunity must explain the economic and policy factors that have influenced individual mobility throughout the history of the United States.

As documented throughout this book, the range of economic variations within internally or externally defined subgroups is the least comprehended factor for people from all populations. Assumptions that all people of color or newcomers come from impoverished backgrounds, or that all whites are rich and powerful, are as damaging as assumptions that all African Americans are lazy, Jews stingy, and Asian newcomers superstudents obedient to the dictates of Confucian cultural systems. Most desegregated schools, workplaces, and neighborhoods bring together people from similar class backgrounds. Even in diverse settings like a large school or workplace, concrete interactions are usually limited to the department or ability track of a particular group. People from similar class backgrounds see those from other races or nationalities whom they encounter daily as being similar to themselves. Group differences may seem irrelevant in these contexts. But like the Borders High School students who view people in different academic tracks as separate and potentially dangerous, or the established residents in Olney and Port Richmond who often have negative encounters with poor people of color, class and race/nationality often combine to create negative stereotypes. It is paramount to bring people across class boundaries when discussing diversity, as well as to recognize that their negative views of those from different groups often come from real-life bad experiences. Programs to encourage interaction and awareness across groups must take class into account, as well as race, ethnicity, or nationality. Bringing people from diverse racial or national backgrounds and different economic groups together must be done carefully, in settings that give no one the advantage.

Crossing the Great Divide

The Changing Relations Project deliberately excluded populations that were completely isolated from people from different groups. Yet the levels of segregation continue to rise, especially for the poor African American community. Such isolation is also increasingly true of Puerto Ricans in Philadelphia. Our research strategy and theoretical position stress that macro- and microlevel analyses are equally important in understanding intergroup relations. It is important to take into account ideas and the socioeconomic structure when analyzing—and especially when attempting to better—intergroup relations. *Both structural inequality and ideas/attitudes about people from different races must be addressed in order to relieve the inequality and intergroup tensions that plague this country.* This is particularly true for populations isolated from people with different class, race, and national backgrounds.

Programs for individuals who have little experience with other groups require slowly developing an understanding about the history and current experiences of people from a given population before bringing strangers together. Exposing persons who regularly work together to additional information about their colleagues is a very different project. As Chapters 5 and 7 (on everyday contacts and simultaneous contradictions) point out, day-to-day interaction with people from different groups is the best way to teach individuals about living in a diverse world. Programs that bring people together on an ongoing basis are far preferable to any form of limited presentation on other cultures, to short-term empowerment, or to cultural-awareness workshops. Bringing people together to work on a common interest is often the best way to expose individuals to diversity.

As we have indicated throughout this book, whites generally avoid the topic of race, and people of color expect racism. Especially in working-class contexts, people are more likely to come together to work toward a common interest than to discuss or celebrate diversity. Projects that involve common goals and issues that concern an entire community are also more likely to attract a range of busy people than are diversity events, which are often seen as peripheral to daily life. Two examples from our research show how otherwise separate communities will come together to fight a common enemy.

Fighting Unfair Real-Estate Practices in Olney

One idea that seemed to capture the interest of both empowerment groups and established components of the community was the movement to stop aggressive, unethical real-estate practices in Olney. Young white diversity seekers organized to fight the constant barrage of solicitation by phone and mail from agents encouraging people to move. They were angry about the use of photos that implied racial change, as well as the practice of "steering" (showing different groups housing in different areas) and consequent block-busting. Many of these activities violated the guidelines of the Human Relations Commission and were subject to penalty.

Believing some members of the traditional civics to be "racist," the group was concerned about making a presentation to them seeking endorsements.

Those involved were delighted when most Olney organizations clearly supported their goals. Information about the group stressed its aim of seeking to maintain the advantages of the community—excellent schools, recreation facilities, and the convenience of its own shopping strip and a small mall—while encouraging sharing between oldtimers and culturally and racially diverse newcomers. The diversity seekers also supported maintaining the existing population mixture. This was to be accomplished by developing a pledge of ethical practices to be signed by the local real-estate agents and by creating procedures for reporting unethical practices and seeking penalties from the Human Relations Commission.

While this issue attracted more interest than any other, there were still splits in points of view between newcomers and longtime residents and between established and empowerment leaders. The first controversy was related to competition over real estate, while the second involved tactics.

When sponsors were sought for the group, citywide Latino leaders, as distant broker–representatives, endorsed the idea. Yet the local working group remained almost all-white. Only one Latina resident came to a meeting, and she had been encouraged by her pastor, who was part of the empowerment network. She expressed her support but never attended another meeting. The Korean fieldworker brokered some endorsements from a Korean real-estate firm specializing in business sales. But no Koreans ever attended sessions to participate in activities involving planning strategy, drafting documents, or signing petitions. No Asian Indian or Portuguese involvement was sought or achieved; these populations included active real-estate agents, some with interests in creating submarkets for their groups.

On two occasions, a woman pointed out indirectly the contradiction of trying to maintain a stable population mixture while newcomer agents carved up submarket territories for other members of their groups. She complained that an Asian Indian real-estate agent had stated that he wanted to make the cluster of blocks near where she lived "his," and that he was engaging in activities to encourage established residents to move and to sell or rent to people from his ethnic community. In fact, the attempt by different immigrant agents to create housing submarkets occurred in several parts of Olney, contradicting the notion of a fair and open market. Recognizing this, however, went against the ideas of empowerment leaders, who held that only established residents were exclusionary and had any sources of power. On both occasions that the issue was raised, an empowerment leader said, in effect: "We can't talk about that. It's getting too close to racism." While the whole purpose of the organization was to promote integrated housing, empowerment leaders often took it for granted that white working-class leaders were racist and that new immigrants were always victims, not perpetrators, of exclusionary policies.

Leaders of the traditional civics endorsed the idea of the new organization and occasionally attended meetings. They, however, like many older established residents, expressed some concern about the tactics being used in reporting real-estate agents who violated the pledge. This involved using the civil-rights apparatus, the same approach that had been taken against them on occasion. They also disliked the implication that local agents, often long-term community presences, were being accused of promoting racism. One empowerment leader recognized this when he said:

> People get upset with the Human Relations Commission legalisms. They don't like their tactics because they don't want to punish people. They just want to be left alone by the realtors.

The attendance of some established leaders weakened over time as they were frustrated in attempts to express concerns about newcomers' actions. Yet they continued to lend the support of their organizations to what was seen as an important goal, as did new immigrant leaders. The group was successful in getting the city Board of Realtors to support the pledge; as a result, they won a citywide award and received newspaper coverage. They continue to work on implementing and monitoring the pledge.

Fighting Drugs in Kensington

Just as the real-estate group in Olney emerged in 1988 as an attempt to organize all factions around an issue of significant mutual interest, a similar group emerged in the Norris Square area in 1989 as an attempt to take back the neighborhood from drug dealers.

Beginning in May 1989, the organization held prayer and observation vigils on different street corners. Three hundred people turned out for the first. As part of a citywide movement, the group adopted the style of other antidrug efforts, wearing hard hats to symbolize their tough stance. The organization developed around the already existing network of Norris Square empowerment groups and churches.

These meetings consistently brought out a large group—more numerous than for any gathering that was not related to an immediate crisis—and they were fairly evenly mixed, except for the limited participation of African Americans. At two weekly meetings over the summer attendance was close to 50, and between 35 and 40 people came regularly. At one large meeting there were 29 Latinos, 3 African Americans, and 20 whites; at another, there were 13 whites, an African American, and 20 Latinos. The latter were evenly divided between established bilingual participants and newcomers who spoke only Spanish. A mixed group of community leaders and ministers from the steering committee stood at the front and translated the speeches.

As in the case of the real-estate group, this organization was split by differences between traditional and empowerment leaders and between established and newcomer interests. One bone of contention was the definition of goals for the group—whether to cooperate with the police to jail drug dealers or emphasize the education of young people. Some organizations opted out of the enterprise because they defined the police as bad and argued that drug sales were a rational economic choice for the poor teenagers who were the breadwinners in many households. To them, priority had to be given to solving the economic problems of the community before drugs could be eliminated through militaristic, punitive actions. In addition, these individuals did not want to collaborate with segments of the coalition that worked in the enterprise zone cleanups. Such activities were seen as encouraging gentrification and hence as opposed to the interests of the poor people in the neighborhood.

While most decisions were arrived at by consensus, hot issues required votes. The different views of whites and Latinos (and the existence of factions within the Latino community) interfered with collective decisions on some issues. One meeting devoted a lot of time to whether the antidrug coalition would help sponsor the Puerto Rican Day parade. Attendees were divided for several reasons. One point of view, held by whites, was that the organization should always present itself as a cross-group coalition and not associate itself with any event that was not integrated. Some Latinos thought the parade represented the conservative faction of the community. In the end the vote was almost tied, but the majority decided not to participate in the parade.

Toward the end of the summer, most staff meetings concentrated on funding, particularly on whether to incorporate or use existing component organizations as fiscal conduits. In spite of all this distraction, however, general meetings remained goal oriented, receiving reports on calls and arrests and information about suspected crack houses. The group continued to conduct vigils and kept many residents regularly involved.

Using Intergroup Projects to Foster Cross-Group Understanding

Both these examples show how people of diverse backgrounds and conflicting interests can come together to fight for a common cause. These coalitions often arise spontaneously and can lead to long-term relationships across groups. Individuals attempting to build community in areas of conflict can use the strategy of bringing residents together to fulfill perceived community needs as a way to bridge group boundaries. In neighborhoods where people have developed group projects, human-relations organizers can use this experience to show similarities and differences among populations from different backgrounds.

Both examples point out problems in building group solidarity. In each case, people from different factions came into the process with negative expectations of those belonging to different groups. Goals held in common helped break down these barriers. Nevertheless, organizers sponsoring intergroup projects must be sensitive to such expectations and prepared to negotiate across the various stereotypes and factional strategies.

Competing agendas affected group process in both cases. Many projects fall apart when different factions work toward separate goals or stress intragroup solidarity instead of coalition efforts. Both funders and project organizers must understand that ongoing coalitions involve constantly encouraging intergroup communication and renegotiating relationships among factions. Ideally, groups should include people considered neutral or fair by all factions to negotiate among diverse interests. Decisions should come from the group, rather than reflecting the opinions of a few vocal or educated members, in order to keep a large part of the community involved. Leaders may need to check continually with various community members to encourage continued participation. Especially in deliberately created groups, ongoing technical assistance is vital to resolve problems and to provide an outside view of group process.

While these efforts can build relationships across groups and break down stereotypes, merely working together may not be enough to surmount some diversity issues. In some cases, human-relations organizers can develop discussions of subgroup identity and expectations as part of work with either spontaneously arising or deliberately created groups. But such discussions of difference should occur only after the group has developed familiarity through working together. Like the suggestions for discussions outlined above, these sessions must include historical data and stress sensitivity to the class and national background and everyday experience of group members. Formal discussions of diversity should grow out of the coalition's ongoing work, touching on problems and successes encountered in working together, rather than take place as a separate aspect of the program.

Creating Equality and Bridging Isolation

Improving relationships across groups must involve both changing the structures of inequality by creating real opportunities for people from disadvantaged backgrounds and fostering understanding of the real-life experience of people from different classes, races, nationalities, and neighborhoods. We realize that much energy and significant resources must go into lifting up the African American and Latino populations that Wilson (1987) called the "truly disadvantaged." Neither government nor the private sector is likely to provide the resources to give adequate education, housing, work, and social supports to the entire population. Nor are wholesale approaches to the complex problems of inequality likely to work. Successful programs like Head Start involve consistent, careful effort with individuals. Attempts to correct imbalances across races and nationalities require even more sensitivity and care. The approaches advocated here involve small groups of people working together over long periods. Although these kinds of strategies will not make sweeping changes in society, each small change shifts the balance of intergroup relations slightly. The accumulation of minor alterations in actions and beliefs ultimately creates openings for more radical change.

The process of learning about multiculturalism must also pay attention to the advantaged members of society. Misconceptions about class, race, and immigration abound. Crossing boundaries must also create opportunities for more-advantaged populations to understand the realities of life for new immigrants, poor people of color, and poor whites. This must be done, not simply by presenting them with statistics or creating opportunities to help for a few days, but by encouraging ongoing interaction across groups.

Civil-rights legislation and affirmative action took important steps in opening doors and curtailing some of the discrimination against people of color and women. These laws are significant, and their enforcement is an important part of creating a just society in the United States. But legislation against discrimination only opens doors. People must be prepared to live in a multicultural society, both by giving them the skills to compete in an increasingly complex world and by giving them the flexibility to work with people from different backgrounds.

This book has highlighted the diversity and complexity of U.S. society. Interactions among people from different backgrounds are increasingly complicated and contradictory. The primary lesson for intergroup relations developed from this project is that while common experiences, situations, and strategies exist in every instance, each situation and each context includes its own unique features. Strategies to build community and develop understanding across groups must be tailored for particular situations. Working in multicultural communities requires much more listening and negotiating of meaning and strategy among members than providing information or predefined goals. The Changing Relations Project taught the researchers involved much about different people and different contexts. Developing multicultural community is an ongoing, evolving process that will continually change as the many factors influencing the social structure continue to evolve.

NOTES

CHAPTER 1

1. People admitted to the United States as refugees are sponsored by a private voluntary agency. These agencies contract with the federal government to provide food, shelter, and a variety of social services to refugees when they first arrive in this country. Since the government provides limited funds to the agencies to cover the costs of resettlement, they often place refugees in neighborhoods where housing costs are low. Refugees such as Poles and Soviet Jews who have already established ethnic ties to the United States are often placed in the least expensive sections of those communities. Refugees from Southeast Asia were often settled in poor African American neighborhoods in Philadelphia.

2. Poles have come to the United States since the 1880s in order to earn money to better their lives in Poland. In the early part of this century, the Polish peasant and working classes established a pattern of migrating to other countries for several years to earn money as temporary workers. Many, like the "Birds of Passage" described by Piore (1979) returned to Poland, while others stayed in the United States. This pattern was reestablished when Poland became more open to the West in the 1970s. Poles still come to the United States on visitors' visas, intending to work "under the table" for a few years before returning home. Although U.S. law clearly prohibits people on visitors' visas from working in the United States, the immigration authorities in Philadelphia and the migrants largely ignore this prohibition. Some of these visitors later applied for asylum as refugees after the institution of martial law in Poland in 1981; others applied for legalized status under amnesty provisions of the 1986 Immigration Reform and Control Act. In addition, the United States admitted Poles as both refugees and immigrants during the 1980s.

3. The phenomenon of immigrants bringing in other immigrants is called chain migration, a reference to the common trend of migrants following their friends and relatives to another region or country. U.S. immigration policy has institutionalized this practice by giving the first six preference categories to prospective emigrants who have a relative or an employer sponsoring them.

4. The ideology of the "good immigrant" and its impact on educated refugees is discussed in detail in Schneider 1988b.

CHAPTER 2

1. The only area of the city still undeveloped until after World War II was the Great Northeast, which became an area of quasi-suburban development.

2. A recent study revealed that 25 percent of the population in the region is employed in food-related industries (including agriculture, processing, wholesale, retail, convenience, fast-food, and restaurants). Moreover, 50 percent of the trade sector is related to food markets and restaurants (Koppel 1988).

3. Incidents in the study area will be discussed below. For some descriptions of similar incidents in the southwest of the city, see Adams et al. 1991.

4. For example, one of the central figures in the reform coalition was an officer of the powerful John Wanamaker department store corporation. Today, the chain is in the hands of an international retail conglomerate.

5. One such group was the Greater Philadelphia First Corporation. It played an important role in Wilson Goode's first mayoral campaign, sustaining the alliance between African Americans, downtown elites, and progressives.

6. For example, looking toward the 1991 mayoral election, an informal group was convened. Led by the premier landlord of office space in the city, it included the head of a nationwide service conglomerate (one of the largest corporations headquartered in Philadelphia), a leading lawyer, the president of one of the few local mortgage and investment-banking firms, the head of the Chamber of Commerce, and the president of a major petrochemical firm that had already moved its headquarters outside the city.

7. This has been successful in Boston and San Francisco but not yet in Philadelphia.

8. Outside the study area, Russian Jewish refugees are located in the Jewish Northeast, while Southeast Asians are located among African Americans in West Philadelphia and among whites in South Philadelphia.

9. Since the heart of the Latino spatial community is split into council districts that are either represented by whites in the east or by African Americans in the west, a council seat in a specific district seemed impossible.

10. Governor Robert Casey, sensing an emerging constituency, created a new commission in late 1989. His interest was in part a response to the events of that summer, which involved increasing drug activity and ethnic violence in the Puerto Rican neighborhoods of Philadelphia.

CHAPTER 3

1. Business leaders lament the inability to attract capital to the Golden Block, a Latino-dominated shopping strip. There are no local or national chains that will invest here, and it is hard for the few Latino investors to get loans. Nonetheless, two Hispanic business associations were created by earlier would-be patrons; one was backed by the short-lived minority-business program of the Small Business Administration, the other by one of the downtown groups organized to save Philadelphia.

2. Puerto Ricans are by no means a homogeneous voting bloc. Many registered as Republicans to support Frank Rizzo for mayor in the 1991 primary. This is a result of

anger at Wilson Goode and of a residue of support for Rizzo, which dates back to his patronage of the upwardly mobile merchant-led group, whose members are uncomfortable with the rhetoric of the angry "Independistas." They prefer the image of Puerto Rican Week—with its parade, costumes, music, and big-ticket, exclusive ball—as representing the Puerto Rican presence in the city and reject the notion of an oppressed minority. Since this faction received its first paternalistic support during Rizzo's administration, it remained loyal to him. African Americans see this support for Rizzo as further confirmation of Puerto Ricans' identification with whites.

3. Other cultural organizations include a well-developed group of Latino musicians and two newspapers. One is run by the original, more conservative Puerto Rican organization and emphasizes social activities; the other is operated by a more progressive leadership and includes more international links and political issues.

4. Koreans, not residentially concentrated, are dispersed in several suburban locations. The residential community in the Greater Olney area is the largest in the city, but it serves as a temporary entry point for most newcomers.

CHAPTER 4

1. These neighborhoods are not technically part of North Philadelphia, which as an official planning area contains the western (African American) portion of the area north of the center.

2. During World War II, the Olney area was reputed to have been a center of pro-Nazi German-American Bund activity.

3. It is one of only two areas of the city with very strong ethnic reputations. The other is South Philadelphia, which (although mixed) is seen as Italian.

4. As is typical in community discourse, the deterioration of neighborhoods is blamed on the city. Talking about the decline of Logan, a nearby area west of Olney, one resident recognized both the role of the government and of white (and, later, middle-class African American) flight in the process: "When they [Jews] left, they primarily sold to middle- and upper-income African Americans. And they had to be upper-income to afford the houses, and they kept the places lovely, but somehow the state and city got in there and people abandoned Logan. It's one of the worst areas in the city. . . . A lot was caused by white flight and now . . . flight by the African Americans who have made it and can afford to move." The allusion to government involvement refers to refugee placement, housing programs, and the foot-dragging policy toward an area that is built on sinking landfill and from which residents were supposed to be moved with government support.

5. Two of them had spun off from others as a result of feuds among leaders.

6. Some conflicts in the city attributed to teenage vandalism have nothing to do with race or ethnicity; they concern, rather, keeping outsider lifestyles and class threats away. For example, in Manayunk white working-class youths were committing acts of harassment and vandalism against the upscale white businesses and residents who were "gentrifying" the area. They often shouted "Yuppie Go Home" (see "Chic Shock in Manayunk," *Philadelphia Inquirer*, April 12, 1991).

7. His activism has caused some concern among the elderly, white, established residents who regularly attend his services.

8. The Chicago activist Saul Alinsky developed a set of community-organizing principles. His model has been refined in several manuals of community organization.

9. Irish American and Italian American representatives from city organizations often came to speak and to respond to community complaints. They were also greeted with loud and hostile comments and complaints.

10. Kensington, always a mill town, had been the site of conflict between established English workers and new Irish and German Catholic upstarts in the mid-nineteenth century (Davis and Haller 1970).

11. During this period of early community development block grant funding, housing rehabilitation was seen as the key to saving communities.

12. Many people comment that housing has become more overcrowded in Kensington. Extended families (and even nonrelated households) share single units, and "near homelessness" increases in Philadelphia, where poor households pay an average of 58 percent of their incomes for housing.

13. "Rushing" is an attack on one teenager by a gang protecting turf or school loyalty. It takes place in neighborhoods to bar outsiders; it often occurs on the public transportation system to act out interschool gang conflicts.

14. In 1988, he did try to help a school to fight overcrowding by coming to a parents' meeting and then by leading a protest march to the school district headquarters.

15. The latter include the Greater Philadelphia First Corporation, related to the Chamber of Commerce and the Urban Coalition. The list of corporate and foundation contributors to the Urban Coalition reads like a Who's-Who of corporate Philadelphia.

16. African Americans constitute a small population in the westernmost part of Kensington. They also make up an established multigenerational community in the heart of the neighborhood. African Americans tend to be linked to churches and organizations outside Kensington proper, as they are in Olney. When the representation of African American leaders is needed at a symbolic event, it is often hard to achieve.

CHAPTER 5

1. Puerto Rican children are often sent to live with close family on the island for safety or to find spouses.

2. Kae Young Park (1990) has demonstrated that migration has also shifted Korean kinship away from a patrilateral emphasis. Women now often serve as U.S. anchors, bringing in their siblings and parents one family at a time.

3. One Indian family who moved to the suburbs turned their house over to the wife's parents, who had just emigrated. A Brazilian woman who moved to the suburbs turned her house over to her sister. A Filipino family moved to a bigger house and gave the original house to the wife's incoming parents.

4. Small evangelical Protestant movements also provided the major financial and social support for many Puerto Rican families.

5. Of the families we interviewed, seven were intermarried across the four major categories: one African American/white, two African American/Latino, three white/Latino, and one Latino/Asian. Many of the aspiring middle-class white parents had African American and Hispanic nieces and nephews, as well as sons-in-law; almost half

of the Latinos we came to know well were themselves intermarried to European Americans or African Americans or had siblings who were.

6. McCullough's 1991 work on friendships among white and African American women reveals the high degree of effort entailed in dealing with these tensions to make long term relationships work.

7. Out of 50 businesses, 21 were owned by Koreans, 12 by European Americans, 5 by Latinos, and 1 each by Palestinians and Chinese; 5 were owned by chains, and 5 were in transition.

8. Actually the school contains few students from the neighborhood and many from outside the area. In 1988, a new principal and new practices and procedures were reported to have "turned the school around" from a chaotic environment to a good setting for learning. This was referred to by everyone as "the change," and it may affect the school's reputation and local recruitment.

9. Koreans command other spaces, as do each Southeast Asian group and Asian Indians. African Americans (50 percent of the school) are divided into several clusters. Some of them associate with more-established Latinos who wear gold, dress similarly, and like the same music as African Americans and are reported as walking and talking like them. Some people suspect them of being involved in drugs.

10. This violence was unusual, since segregation works against intergroup violence in the school. Even the use of epithets is rare between groups, and most of the fights occur within groups. When we first heard about it we were told that people could not believe there was an Asian perpetrator, given the model image of Asians, so everybody told the story the other way around.

Yet the incident was not surprising, since the only significant adolescent/gang conflict in the area occurs between the poorer Asians (mostly Cambodian refugees) and African Americans. Both groups are gang organized. During fieldwork, there were three incidents of violence between the two groups—this one, one in an elementary school, and one at a fair.

11. The program recruits good students to the school by telling them they will have advantages in getting college scholarships and admission compared to students from the more competitive magnet programs. The group we worked with included 3 newcomer Latinos, 1 Portuguese, 1 established European American, 2 Vietnamese, 2 Koreans, and 1 African American/Hispanic. The top 10 students in the graduating class included 4 African Americans, 1 African American/Latino, 2 Vietnamese, 2 Koreans, and 1 European American.

CHAPTER 6

1. William Penn offered refuge to many people, including Germans. This boy's ancestors were probably part of a historic population originally invited by Penn.

2. Parents buy low-cost insurance policies for their children, which allow them to participate in classes and to qualify for college scholarships when they are older.

3. Moneys were given to community groups to develop programs to create ongoing structures that would help people get along together. Grant criteria stressed that proposals must focus on reducing conflict between generations, races, newcomers and oldtimers, or those generated by gentrification (class was never mentioned). In addition,

several components had to be involved in the planning: clergy, residents, schools, and businesspeople.

4. Only one established ethnic segment of the parish had a performance group—Irish step dancers.

5. Established women tend to wear casual clothing (often slacks and sweaters), while Korean women dress in designer clothes made in Korea, which they consider to be of higher quality than U.S. garments. Another established woman asked her Korean friend about the price of a sweater and was shocked to learn that it cost more than all of her own clothing purchases for the year.

6. This incident occurred before we began fieldwork, but the repercussions are still felt. We have pieced the event together through retrospective interviews.

CHAPTER 7

1. The theoretical underpinnings for this chapter are described in Schneider 1989.

2. The United States has a long history of resenting immigrants in its midst. In the first decades of the twentieth century, the Know-Nothings still fought for immigration restrictions, arguing that immigrants took away their jobs. The Dillingham Commission spent three years compiling a 42-volume report that attempted to document the inferiority of immigrants from southern and eastern Europe to their western European forerunners. The immigration restrictions of the 1920s resulted from these arguments.

3. See Schneider 1988a for full discussion of this topic.

4. Ehrenreich (1990) and Newman (1989) discuss middle-class expectations in the United States and ways that changing economic conditions have affected middle-class ideology.

BIBLIOGRAPHY

PRIMARY SOURCES

Barrientos, Tanya. "Getting the Facts Right: A New Guide on Puerto Rico." *The Philadelphia Inquirer*, February 21, 1991.

Binzen, Peter. " A Quiet Influence on Phila.'s Agenda." *Philadelphia Inquirer*, November 5, 1990.

Boldt, David. "The Main Line Isn't the Mainline AND That's the Story of Philadelphia." *Philadelphia Inquirer*, March 24, 1991.

Borowski, Neill, "Minorities Account for Area Population Gain." *Philadelphia Inquirer*, February 20, 1991.

Borowski, Neill, and Murray Dubin. "Black Segregation Up in Phila., Census Shows." The *Philadelphia Inquirer*, April 11, 1991.

Carvajal, Doreen. "DA Promises Review of Daily Case at Request of Puerto Rican Groups." *Philadelphia Inquirer*, August 4, 1989.

———. "Chic Shock in Manayunk." The *Philadelphia Inquirer*, April 12, 1991.

Carvajal, Doreen, and Neill Borowski. "Asians, Latinos Flock to Philadelphia." The *Philadelphia Inquirer*, March 3, 1991.

Dubin, Murray. "Hispanic Group Breaks Ties to Mayor." *Philadelphia Inquirer*, March 29, 1989.

———. "Tragic Death Also Takes Toll on Accused, Family." *Philadelphia Inquirer*, August 6, 1989.

———. "City Report on Latinos is Delayed." The *Philadelphia Inquirer*, December 9, 1990.

———. "Balch Exhibit Focuses on Koreans." The *Philadelphia Inquirer*, May 29, 1991.

Dubin, Murray, and Neill Borowski. "Decades of Flight Turning N. Phila. into Ghost Town." *Philadelphia Inquirer*, April 12, 1991.

Duster, Troy. "They're Taking Over! And Other Myths about Race on Campus." *Mother Jones* (September–October 1991): 30–33, 63–64.

Ethnovision. 1987. *I'm Not Prejudiced, But . . .* (video). Philadelphia: Ethnovision.

Fazllolah, Mark. "Integration Uneven in the Suburbs." *Philadelphia Inquirer*, October 3, 1993.

Gonzales, Patrisia. "A Latino Firm Guards Its Turf." *Philadelphia Inquirer*, October 11, 1987.

King, Martin Luther, Jr. "I Have a Dream." Address at the Lincoln Memorial, Wasington, D.C., August 28, 1963.

Lazarus, Emma. "The New Colossus." *Poems*, 1889.

Lipson, D. Herbert. "Off the Cuff." *Philadelphia Magazine* (September 1989).

Logan, Joe. "Study Criticizes 'Racial Divisiveness' of Radio Talk Shows." *Philadelphia Inquirer*, November 8, 1990.

Morgan, P. "The Last L . . . " *Philadelphia Magazine*, (August 1989).

Peirce, Neal. "The City's Crisis Has Many Fathers." *Philadelphia Inquirer*, September 17, 1990.

Philadelphia Inquirer. Metropolitan Business Report. September 12, 1988.

Philadelphia Inquirer. Report on Early Census Statistics. September 16, 1990.

Power, Edward. "Asian Immigrants Lend New Life to City's Sewing Industry." *Philadelphia Inquirer*, February 28, 1988.

Stains, Lawrence. "After the Fall." *Philadelphia Magazine* (April 1991).

Terry, Robert, and Doreen Carvajal. "Puerto Rican Leaders Vent Anger over Killing." *Philadelphia Inquirer*, July 13, 1989.

United States Senate, Subcommittee on Immigration and Naturalization, hearings. *Immigration*, Part I, February 24, 1965. Washington, D.C.

Wallis, Jim. "America's Original Sin." In *America's Original Sin: A Study Guide on White Racism*. Special Issue, *Sojourners* 16, no. 10:6–9.

REFERENCES

Adams, Carolyn, David Bartelt, David Elesh, Ira Goldstein, Nancy Kleniewski, and William Yancey. 1991. *Philadelphia: Neighborhoods, Division, and Conflict in a Postindustrial City*. Philadelphia: Temple University Press.

Allport, Gordon. 1988. *The Nature of Prejudice*. Reading, Mass.: Addison-Wesley.

Anderson, Benedict. 1983. *Imagined Communities: Reflections on the Origin and Spread of Nationalism*. London: Verso.

Anderson, Eli. 1990. *Streetwise: Race, Class, and Change in an Urban Community*. Chicago: University of Chicago Press.

Bartelt, David, and George Leon. 1986. "Differential Decline: The Neighborhood Context of Abandonment." *Housing and Society* 13:81–106.

Bell, Derrick. 1987. *And We Are Not Saved: The Elusive Quest for Racial Justice*. New York: Basic Books.

Berson, Lenora. 1982. "The Reform Period." In John Raines, Lenora Berson, and David Gracie, eds., *Capital and Community Conflict*. Philadelphia: Temple University Press.

Binzen, Peter. 1970. *Whitetown USA*. New York: Random House.

Blauner, Bob. 1989. *Black Lives, White Lives: Three Decades of Race Relations in America*. Berkeley and Los Angeles: University of California Press.

Blejwas, Stanislaus. 1981. "Old and New Polonias: Tensions within an Ethnic Community." *Polish American Studies* 38, no. 2:55–83.

Bodnar, John, Michael Weber, and Roger Simon. 1979. "Migration, Kinship, and Urban

Adjustment: Blacks and Poles in Pittsburgh, 1900–1930." *Journal of American History* 66, no. 3:548–65.

———. 1983. *Lives of Their Own: Blacks, Italians, and Poles in Pittsburgh, 1900–1960.* Champaign: University of Illinois Press.

Bott, Elizabeth. 1957. *Family and Social Network.* London: Tavistock.

Brooks, Roy. 1990. *Rethinking the American Race Problem.* Berkeley and Los Angeles: University of California Press.

Byler, Janet, and Douglas Bennett. 1984. *Employment Trends in Southeastern Pennsylvania, 1972–1982.* Working Paper 11. Philadelphia: Institute for Public Policy Studies, Temple University.

Carmichael, Stokely, and Charles V. Hamilton. 1967. *Black Power: The Politics of Liberation in America.* New York: Random House.

Carter, Stephen. 1991. *Refelctions of an Affirmative Action Baby.* New York: Basic Books.

Cohen, Carole. 1994. "Facing Job Loss: Changing Relations in a Multicultural Urban Factory." In Louise Lamphere, Alex Stepick, and Guillermo Grenier, eds., *Newcomers in the Workplace: Immigrants and the Restructuring of the U.S. Economy.* Philadelphia: Temple University Press.

Cruse, Harold. 1987. *Plural but Equal: A Critical Study of Blacks and Minorities and America's Plural Society.* New York: William Morrow.

Davis, Allen F., and Mark H. Haller, eds. 1970. *The Peoples of Philadelphia: A History of Ethnic Groups and Lower-Class Life, 1790–1940.* Philadelphia: Temple University Press.

Dewart, Janet. 1989. *The State of Black America, 1989.* New York: National Urban League.

di Leonardo, Micaela. 1984. *The Varieties of Ethnic Experience: Kinship, Class, and Gender among California Italian-Americans.* Ithaca, N.Y.: Cornell University Press.

Dominguez, Virginia. 1986. *White By Definition: Social Classification in Creole Louisiana.* New Brunswick, N.J.: Rutgers University Press.

Ehrenreich, Barbara. 1990. *Fear of Falling: The Inner Life of the Middle Class.* New York: Harper Perennial.

Ericsen, Eugene, David Bartelt, Patrick Feeney, Gerald Foeman, Sherri Grasmuck, Maureen Martella, William Rickle, Robert Spencer, and David Webb. 1985. *The State of Puerto Rican Philadelphia.* Philadelphia: Institute for Public Policy Studies, Temple University.

Fields, Barbara. 1990. "Slavery, Race, and Ideology in the United States of America." *New Left Review,* May–June: 95–118.

Foner, Nancy. 1987. "The Jamaicans: Race and Ethnicity Among Migrants in New York City." In Nancy Foner, ed., *New Immigrants in New York.* New York: Columbia University Press, 195–218.

Forsythe, Dennis. 1979. "Race Relations from Liberal, Black, and Marxist Perspectives." In Cora Bagley Marrett and Cheryl Leggon, eds., *Research on Race and Ethnic Relations: A Research Annual,* vol. 1, 65–86.

Gans, Herbert. 1982. "Symbolic Ethnicity: The Future of Ethnic Groups and Cultures in America." In Norman Yetman and C. Hay Steele, eds., *Majority and Minority:*

The Dynamics of Race and Ethnicity in American Life. Newton, Mass.: Allyn and Bacon, 495–508.

Gaymon, William, and John Garrett. 1975. "A Blueprint for a Pluralistic Society." *Journal of Ethnic Studies* 3, no. 3:57–69.

Gitelman, Zvi. 1984. "Soviet Jewish Immigrants to the United States: Profiles, Problems, and Prospects." In Robert O. Freedman, ed., *Soviet Jewry in the Decisive Decade, 1971–80.* Durham, N.C.: Duke University Press, 89–98.

Glazer, Nathan, and Daniel Patrick Moynihan. 1970. *Beyond the Melting Pot.* 2d ed. Cambridge, Mass.: MIT Press.

———. 1975. *Ethnicity Theory and Experiences.* Cambridge, Mass.: Harvard University Press.

Glick-Schiller, Nina, and Georges Fouran. 1990. " 'Everwhere We Go, We Are in Danger': Ti Manno and the Emergence of Haitian Transnational Identity." *American Ethnologist* 17, no. 2:329–47.

Golab, Caroline. 1977. *Immigrant Destinations.* Philadelphia: Temple University Press.

Goldsmith, William W., and Edward J. Blakely. 1992. *Separate Societies: Poverty and Inequality in U.S. Cities.* Philadelphia: Temple University Press.

Goldstein, Ira. 1986. "The Wrong Side of the Tracts: A Study of Residential Segregation in Philadelphia, 1930–80." Doctoral dissertation, Temple University.

Goode, Judith. 1985. "The Formation of the Puerto Rican Community in North Philadelphia, 1950–1985." Paper presented at the North Philadelphia Conference, Urban Studies Program and Institute for Public Policy Studies, Temple University, April.

———. 1989. "Relating to the Human Relations Institutions in the City of Brotherly Love." Paper presented at the American Ethnological Society/Society for Applied Anthropology Joint Meetings, Sante Fe, April.

———. 1990. "A Wary Welcome to the Neighborhood: Community Responses to Immigrants." *Urban Anthropology* 19:125–53.

———. 1994. "Encounters over the Counter: Workers, Bosses, and Customers in a Multi-Cultural Shopping Strip." In Louise Lamphere, Alex Stepick, and Guillermo Grenier, eds., *Newcomers in the Workplace: Immigrants and the Restructuring of the U.S. Economy.* Philadelphia: Temple University Press.

Goode, Judith, Karen Curtis, and Janet Theophano. 1984. "Meal Formats, Meal Cycles, and Menu Negotiations in the Maintenance of an Italian American Community." In Mary Douglas, ed., *Food and the Social Order.* New York: Basic Books, 135–99.

Goode, Judith, Jo Anne Schneider, and Suzanne Blanc. 1992. "Transcending Boundaries and Closing Ranks: How Schools Shape Interrelations." In Louise Lamphere, ed., *Structuring Diversity.* Chicago: University of Chicago Press.

Gordon, David M., Richard Edwards, and Michael Reich. 1982. *Segmented Work, Divided Workers: The Historical Transformations of Labor in the United States.* Cambridge: Cambridge University Press.

Gould, Stephen Jay. 1981. *The Mismeasure of Man.* New York: Norton.

Grasmuck, Sherri. 1984. "Immigration, Ethnic Stratification, and Native Working Class Discipline: Comparison of Documented and Undocumented Dominicans." *International Migration Review* 18, no. 3:692–713.

Greeley, Andrew. 1974. *Ethnicity in the United States: A Preliminary Reconnaisance.* New York: John Wiley.

———. 1975. *Why Can't They Be Like Us? America's White Ethnic Groups.* New York: Dutton.

Greenburg, Stephanie. 1981. "Industrial Location and Ethnic Residential Patterns in an Industrializing City: Philadelphia, 1880." In Theodore Hershberg ed., *Philadelphia: Work, Space, Family, and Group Experience in the Nineteenth Century.* New York: Oxford University Press.

Haines, Pamela. 1982. "Loss in the Garment Industry." In John Raines, Lenora Berson, and David Gracie, eds., *Capital and Community in Conflict.* Philadelphia: Temple University Press.

Handlin, Oscar. 1951. *The Uprooted: The Epic Story of the Great Migration That Made the American People.* Boston: Little, Brown.

Hawks, Irene Kaminsky. 1977. "The New Immigrant: A Study of the Vocational Adjustment of Soviet Jews." *Journal of Jewish Communal Service* 54, no. 2:161–65.

Hayes-Bautista, David, and Jorge Chapa. 1987. "Latino Terminology: Conceptual Bases for Standardized Terminology." *American Journal of Public Health* 77, no. 1:61–68.

Hector, Michael. 1975. *Internal Colonialism: The Celtic Fringe in British National Development, 1536–1966.* Berkeley and Los Angeles: University of California Press.

Hershberg, Theodore, ed. 1981. *Philadelphia: Work, Space, Family, and Group Experience in the Nineteenth Century.* New York: Oxford University Press.

Hershberg, Theodore, Alan Burstein, Eugene Ericksen, Stephanie Greenburg, and William Yancey. 1979. "A Tale of Three Cities: Blacks and Immigrants in Philadelphia, 1850–1880, 1930, and 1970." *Annals of the American Association of Political and Social Science,* no. 441:55–81.

Hobsbawm, Eric, and Terence Ranger, eds. 1983. *The Invention of Tradition.* Cambridge: Cambridge University Press.

Hochner, Arthur, Cherylyn Granrose, Judith Goode, Elaine Simon, and Eileen Appelbaum. 1988. *Jobsaving Strategies in the Supermarket Industry: Worker Ownership and QWL.* Kalamazoo, Mich.: Upjohn Institute for Labor Studies.

Hochner, Arthur, and Ira Zibman. 1982. "Absentee Owners and Job Losses." In John Raines, Lenora Berson, and David Gracie, eds., *Capital and Community in Conflict.* Philadelphia: Temple University Press.

Hourwich, Isaac A. 1912. *Immigrants as Labor.* New York: Putnam.

Hughes, Mark Alan. 1989. *Poverty in Cities.* Washington, D.C.: National League of Cities.

Hurh, Won Moo, and Kwang Chung Kim. 1984. "Adhesive Sociocultural Adaptation of Korean Immigrants in the U.S.: An Alternative Strategy of Minority Adaptation." *International Migration Review* 18, no. 2:188–216.

Kerner Commission. [1968] 1988. *The Kerner Report: The 1968 Report of the National Advisory Commission on Civil Disorders.* New York: Pantheon.

Kleeman, Janice. 1985. "Polish American Assimilation: The Interaction of Opportunity and Attitude." *Polish American Studies* 42, no. 1:11–26.

Koppel, Ross. 1988. "Agenda for Growth: The Impact of Food and Agriculture on the Economy of the Delaware Valley." Philadelphia: Mellon Bank Food and Agriculture Task Force.

Koss, Joan. 1965. "Puerto Ricans in Philadelphia: Migration and Accomodation." Doctoral dissertation, University of Pennsylvania.

Kotlowitz, Alex. 1991. *There Are No Children Here: The Story of Two Boys Growing Up in the Other America*. New York: Doubleday.

Leacock, Eleanor. 1969. *Teaching and Learning in City Schools*. New York: Basic Books.

Lieberson, Stanley. 1980. *A Piece of the Pie: Black and White Immigrants since 1880*. Berkeley and Los Angeles: University of California Press.

Light, Ivan. 1981. "Ethnic Succession." In Charles Keyes, ed., *Ethnic Change*. Seattle: University of Washington Press, 53–86.

Light, Ivan, and Edna Bonacich. 1988. *Immigrant Entrepreneurs: Koreans in Los Angeles, 1965–82*. Berkeley and Los Angeles: University of California Press.

Lopata, Helena Znaniecki. 1976. *Polish Americans: Status Competition in an Ethnic Community*. Englewood Cliffs, N.J.: Prentice-Hall.

Lowy, Richard. 1991. "Yuppie Racism: Race Relations in the 1980s." *Journal of Black Studies* 21, no. 4:445–64.

Macdonald, John, and Leatrice Macdonald. 1964. "Chain Migration, Ethnic Neighborhood Formation, and Social Networks." *Milbank Memorial Fund Quarterly* 42:82–91.

Mack, Raymond W. 1963. *Race, Class, and Power*. New York: American.

Majetco, Alexander. 1974. *Social Change and Stratification in Eastern Europe: An Interpretive Analysis of Poland and Her Neighbors*. New York: Praeger.

Marable, Manning. 1983. *How Capitalism Underdeveloped Black America*. Boston: South End Press.

———. 1992. *The Crisis of Color and Democracy: Essays on Race, Class, and Power*. Monroe, Maine: Common Courage Press.

Marger, Martin. 1991. *Race and Ethnic Relations: American and Global Perspectives*. Belmont, Calif.: Wadsworth.

Marshall, Adriana. 1987. "New Immigrants in New York's Economy." In Nancy Foner, ed., *New Immigrants in New York*. New York: Columbia University Press, 79–102.

McCullough, Mary. 1991. "Black and White Women's Friendships: Claiming the Margins." Doctoral dissertation, Temple University.

Montagu, Ashley. 1963. *Race, Science, and Humanity*. Princeton, N.J.: D. Van Nostrand.

———. 1979. *What We Know About Race*. New York: Anti-Defamation League of B'nai B'rith.

Mostwin, Danuta. 1980. *The Transplanted Family: A Study of Social Adjustment of the Polish Immigrant Family to the United States after the Second World War*. New York: Arno Press.

Myrdal, Gunnar. 1944. *An American Dilemma, the Negro Problem and Modern Democracy*. New York: Harper and Bros.

National Institute Against Prejudice and Violence. 1986. *Striking Back at Bigotry: Remedies under Federal and State Law for Violence Motivated by Racial, Relgious, and Ethnic Prejudice*. Baltimore.

Newman, Katherine. 1989. *Falling from Grace: The Experience of Downward Mobility in the American Middle Class*. New York: Vintage Books.

Ninivaggi, Cynthia Carter. 1994. "Poverty and Politics: Practice and Ideology among Small Business Owners in an Urban Philadelphia Enterprise Zone." In Louise

Lamphere, Alex Stepick, and Guillermo Grenier, eds., *Newcomers in the Workplace: Immigrants and the Reconstructuring of the U.S. Economy*. Philadelphia: Temple University Press.

Novak, Michael. 1971. *The Rise of the Unmeltable Ethnics: Politics and Culture in the 70s*. New York: Macmillan.

Obidinsky, Eugene. 1985. "Beyond Hansen's Law: Fourth Generation Polonian Identity." *Polish American Studies* 42, no. 1:27–42.

Omi, Michael, and Howard Winant. 1986. *Racial Formation in the United States: From the 1960s to the 1980s*. New York: Routledge.

Padilla, Felix. 1985. *Latino Ethnic Consciousness: The Case of Mexican Americans and Puerto Ricans in Chicago*. Notre Dame, Ind: Notre Dame University Press.

Panish, Paul. 1981. *Exit Visa: The Emigration of the Soviet Jews*. New York: Coward, McCann and Geoghegan.

Park, Kae Young. 1990. "The Korean American Dream." Doctoral dissertation, City University of New York.

Park, Robert. 1928. "Human Migration and Marginal Man." *American Journal of Sociology* 33, no. 6:881–93.

Pennsylvania Economy League. 1986. *Taxes in Philadelphia Compared to Other Large Cities, 1986*. Philadelphia: Pennsylvania Economy League, Eastern Division.

Peshkin, Alan. 1991. *The Color of Strangers, The Color of Friends: The Play of Ethnicity in School and Community*. Chicago: The University of Chicago Press.

Petras, Elizabeth. 1990. Personal communication, August.

Piore, Michael. 1979. *Birds of Passage: Migrant Labor and Industrial Societies*. Cambridge: Cambridge University Press.

Portes, Alejandro, and Robert Bach. 1985. *Latin Journey*. Berkeley and Los Angeles: University of California Press.

Portes, Alejandro, and Ruben Rumbaut. 1990. *Immigrant America: A Portrait*. Berkeley and Los Angeles: University of California Press.

Powdermaker, Hortense. 1944. *Probing Our Prejudices: A Unit for High School Students*. New York: Harper and Bros.

Pyong Gap, Min. 1989. "Some Possible Functions of Ethnic Business for an Immigrant Community: Koreans in Los Angeles." Doctoral dissertation, City University of New York.

Radzialowski, Thadeus. 1974. "The View from a Polish Ghetto: Some Observations on the First Hundred Years in Detroit." *Ethnicity* 1:125–50.

Reich, Michael. 1981. *Racial Inequality: A Political Economic Analysis*. Princeton: Princeton University Press.

Rodriguez, Clara. 1989. *Puerto Ricans Born in the United States*. Boston: Unwin Hyman.

Sandberg, Neil. 1974. "The Changing Polish American." *Polish American Studies* 31, no. 1:5–14.

Sassen-Koob, Saskia. 1980. "Immigrant and Minority Workers in the Organization of the Labor Process." *Journal of Ethnic Studies* 8, no. 1:1–34.

Schneider, Jo Anne. 1986. "Immigrant Group/Ethnic Group: Polish Refugees and the Polish American Community." Unpublished paper presented at the 85th Annual Meeting of the American Anthropological Society, Philadelphia, December.

————. 1988a. "In the Big Village: Economic Adjustment and Identity Formation for Eastern European Refugees in Philadelphia, Pa." Doctoral dissertation, Temple University.

————. 1988b. "Fieval Is an Engineer: Immigrant Ideology and Economic Absorption of Eastern European Refugees." Paper presented at the 87th Annual American Anthropological Association Meeting, Phoenix, November.

————. 1989. "Dialectics of Race and Nationality: Everyday Contradictions Among Philadelphia Working Class Youth." Manuscript.

————. 1990a. "Patterns for Getting By: The Role of Household Status and Industry in Polish Women's Employment Patterns in Delaware County, Pa., 1900–1930." *Pennsylvania Magazine of History and Biography* 114, no. 4:517–41.

————. 1990b. "Defining Boundaries, Creating Contexts: Puerto Rican and Polish Presentation of Group Identity Through Ethnic Parades." *Journal of Ethnic Studies* 18, no. 1:33–58.

Scott, James. 1985. *Weapons of the Weak: Everyday Forms of Peasant Resistance.* New Haven: Yale University Press.

Seder, Jean. 1990. *Voices of Kensington: Vanishing Mills, Vanishing Neighborhoods.* McLean, Va.: EPM Publications.

Simon, Rita. 1985. *New Lives: The Adjustment of Soviet Jewish Immigrants in the United States and Israel.* Lexington, Mass.: Lexington Books.

Sowell, Thomas. 1981. *Ethnic America: A History.* New York: Basic Books.

Stafford, Susan Buchanan. 1987. "The Hatians: The Cultural Meaning of Race and Ethnicity." In Nancy Foner, ed., *New Immigrants in New York.* New York: Columbia University Press, 131–58.

Steele, Shelby. 1990. *The Content of Our Character.* New York: St. Martin's Press.

Steinberg, Stephen. 1981. *The Ethnic Myth: Race, Ethnicity, and Class in America.* New York: Atheneum.

Summers, Anita, and Thomas Luce. 1988. *Economic Report on the Philadelphia Metropolitan Area, 1988.* Philadelphia: University of Pennsylvania Press.

Susser, Ida. 1982. *Norman Street: Poverty and Politics in an Urban Neighborhood.* New York: Oxford University Press.

Symmons-Symonolwicz, Konstantin. 1979. *Ze Studiow nad Polonia Amerykanska* (The study of American Polonia). Warsaw: Ludowa Sp. Odzienlnia Wydawnicza.

————. 1983. "Is There a Polonian Culture?" *Polish American Studies* 40, no. 1:89–90.

Taras, Piotr. 1982. "The Dispute Over Polonian Culture." *Polish American Studies* 39, no. 1:38–54.

Thomas, William Isaac, and Florian Znaniecki. 1927. *The Polish Peasant in Europe and America,* 2 vols. 2nd ed. New York: Knopf.

Tidwell, Billy. 1990. *The Price: The Study of the Costs of Racism in America.* New York: National Urban League.

Trevino, Fernando. 1987. "Standardized Terminology for Hispanic Populations." *American Journal of Public Health* 77, no. 1:69–71.

Warner, Samuel Bass. 1968. *The Private City: Philadelphia in Three Periods of Its Growth.* Philadelphia: University of Pennsylvania Press.

Waters, Mary. 1990. *Ethnic Options: Choosing Identities in America.* Berkeley and Los Angeles: University of California Press.

West, Cornel. 1991. *The Ethical Dimensions of Marxist Thought.* New York: Monthly Review Press.

———. 1993a. *Beyond Eurocentrism and Multiculturalism.* Monroe, Maine: Common Courage Press.

———. 1993b. *Race Matters.* Boston: Beacon Press.

Williams, Raymond. 1977. *Marxism and Literature.* London: Oxford University Press.

Wilson, William Julius. 1978. *The Declining Significance of Race.* Chicago: University of Chicago Press.

———. 1987. *The Truly Disadvantaged: The Inner City, the Underclass, and Public Policy.* Chicago: University of Chicago Press.

Yancey, William, Eugene Ericksen, and Richard Juliani. 1976. "Emergent Ethnicity, Review and Reformulation." *American Sociological Review* 41: 391–402.

Yancey, William, Eugene Ericksen, and George Leon. 1985. "The Structure of Pluralism: 'We're all Italian Around Here, Aren't We Mrs. O'Brien?' " In Richard Alba, ed., *Ethnicity and Race in the U.S.A.: Toward the 21st Century.* New York: Routledge and Kegan Paul, 94–116.

Young, Robert J. 1989. "What Kinds of Immigrants Have Come to the Philadelphia Area, Where Did They Settle, and How Are They Doing?" Paper presented at the Conference Who Are These Strangers Among Us? at the Balch Institute, Philadelphia, September.

INDEX

Adams et al., 32, 34, 35, 42, 45, 46, 48, 60
Affirmative Action, 141, 153, 216–17
African Americans: and ethnicity, 173, 218–21, 223; and fear of racism, 162; and Great Migration, 34; and human relations events, 201; and industrial employment, 35; in Kensington, 125–27; and new immigrants, 4, 227–28; in Olney, 107–9; place in economy, 12–14; political organization of, 48; political power of, 221–22; population of, 34–35; in Port Richmond, 121; relationships with Koreans, 58, 75, 84; relationships with whites, 64; and segregation, 3–4, 40–43, 254–55. *See also* racial dyad, racial politics
Alinsky, Saul, 102, 114
Allport, Gordon, 20–21, 64
Anderson, Eli, 13, 223
Asian Indians, in Olney, 109–49
Asians: in labor force, 37, 39–40, 54; as label, 69; in Olney, 109; as "model immigrants," 73; population of, 52; spatial clustering, 55

Barrientos, Tanya, 68
Bartelt, David, and George Leon, 125
Bell, Derrick, 13, 223
Berson, Lenora, 45
Binzen, Peter, 34, 46
Blejwas, Stanislaus, 90, 91

Bodnar, John, Michael Weber, and Roger Simon, 90
Boldt, David, 31, 136
Borowski, Neill, 49, 52
Brooks, Roy, 249
Byler, Janet, and Douglas Bennett, 35

Cambodians, in Olney, 109
Carmichael, Stokely, and Charles V. Hamilton, 17–18
Carter, Stephen, 13
Carvajal, Doreen, and Neill Borowski, 51, 104
categories of difference: Asian label, 69; color line, 94, 150; Latino label, 69, 82; macro categories, 68–70; maximizing difference in conflicts, 149; resisting labels, 69; variation between neighborhoods, 134
Central Americans, in Olney, 109
Changing Relations Project, xi–xii, 29
children: babysitting, 141, 146–47; crossing boundaries, 183; as intergroup brokers, 146–48; in intergroup relations, 248–49
churches: Korean, 88–89; in Port Richmond, 119, 122; Puerto Rican, 78; social relations of, 139–40, 141, 151
Cohen, Carole, 39, 154
Colombians, in Olney, 109
community empowerment groups, 101–3, 170; funding of, 102; in Kensington, 128–30; leadership and staffing of, 102;

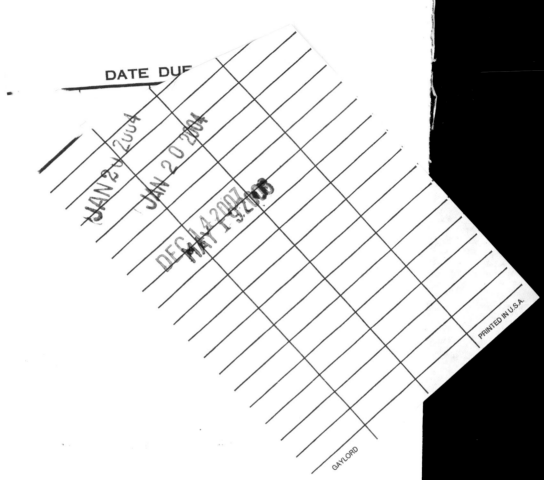
917-209-1098